Trusting Spirit now

Life Through the Eyes of an Energy Intuitive

Judy Rankin Hansen

To Bonnie,

I hear we're a lot
a like — looking forward to
meeting a kindred spirit! Til then
~ love, judy

judy@trustingspiritnow.com
www.TrustingSpiritNow.com

Published by
Spirit Tree Publishing
www.SpiritTreePublishing.com

Library of Congress:
2010915300

Printed in the United States of America
ISBN 978-0-9825878-1-2

Contents

Author's Note and Acknowledgements

   Gratitude—the deep satisfaction of having obtained a great gift—that's the only way I can describe what happened to me in the creation of this volume: I finally came to know myself. As I drove away from my retreat in nature having finished the mass of this work, I felt giddy happy and completely whole for the first time in my life.

   Discovering myself in this quest, I realize how strong my core to living by spirit has always been, and how strong is my desire to exclaim and rejoice about this truth—to live always by the guiding light of spirit—that sacred gift we can always, always trust. The thing that I love best about myself is that I really do know this, and with this confidence, I feel completely capable to do anything that comes my way. Even when I don't know how, I trust that spirit does.

   I wrote the design chapters of this book in the summer of 2001 while on a month-long solo with spirit in nature. In the winter following while feeling particularly inspired one morning, I re-wrote every word in poetry. I had no plans at that time to ever publish the content. I only wished to know for myself what it was that I knew about design. It was in that experiment that I discovered what I knew—what I call the science behind Feng Shui—the energy of spirit radiating within and without our dwelling places.

   I returned to my work as a designer for a few more years, then in January, 2009, I switched the channel on my career: the daily messages from spirit were asking me to organize myself as a writer, and I could no longer justify ignoring their pleas.

   The opposition began immediately, reminding me that I was not trained as a writer, and that no one would ever read my books. But I continued writing anyway, guided by inspiration and a very strong will.

I took my seven-year old firstborn out of the drawer and looked her over. I immediately knew I could not share this majesty — bringing spirit into homes — and then have the people who live there mess it up due to their lack of consciousness for accessing spirit in the rest of their lives; I knew then I had to tell the rest of my spirit story.

I checked myself into a beautiful lodge right on the stream in Zion's National Park. I told the clerk I would need five days, and I told God I was going to add eleven more chapters in that five days — everything that would be needed to round out the perfect life with spirit in a perfectly spirit-filled home. I pleaded for heaven's help, and inspiration began pouring out immediately. I wrote hour after long hour from the moment I arrived, and the last words were added exactly at checkout time on the fifth day. Every subject, every title, and every word came to me from spirit and from deep within my soul's experience; I was merely the scribe.

The next twenty months were spent experiencing life on a deeper level — learning the lessons I would need in order to clarify the messages, as well as in editing and gaining the courage to actually put my life out there in public. Most every day I fought the adversary shouting in my head, telling me I couldn't do it. Everyday I continued to work those long hours, renewing my courage as supportive associates always reminded me I was teaching something very special.

I now know more than ever the mission I have chosen is right on target — all the lessons of my entire life were lined up in perfect order to lead me to comprehend this one great principle: trusting spirit, starting right now!

I give thanks to my housemates — Tiffany, Tara, and my loving husband Don Hansen — who have shared my enthusiasm and supported me in every way.

None of these writings would be more than a dream and a longing in my heart had I not been guided to my good friend, Debi Jones. As we sat on my sofa sharing these truths for hours at a time, the door was literally opened for my writings to begin. I know she was sent from above to be my earthly angel.

I told Father in Heaven I would write but He would have to take care of the rest, and so He did. Marnie Pehrson miraculously came into my life at the perfect moment, and with her wisdom, guidance, and unconditionally loving encouragement, as well as skills as a publisher, this book is now a reality. Also a special thank you to Wayne Harding for his artistic magic in being the hands that create what my eyes envision.

I thank Lisa Preston for teaching me structured organizational skills, and for ways of thinking and writing so that everyone, everywhere can understand. Thank you Melanie, Don, Whitney, and Janice for your very wise editing suggestions too.

I thank my good friend, April Bardsley, for inspiring me to a greater spiritual enlightenment, for your content advice, as well as your love, encouragement, and wisdom.

Thank you to my precious children Melanie, Ryan, Jamie, Jeffrey, Tara, and Tiffany who always believe in me and cheer for me along my way.

Thanks to my team of angels from heaven who continue to inspire me and keep my life intact and on track. So much love from all of you has kept me smiling no matter what.

I thank my Heavenly Father and my Savior for teaching me, for trusting me, for loving me, and for allowing me to understand and share the simplicity of the mysteries of life in this one common denominator — spirit — from which everything makes a whole lot more sense.

Thank you and bless you to everyone who reads this book: may my innocent beliefs in the absolute power of spirit bring clarity to all that you already know, and give you courage to rise above the things of this world, and seek for the things of a better.

Introduction

Spirit is the panacea for all our problems — the Holy Grail — the ultimate prize each of us is seeking to obtain through all our choices, yet unobservant human beings are needlessly suffering — starving themselves of the very essence from which they are made. We were created *first* from spirit, and we must learn to keep that lifeline open to our source, where we find all the magic of life's goodness ready and waiting to serve and bless us with everything our heart desires.

To return to spirit is the ultimate quest of life — to find that elusive pasture of peace, that out of the body shift into a happier, holier experience. There are plenty of impostors willing to offer you the goods, but you want the *real thing*, which is what this book clearly explains. People choose alcohol, drugs, sex, extreme sports, as well as many other more lovely and soulful connections to create an escape from the body into the realm of what they hope to discover as *spirit*. When people choose any of these quick escapes, what they are really seeking is to be able to feel their heart and verify they are indeed alive in a world that offers far too little joy. They also want to know the truth about who and what they are and how to achieve those natural highs bringing enduring climaxes of the heart through every day choices.

To put it simply, I have discovered *spirit* as a state of instant happiness by living in a world of childlike innocence. I see spirit in *everything*. I've been a truth-seeker looking through spiritual eyes my whole life and the longer I live, the more I love my trusting, teachable heart. I know the way to find and feel that sacred state of joy — *spirit* — no matter what is going on around me.

From my earliest days of lying on the grass observing the shapes of clouds in the sky, I have sought to know how and why everything works, especially when it comes to the subject of *spirit*. Driven to understand the nature of God and man's relationship with Him as well as all the workings of heaven and earth, I have lived by faith and hope, but still always wanting more. I wanted proof—which is exactly what I have discovered.

This is a book of grand *ah-ha* moments: mine as I have come to know the depths of the energy I call *spirit*, and yours as you relate to them and realize that they make perfect sense of your life too. Throughout my days of seeking truth from a wide-open heart, I have been abundantly and deeply blessed to know of the *goodness and mysteries of God*. The reality of these concepts has come to me from *spirit*, from my connection to that very misunderstood, mostly unidentified, and rarely used source of all truth, wisdom, and joy—our very own access to all of heaven while here on earth.

When I was very young, I read a parable of the tree of life, which promised abundant joy and inner peace to those who reach the end of the path leading to it. Being forever childlike and trusting, what some may call naïve or gullible, I have always believed most everything I have learned in a very literal way. If there was to be a great reward at the end of the path, I wanted my prize as soon as I could get there, and I would pay whatever price was required to get there *now*.

Maybe this strong desire to make sense of and find power over what I saw as a dysfunctional world has led me to this sacred garden I know as *living in the world of spirit while yet in the body*. Maybe I chose or was chosen to be a seeker of truth from the beginning, and to grasp the rules of the game that others seemed to miss. However I got to be the way I am, I have always been passionately curious as to why some parts of life work while others sadly lead to dead ends, and why are some people happy and successful while others are living in a

2

fog of misery. Gratefully, now I know.

I have always been in love with children and sunshine and freedom. I don't believe I have ever lost the innocence of my child-like heart. I am always ready to *feel* life, always teachable and forgiving and willing to try again, always with faith that my needs will be met, on time and in abundance, which they have — even in the most unexpected ways.

Life to a child in my day moved at the speed of stillness in nature, where I first became intimate with spirit. Choices were easy when we had all the time in the world to get in touch with and follow our feelings. Nowadays, choices are coming at us faster than ever before, faster than our rational, physical bodies can process them, which makes trusting *spirit as your guide* the lifeline we all must have. Choices made from *information only* can leave us facing some un-welcomed results that painfully affect our spirit — the center of our soul — the place where we long for peace and emotional strength to bring us true, satisfying happiness.

Information includes opinions and other people's experiences, but it may not always be what's best for *you*. Only *spirit* can tell you the answers to those questions concerning what is for your highest good in every situation, thus spirit is the best friend you *need* to get well acquainted with, starting right now.

Spirit is the original home of the soul — the place where all truth is accessed and where truth is delivered immediately, *even as fast as the speed of our computer-age technology.* The trick is in getting to spirit *quickly*, in the very moment that we need to make those choices.

The process of communicating easily with spirit — *all truth in the universe* — takes a little bit of practice and a little bit of time; not all day — just a moment of focused, intentional effort when making a choice, looking into a place that most of us rarely go, probably because most of us simply don't know *how!* Yet *joyfully* surviving on this planet in the age of computer-speed-living *requires* you to have *instant access to spirit* — and that is what I teach.

When you think about living by and trusting spirit as your guide in all of these moment to moment decisions, you might think the process is way over your head, that it takes too much effort, and that such practices are only for *gurus*, not someone as important or busy or clueless to these matters as you might be. Maybe you have your own belief system clearly installed, and you don't want to get confused; you won't — my discoveries are consistent with every belief system on the planet. Just ask yourself this question: do you have a little voice telling you that maybe someday you will find the way to learn how to live from spirit? Well, here is your chance — so take it — right now.

Trusting spirit is not complicated, but it is a deeper way of looking at just about everything you are and everything you are experiencing. *Spirit* is the guiding principle and tool and reality that makes everything perfectly divine, and **using *spirit* to create a better world is *the easiest work you will ever do!***

Dissecting spirit is what I *do.* I reduce everything to its common denominator as the *spirit* — the literal elemental energy of it. Using this gift, I can allow pretty much everything about my life to work the way I innately know *from spirit* that it is meant to work, and I can make those choices instantly, just like the computer's search engine tools. From the vantage of this access to spiritual inspiration, I can always know I am on the right path and have peace and joy as my constant companions, and I will teach you to do the same!

Being so connected to spirit, I feed my soul on sunshine, see vibrations in and talk to all of creation, and heal my body while touching the earth. I play the music my own personal ministering angels enjoy hearing while they are attending to my needs, protecting me, and watching over all my things. I

4

recognize spiritual guides and butlers as my personal assistants who assist in every detail of my efforts and tell me which way to go for my highest good in every decision. With an intense connection to spirit, all of my personal possessions emit *life-giving energy* through the materials they are made of and the life I have created with them.

Tuning into spirit to find my peaceful center, I feel the presence of an artist's heart in his work and I get high just walking into a store that sells foods and gifts straight from nature. I recognize the message in and purpose of all apparent illness and how to send it out of my body and yours. I see patterns of vibrations in the repeated experiences of others and guide them to the lessons they need to learn from them, after which all suffering can stop.

I know the healing power of the atonement of Christ and how to literally see darkness changed to light in the whisper of a prayerful heart. All of this comes from an intimate relationship with none other than my dear friend, *spirit*, who is God and all the creations of God, and from the love that *is* God, including you and me.

For many years the events in my life caused me to live in survivor-mode, to feel a need to protect myself from suffering — to hide, to watch, to lock up my heart. Those I loved left me. Over the years, every one and every thing I connected to for love *outside* of myself *left*. I had assumed my identity was from tangibles: other's approval, relationships, physical evidence of myself as a producer — *illusions that will always leave us,* but for so many years and through so much pain I did not understand.

The time came when I was no longer willing to see God through the eyes of others; I had to see Him face to face for myself. No longer willing to live from others perspectives of how my life should look and feel, I had to discover who I was and what was real for me.

There has to come a time for all of us when we no longer

5

look for this loving truthful energy of spirit *outside* of self — in nature or from family, teachers or accolades, though these may be aligned with truth and may guide us in that direction.

The absolute truth is that spirit simply *is* – everywhere – free as the air we breathe — massive and unlimited amounts of it — ready and waiting to be received and to bless us with those natural, joyful highs and perfect solutions to every situation.

This truth is revealed as I honor my own inner knowing — my own personal relationship with God. When I go to spirit — my connection with God — realizing that I too am a *being of spirit* and loving myself unconditionally, there is no need to create artificial protection behind a locked gate to my heart. I am completely safe and free to be myself — however that might look — which is the only way to find happiness.

As you let go of all that you are *not*, you will see and know only who and what you *are* in all your magnificence. And you will have the tools to receive the life that is yours in loving and powerful spirit — always and forever.

On the deepest levels, to succeed in creating a happy life, I must actually *know myself* as this energy of love — *spirit* — no matter where I am and no matter what is going on around me. *Spiritually* empowered living from a clear understanding of our truthful being is the only operating system that works. *This power is the reward for choosing to push past all connections to fear and to be willing to let go of everything you are and everything you possess to get there.* Sound like too high a price? Are you worth it? Is knowing God worth it? Trust me — *you are and it is.*

You can heal your illnesses, your relationships, and your less-than-satisfying producer-minded existence. You can fill your empty wallet and your empty heart with the abundance of a most powerful universe right before your eyes that you never even knew existed. You can feel your heart beating with joy and fill your whole soul with a satisfaction you never knew possible. You can truly learn to *live while you are alive;* indeed,

6

your life is *your own original work of art!*

Trusting Spirit Now is a literary description of how it looks and feels to live from spirit — *the energy of love* — and how that works for me in every possible way. While most teachers tell you *what* you should do to find such personal satisfaction with your life, I will show you *how and why*, in a style that makes sense to everyone, in every culture. In this book you will learn what spirit literally is, how to freely and instantly access it, how joyful and powerful it feels to live from spirit, and how to become intimately connected to it as a physical reality. You will discover that spirit is always here as your constant companion, free for the taking; and once you connect to spirit, you *will* want to take it!

You will learn that you are not alone, that all of heaven is here to help. You will also learn that as you awaken to these truths within yourself, you can bless and heal others. Only when you know the power of spirit for yourself can you know how to successfully use it, giving others permission to do the same.

As I have come to know God more intimately, I wonder if the main difference between Him and His children is this: God *knows* He is love, and knows *how* to use love energy — spirit — to fulfill His purposes.

Being the love — spirit — one hundred percent of the time, never wavering, is perhaps what makes Him God. You can trust in a power that is one hundred percent true to His purpose, *to spirit*. This is perhaps why the elements obeyed to combine and form as the earth at its creation. Trusting love created the universe and keeps it going in divine order, and *trusting spirit will allow our lives to manifest and operate in perfectly divine order too!*

I share these concepts from my lifetime of discerning every experience through the eyes of a very sensitive soul that literally sees and feels spirit filling every particle of life

7

throughout the universe. I explain my theories using many personal and intimate stories. I take you into this vision one element at a time, and by the end, it will all tie together and make perfect sense. From my description of the powers of creation within each of us, to the realization of seeing ourselves as the embodiment of perfectly divine, pure, holy love—**stay with me**. I don't believe you can read this book through without getting the epiphany for yourself.

As you learn to trust spirit as your teacher and guide, everything about your life will finally make sense. All your desires and dreams and relationships will fall into place, and everything you are driven to do and become will make you exquisitely happy and bless the good of the whole human race. Yes, you have a unique and special part to play that is intimately important to the overall plan of the family of God. So begin now living the life you were always meant to live, looking beyond physical appearances of the elements and experiences to recognize the higher purpose and meaning of everything, which always is and always will be defined and clarified as truth when seen from the energy of love in *spirit*.

Chapter 1

The Energy of Creation

*Let me feel the love of the whole world so I can know all the
possibilities for creation,*
A yearning to know all the ways in which life emerges.
Let me be blessed with the gift to see and feel energy
And bring it home to nurture me.
It is truth from Father in Heaven, where all love is created.
It is nurturing from Mother Earth, where all life springs forth,
manifesting in me.
When I am at peace with both worlds, I am one.
I find home — my own sanctuary, new life.
Heaven in one hand, Earth in the other,
Father in Heaven, Mother Earth,
Your Child is born.

My discovery of *all things as energy* began to become very clear to me in my forty-seventh year. It was the summer of 2001, and I decided to spend a month alone in a cabin in the lush, wooded Smoky Mountains near my childhood home in East Tennessee. Somehow I knew it was time to find the answers to my questions, and especially to know how I fit in the big picture called *life on earth*. With nearly half my expected time spent on the planet, and enough pain in my opinion for many lifetimes, I committed to a self-discovery experiment—*a solo with spirit.*

I opened my heart to spirit, to truth, to whatever God, angels, and anyone else who wanted to share might show me. I wanted to know what exactly it was that had guided me through years of what seemed like constant surprises with less than satisfactory results, always leaving me somewhere just out of the reach of my dreams.

Lounging in the morning mists and the sunny afternoons watching baby bears climb wild cherry trees, with spirals of paper and pens in hand and all the time in the world, I poured out the prayers of my desperate soul. I wrote every message, every word, and every thought and feeling that entered my mind and heart—in vivid detail. My plan was to stay there as long as required to analyze these messages, to make sense of the patterns of my experiences, to understand my nature, to heal from an unsuccessful marriage, to define the magical gift of intuition I had successfully used for so many years in designing and mothering, and most of all *to find my connections to and power over it all*.

What was the essence that I felt within me, the untapped

knowledge that guided me in my experiences of wife and mother and interior designer? How did I know since childhood that I wanted to become a wife, mother, and professional designer? I was always planning on having a family of my own; it was a given. I always loved being with and caring for children. I was good at it and it made me happy. I could and often did create interior design perfection in my sleep; it was so natural to me. I always knew I could do it, but how had I innately known *how* from such an early age? The answers to these questions are what I would eventually learn to call my *inner knowing*.

For most of my life I had been able to instantly explain how to rearrange and give a beautiful face-lift to any space, from the humblest home to the grandest hotel. Something inside me intuitively knew how to align everything to fit in such a way that allowed a powerful and comfortable *feeling* to flow through the spaces. It seemed as if somewhere in my inner wisdom I held an imaginary grid that I could place over any space and innately know how to arrange everything accordingly. This knowledge was more than just a system that could be taught in textbooks, even deeper than intuition.

I have always felt the tangible presence of something moving through my mind, my eyes, my heart, and my hands as I approach design. It was as if I had magic in me and I could *dance* with all the elements of the room, placing everything in such detail that it radiated energy in a balance that made me feel quite satisfied. This real and powerful essence has been with me all my life, but was never taught in all those years earning a university degree.

As I have studied since, I realize this complex system of patterns — that imaginary grid — is consistent with the principles of *Feng Shui*, which was a most joyful revelation. But it is more than that — it is *the science behind it* — the science behind everything I am able to do, innately.

12

The Leap of Faith

Embraced in the warmth of those mountains, I decided to write all of my thoughts and impressions, to know for myself what kind of textbook existed in my own mind and beliefs. Until I wrote everything I felt in my heart, I had no idea what was buried there. Spending that month alone in nature with no one but God and my deepest soul to talk to, all the pieces finally came together.

Most everyone I know has the desire to live from spirit, but they just don't quite trust it yet. They want to and believe they should, but the simple *how to* escapes them.

Trusting spirit may seem like a leap into a black hole because there is no way to define something as ethereal as spirit, no way to draw the walls, nothing to hold onto. By following spirit, we agree to live without knowing how things are going to turn out in the end, as would a scientific explanation of reality. We may not know where spirit is leading. We have to trust in an essence that is so intangible, a feeling that we cannot contain, following one bit of perceived inspiration at a time.

But until you take the leap of faith for yourself, you will not have the keys to open the doors to be with spirit! Know that whatever is holding you back is simply a temporary barrier, like the walls that show up when you are exercising and think you just can't do one more, or when you begin anything new and untested.

Spirit is waiting for you on the other side of that wall, and your resistance to the barrier is simply a gaping fear of your own beautiful and most powerful self! Knowing that, you can tell that terrifying fear (which has no power but what you give it) to be gone. Then take the leap! Let go, trust, and find the tangible presence of spirit, love, and God. As mysterious as it seems, soon you will know for yourself: *powerful, unconditionally loving spirit is the one constant you can always trust to be there for you*, to catch you as you leap into any unknown.

To remember, to know, to create from, and to be *love* is the whole purpose of our lives in this world.

To find our peaceful center—our power place—we must remember that we are the energetic reality of spirit—love. *Remembering that we are love, getting in touch with this valuable, precious truth, we can practice what the Children of God were always meant to do, and be co-creators of life with Him.*

Be at peace; God gave all mankind everything they need, even a lifetime, to figure these things out, and no matter what is going on in your life right now, at least your supply of *spirit energy* is still with you, waiting to be recognized, received, and acted upon. You may be out of money, work, food, friends, and direction, *but you will never be without an abundance of spirit!*

When you remember and re-claim this, all the other things that you feel are yours will begin manifesting too, clear as day. Your gifts are not somewhere *out there*, waiting for you to hopelessly work and search your whole lifetime trying to find them. *The perfect life inherently yours is all around you and inside you right now!* Your joyful, loving life is waiting for you to wake up and see with eternal, spiritual eyes, to recognize and receive what has been there within your grasp all the time! **Love is your birthright, not a reward for your work!**

In the summer at my mountain cabin, I finally let go of all the voices of my intellect—the rules, the beliefs. I chose instead to follow only *spirit*—my gut feelings, inner knowing, my personal guidance system, guardian angels, the Holy Spirit. I returned to the innocence of my inner child self and began life all over again, this time making choices from that deeper awareness of spirit—my *inner knowing.* And the beauty of this mode of operation is that spirit—*love energy*—has never guided me in any way that cannot be supported by the natural laws of God! Spirit has taken me on some pretty interesting adventures, but I am always safe and guided to awesome truths in the end.

14

Aligned with Truth

Being with spirit is the only part of my world that always feels right, where all the parts fit. Choices birthed from that relationship make life work—every time. *With the knowledge of how spirit works, I realized a powerful co-creation with God and no longer struggled as a victim of circumstances and other people's choices.*

The truth is that all of the laws of God *begin* with spirit. **Everything is created from spirit first, then manifest into the physical reality.** It always works this way for everybody and everything, whether or not you are conscious of it.

To experience the energy of creation in life, you first have to get very clear about who you are. You must receive the truth that you are a perfectly divine child of God, and let go of everything that tells you otherwise. *Everything.* You have to accept it on faith until you know it with sure knowledge. The knowledge will come as you *act* on your faith. The power to use spirit means you commit to being a part of this team.

Next you have to spend a lot of time with spirit— practicing. Your very essence, nature, and purpose have roots in this energy of God. You have to learn to hear His voice and feel His comfort in your soul, and this takes time. I am not talking about forever, just as long as it takes. As I spent more and more time with spirit, I then created a daily walk from a spiritual awareness of what was innately true and mine—from what spirit had given me—and it always manifested perfection and served me well.

Thoughts and Beliefs Manifest Creation

During these years of spiritual searching, I received many other forms of inspiration, as if being guided to a deeper awareness of the gifts of spirit. In one very special meditation, I was given a vision. I saw a beautiful temple, and in the center of that temple there was a very sacred chamber filled with intense light. The door to that sacred chamber was open so that I could see inside, but I was not permitted to enter. In the center of that room I saw a tree — a glorious white, glowing tree of *light.*

It seemed that there were walls, but they were not solid physical barriers. Rather they were walls of more light, with no end, as if they were there but at the same time, expanded into the whole universe beyond. There was only white light as far as I could see. The tree seemed to be emanating this light, and on its limbs very special berries grew. These berries were small, about the size of cranberries. They too glowed with brilliant white light, which made them seem to radiate exquisite vibrations.

I saw an angel attending by the door and asked why I could not go into that room. I was sitting on a soft bench just outside and patiently waiting.

"What am I waiting for?"

"You must prepare for a while, for in that room, to even think a thought causes that thought to be **created***, to manifest into a physical reality."*

I could sense the truth of such a powerful energy, as its absolutely breathtakingly glorious presence left me in a state of absolute awe.

Until this vision, I had no idea how quickly *spirit* **obeys** *thoughts and beliefs* **to form** *creations.* Just being in the presence of such spiritual energy, even in a vision, I felt most humbled. There was infinite power in those berries of light — so much so that even to think a thought would cause that thought to manifest into a physical reality.

Additionally, I knew that **the more a person is living in spiritual integrity, and the more the person truly believes and feels emotionally connected to the thought,** *the quicker the light responds to create the thought into a physical reality.*

16

It was obvious to me that I must learn to be careful of my thoughts! I was there to learn an important lesson: I must become consciously aware of all the information going through me. Then I must choose to keep only that which was loving — consistent with the energy of the light berry tree. The rest had to go.

As I reflected on that vision, I had the desire to be as pure as that light so that I could be allowed in the creation room with the tree. I knew I would have to learn to obey spiritual promptings more consistently. I wanted to *bridle* all the messages and questions and desires that were shouting inside me. It would take some time to learn to follow spirit quickly, and I committed right then to do so.

If I had been allowed to enter into the *room of light* at that time, my out-of-control thoughts might have created a monster, and I would have been completely helpless to stop it. Chaos would have instantly manifested everywhere! No, before I could be invited into that room, I had to learn to channel all the negative within me to a safe place outside of my being where it could be re-created into *love* by the powers of the all-encompassing Source of love.

I had to learn to know myself as a worthy daughter of God, to understand and trust myself as a being of love in peaceful co-existence with all of life. When I could reach such an enlightened state, I would have some very interesting experiences in that sacred chamber of spiritual creation. But in the meantime, only deeply peaceful, connected, spiritually centered beings were allowed, and I was just fine with the guardian angels in charge there for making that decision.

Actually, the truth is the light berry tree is working whether or not I am prepared. If I am living with chaos in my thoughts and beliefs, then chaos is *manifesting* in my daily experience of life. Fear of that chaotic creation does not stop the process from working.

In the years since this vision I believe I have learned *how to* experience spiritual cleansing and *how to* identify myself with knowledge of my infinitely valuable worth. I have learned my worth and nature as a child of God — that I am created *from* God and of the same elements as God is, though I am but a child. I have the same gifts of love and the same power to create life, which I get to *develop* while in this mortality.

I have developed a personal relationship with God, not through others and what they tell me or how others tell me it works. During my leap of faith, I went to the Source myself — alone. Everything else was no longer trustworthy, and nothing but God himself would do to teach and heal me! In my innocent search for healing, for worth and identity, I learned that I am a part of God, and I always will be! **My umbilical cord to God will never be cut!** Being one with spirit is my reality for a peaceful co-existence and co-creation with all of life. *Trusting spirit, I can do anything.*

Personal Accountability

Once while in a deep spiritual contemplation of these principles of energetic creation, I reflected on some memories from my childhood. I wondered if these creation principles had caused me to play a part in my own demise, which I recalled in those memories. I questioned how certain abusive things had happened to me in my earlier years, and I wondered if those things caused me to feel the need to prove myself *worthy* of love.

In that spiritual exploration of self, I witnessed that I had actually been the one who was the creator of that belief. Yes, bad things did happen to me from others, but I made the choice to believe less of myself because of their bad choices.

Then because of my beliefs, which were created from an innate need for survival, consequences happened. Choices were formed in my own mind. No one else made me choose those beliefs of being personally unworthy of love. Being unworthy of love may never have entered the minds of those who caused such beliefs. It is more likely such abusive actions from others resulted from their own lack of self-worth. I was the one who had put such demands on my own self, forcing myself to work hard to prove I had worth, because of the beliefs formed in those early childhood less-than-love experiences.

In this same meditation, I realized that I was also the innocent child, the frightened spirit who had to constantly meet the demands of myself as the slave-driving master, forcing myself to live every action with the motive that it would make me worthy of love. My child-self was worn out and yet continued to serve that master. I learned some great truths about the power of creation when I realized that both characters in this story were me: the slave and the master.

I felt the ignorance of being such a master, and the wear and tear on my spirit of being the slave. When I realized the harm this duality had caused me, I dissolved into sobs of deep grieving. I knew that I could never redeem myself from such an ignorant, blind way of running my time on earth. I stayed with those feelings of grief for a while, then vowed to never again let anyone or anything treat my sweet innocent heart in that way.

The *slave-self* awakened, realizing the truth of herself as worthy of unconditional love. The *master-self* repented of expecting she would ever again have to do anything that was out of alignment with her spirit. They became one powerful, clear spirit—one loving awake-in-the-light being, ready to always live from the spirit of *love*.

Since that and many similar healing experiences, I only allow that I treat myself kindly and go where I know the circumstances will allow me to choose peacefulness. *I came from love, and love is what I am and where I live.* Anything less than that is abusive to my real self. I must honor my own feelings, and insist on allowing the same to others. (In my defense,

19

as a child this was a mode of survival. If anyone had shown me my intrinsically valuable worth, I believe I would have spontaneously taken it.)

You may wonder if it is really possible to operate from spirit. Yes! Spirit is working, twenty-four seven, whether you are aware of it and operating from a source of self-loving power or letting the power of creation run blindly on its own. But herein lies the greatest gift: *from a place of spiritual awareness, everything wonderful and a part of your highest good can be manifested.*

My spirit wanted to know my worth, and so by taking my questions to God (spirit), I discovered and now share the truth of my worthiness. Such experiences as these and a lifetime of others have shown me how to practice the power of *spiritual creation.*

I am learning to manage my experiences, one day and one question at a time, from the spiritual plateau. In spirit I can see with *eternal* eyes. I am here in this mortality to practice being a creator — a god — not of the whole world, as does our Father, but of *my own* world.

When I use the tools to elevate myself into the spiritual realm, I make all choices from the space of *spirit.* In spirit, I always have satisfying experiences in my relationship with self as well as with others who walk my path with me. I get to *know* the godliness in myself and to *feel* the joy of a most creative, peaceful and loving life — the state of being I believe is true *charity.*

Creation comes from spiritual feelings — *knowings,* as I call them. No matter what is your *experience* right now, know that *you* have created it. It's the physical manifestation of the feelings you have generated. It's what you have attracted that is the perfect fit to the messages you have been *broadcasting* from your own spirit-energy channel, like I did with worthiness issues as a child. *Whether or not you want to believe this, it is working, just the same.*

Identifying Feelings as Energy Forms

To show how this works, let's experiment with positive and negative energy vibes, and I will explain how to delete the negatives and live only with positives.

First, consider anything negative that is going on in your life right now—something unpleasant. It may be some issue that you are facing which you would like to resolve into a more peaceful experience. For me, that might be a pain in my back. Now ask yourself to put a voice to that issue or thing. What is it saying to you? What is its message?

Next, ask how does this make me feel? What does it bring up? It could be called stress, fear, or frustration. Maybe the voice is saying, *I am angry*, or *I am terrified*, or in my case, lower back pain may be saying I feel unsupported. If this issue were true, what would that mean? Face the worst possibility!

Continue dissecting the issue and its possible meanings as if it were a form of matter—the words and shapes and colors that would make it a real entity. Make a list. Paint a picture of it and take a good long look into its meanings and messages. What is it trying to tell you? Mine may be saying I need others to believe me, or to believe *in* me, that my own love for myself from a partnership from God is not enough. (Rubbish!)

Know that whatever that message is for you, it isn't true either, because it is *negative* and that is not love, or truth. But you have to discover the message anyway to then reverse it. I can admit I was allowing the opinions of others to influence my feelings for self. When I recognize this and exchange the false belief for a truth, I feel the love flowing back into my body, healing my back pain in the process. Turning false beliefs around allows you to see any issue as the gift of love it is. Back pain, in my case, is here to remind me that I am truly loved and whole just as I am, no matter what anyone else says or doesn't say or do.

21

If the message I feel is *I need to be loved from others*, I further decide what *needing to be loved* would look like. I imagine it as a foreign object—outside of myself. Perhaps I would paint it as a red vibration with a pulsating shape going on, with lines like arms reaching out to grab me (I have a vivid imagination.) I then imagine the container such an entity could be packaged in, such as a leather pouch in which it dissolves into the darkness.

As I use my imagination to create a separate identity for this negative feeling, I see *needing to be loved by others* as an identifiable form of energy, outside of the being known as *me*, and with absolutely nothing to do with me. For some reason which I am about to discover, I am simply the *target* of that foreign energy.

Next I may run that identifiable energy form—*needing to be loved by others*—past my own heart, my center of truth, my connection with God. In that space, what do things look and feel like? In every case, as my heart radiates the truth that I am a perfect and loving child of God, I immediately know the truth. I find that the negative energy is *not* truth at all. Now that I realize it is outside of me, and that it is not the truth about me, the *sting* of that false belief dissipates immediately.

As you do this exercise with your own discomforts, you will quickly return to your own loving center. While remaining in this sacred space, pray to recognize a thought or belief from your past experience that created the current experience of *needing to be loved by others* (or whatever your issue made you feel like.)

As I reflected on my past, I could easily see that my experiences of being controlled by others created my way of thinking that I needed their approval in order to feel safe, to feel what I thought was love. In all cases, **thoughts or beliefs from the past create what shows up in the present!**

Something about the past caused you and me to resist the truth that we could be worthy of being totally and completely loved just as we are. At the point of realization of such, we simply make a choice to *forgive* all that caused the false belief, and then to accept the truth about ourselves: we are beings of pure love. Once received, this new and truer belief acts to attract more of love into our experience.

Recognizing and applying these truths creates a whole new and powerfully peaceful way of handling life. Shifting our perspective to what we want, what is *truth*, what is *loving*, those better experiences will manifest now.

How much time do you spend focusing on the negatives, what I call the *not-love energy*? For every moment you spend in that kind of energy, you are *multiplying* the opportunities for those kinds of experiences to show up in your life, because that's what is broadcasting from your spirit channel.

Take all *not-love experiences* to the deeper levels of compassion. Learn what they are here to teach you. Accept the gifts of these apparently negative realities. Forgive all involved in the complex thought patterns around the beliefs.

Seeing and believing the *love reality* allows more of real love into your experience. The principle of spiritual creation is true, and using the patterns explained here to manage in a better way does actually work in everyday life with everyday people!

Recognizing Love Energy

To understand this principle further, notice something that brings you joy — a person, a thing, a situation, a place. I will call this a *loving* feeling. For me, it may be sitting in a warm secluded place in nature or watching a baby's peaceful face. Just think of your own connection to joy: what brings you loving feelings.

Now go deeper by asking to discover the roots of your connection to that source of love. Spend some time in gratitude for whatever brought you to this feeling. For me it was the safety I found in nature and the wish to be loved and protected always as babies are. Notice your own feelings and connections to gratitude for love. Hold the feelings of your connection to love, allowing that energy of gratitude to swell in your heart. Give it a few minutes to magnify and you will feel the spirit of joyfulness, *which is a signal that God's spirit is in you.*

This form of love energy—spirit—seems so real it's tangible. Consider it to be real and tangible, as if an angel appeared with a glowing star in her hands and dropped it into your heart. You can feel it, see it, hear it, taste it, or maybe even breathe it—all physically. You can *celebrate its reality,* which causes you to *receive* this energy. This is the point when it actually enters your heart, allowing it to raise your own body's vibrations to a higher spiritual realm.

I identify this feeling as a literal essence, like a chemical reaction in the body. It becomes a part of you, and then it becomes the same as you—the en*light*ened version of you. You are becoming more like God, with more of His love—spirit—shining in your soul. As you repeat this experience over and over, you become even more refined in spirit, feeling more peaceful each time you accept the gifts of the presence of *spirit.*

Again, this joyful, creative, healing energy I call spirit comes *from* God and His creations, but **it is all around you and in you all the time,** *not* **far away and** *not* **difficult to access.** I want you to believe this and to know this! This is the creative power of the energy of truth, or love. When you receive love as a part of you—what you are made of—it will glow in your face and lead your heart to make choices that will bring more of this light into your life, raising you higher and higher, brighter and brighter with each new experience.

How It Works

An example of the application of these truths comes from a client of mine. She felt like her control over a business venture was being stripped away by her partner, a guy who wanted more of a share in the management of everything she was used to doing quite capably all on her own. Her experience with her partner was that she could not trust him. What was she to do—submit with a smile, leaving hurt and fear to invade her peace?

It's just negative energy, I told her. It's not the truth of who you are. **Truth leaves you feeling good, not gripped in fear!**

What shall we call this energy? I asked her to describe it. My client began to explain how she felt: *Fear of loss of control. Need to take care of everything myself. Lack of trust for men. Men can't handle things as well as women.*

We named it by these phrases, so that it became an identity of its own. This sort of labeling takes the feeling *out of the body* and puts it into a category of energy outside of the person. Since all energy has a power with creative life force—a purpose—it will show up over and over again until you identify and deal with it, so you may as well do it now!

As this lady named the energy, she could look at it outside of herself. *It* was not really *her* of course. As I asked her to recall other times in her past when she felt this way, she began to admit that her father behaved just like her partner. I then asked, *what did your mother do when your father was irresponsible?* My client replied that her mother did nothing!

How did that affect my client? It made her very frustrated, and in some place in the mind of my client's childhood, she made a judgment that men cannot be trusted, and that she was the only one who could handle things right in a partnership with a man.

In the very moment of making that limited perspective judgment, she took on the *belief* that it was a universal law: *all men are like my dad.* From that moment to this, that is the exact experience she has allowed to be in her path. Once she discovered the false belief, she used techniques of forgiveness and love to change those old patterns, which then allowed the outcome of her experiences to dramatically change for the better.

This is a very common example showing that we are not usually consciously aware of what we are creating or attracting into our lives. A subconscious belief actually directs our experience, while conscious awareness — authenticity — allows us to make choices to insure things go better in the future.

Reverse this concept to look at all the good things in your life, and go back in your history to see if you did not always deeply believe that these good things you now have should and would come to you.

Energetic Cords

Imagine that your spirit creates cords from you to things and people you interact with. These *ethereal cords* allow information to flow back and forth between the two forces connected by the cord. Imagine that with every interaction in which you participate, this open line of communication is suddenly created, allowing you to give and receive thoughts. This cord allows you to connect to people, to understand the messages of any experience — what she said, what he wants, what I think happened, what I *think* about what happened.

All of that information is *judgment* of that situation, according to how you experienced it. You go through life creating a cord with every judgment you make, which somehow allows you to access the information as you *assume* you might need it. These cords give you some kind of ownership of what happened, as if to allow you to remain the *manager* of it all.

Imagine a complex web of spiritual cords that represent the path of your life on earth. All of the designs within that web are possibly what you think of as *your life*, and what you assume is the *real you*. It feels so real, so tangible. It's your *story*. But *none* of this is the real you! It is simply your *experience of you*, here to teach you, to allow you to learn.

We humans are the highest form of creation, and with our creation came intricate systems of biology in our being: skin, muscles, organs, parts that work together to allow us to live here. But that is not *who* or *what* we really are. Those intricate biological systems are the *physical representation* of our most incredible *spiritual origins*.

We are innately magnificent *spiritual* beings, born to have a *physical* experience, born to create love in physical expressions. Why would this be so important that whole worlds of life forms have been created to set the stage for this grand experience? *And why do we so easily forget that which we cannot see, feel, touch, taste or otherwise control with our physical senses?*

Birthing Creation from Inner Knowing

The power of our spiritual presence increases with each exercise of *faith* into these spiritual dimensions. We begin innocently and with little evidence, but with time and practice, we can learn to know and manage *spirit*, even though we are essentially physically blind to the spiritual reality. Managing spirit is not about seeing or touching a physical element, for spirit is not about seeing and touching. It is the deeper sense — *the sixth sense*, the *inner knowings*, the energy *behind* the tangible elements — that which you cannot hold in your hands, but only know somewhere deep within your heart.

The highest form of creation I have ever experienced was to mother a child. From my own creative organs and from a spirit much more powerful than any conscious awareness, human life reproduced through my body and soul six times. It was magnificent and joyful in every way. It was natural to my feminine spirit and in divine order with my body and my inner knowing.

While I knew little of birthing in the beginning, with my desire to live in tune with all that is natural, I learned easily and timely from wise teachers ways to carry and deliver in pure light and joy with little if any pain. I learned that pain comes from fear, so by releasing fear I learned to experience childbirth as a glorious channel of spiritual creation in partnership with heaven.

Each baby came with a unique and individual spirit and life purpose. All came as love and expanded my aura of love with theirs. To have these children was the truthful manifestation of a lifelong *inner knowing*.

Our inner longings are real—signals of our higher purpose. **The joyful blessing of the energy of creation is to see your dreams come true.** I traveled the path from a time years before when a magnificent spiritual experience caused me to know I had six children who wanted me to be their mother. Through those next many years until they were all born, I held onto a deep belief that all those babies were coming to this earth through my body. And I learned some of life's greatest lessons as I overcame all the obstacles that were in the way of seeing this dream to fruition.

I am still in awe that my *spiritual belief* became a *physical reality*. That is the essence of a life well lived: to follow your path making choices according to the spiritual inspirations you know in your heart. *To always honor your heart brings joy and rejoicing in the beauty of your creations.*

In every man and woman there is reproductive life force—seeds that exist—his sperm and her eggs. Women are born with these seeds already within us, while men's

28

are produced throughout life. These reproductive seeds are perhaps symbolic of the seeds of all our creations, ready and waiting to incarnate.

In a woman, her physical *seeds* drop through the fallopian tubes and into the womb—her sacred space. There they are nurtured in embryo, to blossom and grow and to eventually be birthed. Each new creation is then nurtured in life, to blossom and grow to be all that she came here to be.

Men and women you see are **creators**—*life givers*—full of *life force*. This process of creation from spirit is not just about birthing babies. It is about birthing from the inner knowing soul: ideas that won't leave you alone, inventions, connections, art forms, gardens, poems, smiles, a hand to hold, a perfect day, a happy relationship.

Creation energy has as many different possibilities as all the longings in the lives of all the many men and women themselves. **Real joy in creativity is doing and being what we came here to do and be!**

What will I create with my precious seeds? What is within me now that I call my inner knowing? These seeds—these *knowings*—are my creations and are waiting to be birthed. My seeds, which were given to me even before I incarnated, have always existed in the form of *spirit*—*love* energy—with express purposes—an essential part of the plan of my life. Since these seeds already exist as a living form of energy, they must be a part of the original creations of Father in Heaven, just like each part of every element of our mortal lives.

Again, our very existence here on earth with these desires (seeds) testifies that we have a divine purpose to fulfill. These seeds are *made* from love. **There is nothing but love in a seed within me, and experiencing the energy of creation is the** *procreation* **of that love!**

I consider the repercussions of the love that is radiating out from my own creative self. My being—the magnificent

29

creation that brings forth life—continues to reproduce through my creations, over and over and over. Each of my creations goes on to multiply in all that it represents—the ripple effect. So with my creations, I multiply the good I exponentially create many times over with each new life form (idea). Oh my, **that is enough love to light up the whole world, just from me!** Our purpose and being in life is truly divine!

Creating from Truth and the Ripple Effect

I noticed a powerful example of this concept with my oldest child. As my first-born, being around me during those child-birthing years, she was impressed with *my* personal beliefs. Watching me managing my health in the most natural ways possible through five more pregnancies and deliveries, she learned my belief system that childbirth is the most natural thing in the world for a woman to do. My beliefs sprang from an innate desire to live at one with the earth and all it offers. Some portion of her beliefs came from the examples I showed in day-to-day living.

It surprised me yet validated the personal-creation principles when my daughter followed this belief system and delivered her own four babies naturally. She enjoyed feeling every moment of the overwhelming joy such natural child birthing allows. She did not buy into the common belief that with birthing comes suffering. Even though she had witnessed others suffering through childbirth, such as in movies and school videos, she had an *over-riding and more truthful belief*, well set in her mind from a lifetime of personal example. Her trust in what she had witnessed spiritually created her deep belief, which then guided the choices and outcome of her own experience.

I have given consistent effort over the years to teach my children the power of their beliefs and intentions. I have taught through my example that everything about the body is natural and normal, even beautiful. But until I witnessed this amazing result with my daughter's natural child birthing, it was hard to know if the lessons of example really work, and of course it shows up in so many beautiful ways in all of my children's lives.

Being a parent is a most sacred responsibility. What we believe is what we teach. What we teach becomes our children's experience. We should be very clear that what we believe is truth. The energy of creation continues like the ripple effect as we pass our beliefs to our children and successive generations.

To take this symbolism personally and literally, contemplate your own hearts deepest desires. What do you naturally and simply love? Discovering or realizing such may take a little time, but in all its magnificence, this is what you are here to create! *You must believe this can happen.* Hold onto that belief, treasure it, and live in faith knowing it will manifest. Never doubt it and never give up! From time to time, ask what you could be doing to manifest those desires, while remaining absolutely sure that your creation will be delivered. RELAX

While you wait, your creation gets bigger and bigger, kept warm, nurtured, safe, and alive. This new *baby* is literally energetically growing from your personal faith (your womb) where it will stay until it is ready to be born—perfect in every way. This new life can do anything you want it to do. This new child has your DNA! **Whatever you believe, want, and know from spirit is vibrating life right now in your creative seed, and that is exactly what you will birth.**

I believe I am here on earth to have this creative experience of acknowledging the feelings of my heart. I must hold onto them through thick and thin until they are realities. **I get to continue creating over and over throughout my lifetime, the sum of which is *my contribution to humanity* and my chance to experience being a creator in this physical realm.**

Honoring Your Own Seeds of Creation

So what am I creating with my seeds? As I notice a *desire* for something from within, I know my seed is ready. Anticipation is building within me, and vast amounts of extra energy are available. The longing is powerful, though it may not be instantly recognized for what it is. It may feel like a desire to go somewhere, to be with someone, to eat something, or if we are not paying attention and ignore the impression, it may feel like discontentment, or even frustration. Pay attention to the signals of the energy of spirit!

We can allow our lives to run our creative forces blindly from the subconscious, and they will whether or not we like the results; or we can become aware of our feelings, thoughts, and beliefs, and generate their procreation accordingly. *As a man thinketh, so is he.*

Whenever I hear someone speak of the law of attraction, they are always suggesting that if you believe this law, you can make anything in the world happen that you want to have happen—no parameters given, and it is usually about creating worldly acquisitions and power.

Well, that is a little deceptive, and I will explain why. It is true that you can attract whatever you believe strongly enough, but know that those things, while very enticing to the mind, *may not continue to make you happy.*

Happiness comes from being aligned with spirit, living in the abundance of spirit, and there is no *spirit* in material possessions as such. These much-publicized laws of creation through belief have the basic principles right, but please remember to use them *to create what it is you came here to create*, for that is the only way you will ever be *satisfied* with your creations!

When you create from spirit, you will feel joy in the alignment with such truth. You are here to manifest a certain spiritually designed life, and that is why the laws exist – to guide you to that alignment!

You have the seeds for your ultimate life already within you! When you become aware through epiphany and introspection of these natural traits, gifts, and paths, and then if you consciously and emotionally accept and put your beliefs and energies in those areas, you will succeed magnificently, even spontaneously in their manifestation. Spirit is so much easier to manage than anything in the physical realm. **Spirit obeys truth immediately.** Discover the truth, and all you have to do is hold true to the beliefs and they respond. (Could these truths be the same basic principles God used when he spoke the word from spirit and created the world?)

Conscious creation begins when my creative energy (desire) shows up. I relax into my spirit and ask, *what am I to do with this energy, naturally mine?* What do I *know* I get to use my energy for? What are my desires, my needs, my wants, and my gifts?

questions

I know the answers by noticing what I am passionate about, even a little bit. What is my platform? What do I believe in? What do I want to change in the world? What is not right that I want to make right? I must start my conscious creations by noticing these inner longings and knowings about myself, honoring these parts that are very real within me, allowing them to surface and then to manifest.

For example, when I feel an unidentified energy occurring in my body, I relax into meditation and ask, *what do I want right now?* What difference do I want to make in myself, in my family, in the world? I notice the answer to that question in this very moment from whatever comes immediately to mind — the first and deepest feeling or thought. *Not as concept - but as presence.*

Right now for me that would be something like this: *I would like to never again see a child crying because of an adult yelling at them or hitting them or in any way damaging their innocence or causing their self-worth to be lessened.* This is my greatest wish. I

33

know this is true because of how intense my reactions are when I see abuse in any form.

I also know because of how I feel when I see the opposite, when an adult lovingly cares for a child and how precious that is to watch. Uncle Remus is a hero. Watching him in *Song of the South*, I fell in love with the kindness and understanding this historically inspired figure represents. He always seemed to know what to do and say from a heart full of compassion, and it always served to heal the child with love. I honor such actions with the deepest gratitude.

Next I ask, what gifts do I possess that can express this passion? I could teach at the women's crisis center, whisper the truth of their loving natures while rocking the newborns at the hospital, and guide others who come to me for spiritual meditations to healing. I have organized and serve in a mentoring program for motherless children in my community. All of these will bring me joy, as does writing, because all of these ideas come from spirit.

With my writing, I teach the worth of the human spirit, the innocence of children *of all ages*, and of our connections to higher powers where creative energy can be directed for the greater good. I am intuitively connected to the child in every body, even *grown up* bodies. I see the innocence in each and abhor any abuse of that innocence, including between adults. I innately desire to protect, empower and allow the perfection of each of God's children. I innately desire to protect and empower the innocent beliefs, inner longings and knowings of the child within myself! This is the main purpose for writing my books and for most of the work I do: to *celebrate* the innocence and perfection of each child of God.

The greater vision of conscious creation for anyone is that we make choices of how we experience meaning in our lives from an *inner spiritual awareness*, and not just from the material world of *physical* desires, appetites, and attachments, which do not endure the test of time. *We must consciously create on the highest possible level based on a connection of our spirit with God.*

Inner Passions

Another example of getting in touch with my *inner knowing* is recognizing my passion for clean water. I crave pure water, which carries the energies of Mother Earth to hydrate everyone and everything on and about the earth. The sensitivity of water as an element of spirit is very clear to me. And since water is mostly what our bodies are made of, we are very much and literally spiritually connected to water (our sister,) whether or not we are consciously aware of this connection. Water and me, being mostly made of water, radiate the same energy! Water is a life form that radiates purity, as does the real self that we all are. I know I am spiritually connected to water, as are most people.

I fell in love with water as a child playing by the creeks, as a teen at the lake, and by the rivers and waterfalls in the Great Smoky Mountains by which I lived. I learned to love the fragrance of water, the feel of it on my body, and especially the sound of water falling. Whenever I am near clear and pristine waters, I want to immerse myself in them, so powerful is my connection. Water brings healing energy to me instantly and powerfully, body and soul.

I have read that *the voice of God is like the sound of many waters.* When I was under Niagara Falls for the first time, I knew what that verse meant. The majesty of the sounds of all that water falling drowns out all other sounds. I was right in front of someone on the boat at the base of the falls, talking loudly, and yet could hear nothing of my own voice. At the same time, the sound of those falling waters completely calmed my whole being. I was giddy happy just standing in that space,

35

and it got better by the minute.

This is exactly what happens when I connect to God in meditation—I hear *only that voice*, and I feel perfectly *calm all over*. So God's spirit is in the water, and water radiates the same kind of energy as God? That makes sense, as I know that we are all made from the same basic elements of love: God, me, and all of the waters are one in spirit. *Of course I would feel connected to water.* While I know God radiates so much more of it than I do or water does, it is the same *element – spirit*. **As God's creation, water is full of spirit, and that is why it makes me feel so good.**

I want to see and enjoy pure clean water everywhere, from the springs to the waters that fall into the oceans and all the lakes and seas on the planet. My sensitive body knew immediately when chlorine and other chemicals started to be added to the public water system, and I immediately chose to buy spring water to drink. Pure waters are our gift and our blessing, and we must honor them.

How do I use this passionate energy for pure water when it swells up within me? I spend time by waters allowing the energy emitted to spiritually and emotionally heal me. I go into meditations regularly to visualize the waters of this earth being healed, purified, cared for, enlightened, and I see the Earth's waters sparkling and clear, blessing all of life in return.

Sending blessings to the waters in this way is a matter of simply visualizing them as they run all through and across the earth, like the blood veins running through our bodies. I then send love and gratitude towards these life forms. I feel it even as if these flowing streams and lakes and oceans are my own body, as I send my loving desires and beliefs that the water be loved and healed.

I see the water in its perfection as originally created, just as I see people in their perfection, looking past the baggage. I see the waters of the earth as they truly are in their natural state, without the muck that has adulterated them over the years. With my clear intention of water *being what it is*, with loving gratitude—and not what man has made it—I am literally *allowing* the waters to return to their true and natural state of being, and also to be protected to remain such forever.

The spiritual power of my passionate feelings is shared with the waters, giving them a spiritual *shield* of sorts, which repels, even blocks, those who would contaminate their purity. I also ask for angels to attend to this process with me, multiplying the effects of my desires exponentially. I invite all others with the same passion to join me in such meditations.

As I said, spirit is more powerful than any physical reality, and more good can be accomplished spiritually through these *prayers and blessings* than all our political efforts combined. In fact, we can affect governmental choices with our deep spiritual thoughts.

What we focus on, we get more of. Tell a child that he is good, wonderful, and perfect, that he brings you joy, (and *feel* that joy as you say it), and he will want to please you and do everything in his power to prove you right. If we focus on the offenders and the pollution, we will generate more of the same yuck. Focus on pure water (showing faith) and allow it to become pure. If there is anything more that I should do to help, spirit will tell me, and I will obey. But for now, meditations and blessings are helping, allowing miracles to manifest.

Intention, desire, and inner passion are the most powerful, spontaneous form of creative energy. As I have said, our souls have these longings already within, waiting to be expressed as part of what we came here to do--just notice that. Water represents cleansing, oneness with God, and the purity of the human spirit. My connection to water is a strength and example as I share this perspective of the divinity of each human soul with others.

When a creation is a part of my heart and soul, and I am

wanting it; *it* already exists—present tense. *It* is alive. It always has been. It was created long ago, maybe even before I came here, when I spiritually planned this experience I call my life. So by honoring it, *it* will manifest. There is not much I can do to stop it. The energy of it will build within me until it awakens my attention. *It* is mine, and I have to act on it.

This is the point of origination for everything I am here to create—all from inner knowing and spiritual confirmation. **I came to give what is within me to give, and to do so is the only way I will ever be truly happy.**

I may ask, who am I to think I can make a difference? There are so many more capable than me who can do it better. But that is not the point; I AM, and by being such, I matter! My feelings must be manifest! I get to express what is within *me* that wants to be born, and not from what others are creating. It isn't so much about how others judge my contribution, or if I change the whole world. **It's about me, being myself!**

Joy only comes when I am experiencing my own creative path, accepting what I know is mine to claim and be. **Honoring the voices within, birthing creations, those creations will birth me!**

Alignment of Energies

The opposite is also true. When I am not feeling joyful, when I am feeling confused or depressed, I know I am not doing what I was born to do at this time—not honoring my purpose. The discontent is a *signal* that I need to reconnect with my inner knowing and begin again doing what I get to do, by noticing what makes me happy again when I do it.

If I know I have a book to write and then avoid writing, doing everything *but* writing, I will feel depressed. When I notice I'm feeling depressed, I recognize this as an energy form of being out of alignment with my truth, my knowing. I ask what is my purpose right now? *Is it to write?* I make a simple choice to return to writing, and I immediately feel great again. The energy of being discontented disappears, replaced instead with *life-generating energy* that lifts my soul. **There is never any feeling of depression when I am living true to myself, in love with my life.**

To further explain, compare this to the issue of PMS: midway through a woman's cycle her egg (seed of creation) drops into the uterus, ready for fertilization by sperm (your own passionate desires). This is powerful abundant life-generating energy! If it has to just sit there and wait for you to recognize the message of what you are to be doing, it will make you feel and act quite crazy. **Spirit speaking within you is something you should not ignore!**

People who honor their inner knowing exude energy in their work. They love what they do because they have chosen to do what they love, by being in touch with their *inner knowing.* For example, you can tell which schoolteachers love what they do, and which are just going to their jobs. The teachers who love their profession represent the most incredible gifts to our children during their formative school years. They give from the heart and make learning easy and exciting, because it comes from *love* – love of self by honoring inner knowing. (I don't think they are doing it for the money!)

Among other things, I am passionate about designing. When I work in design, I have a blast. I am in my element— my *knowing* place. I feel terrific. I make myself happy and I make my clients happy because I am designing *from spirit.* I am a lucky one. When I act in *alignment with my knowing.* I am blessed, and I can bless others!

I choose to live in joy, so I must be in touch with *who I am, what I came here to do,* and *get on with creating such a life.* **This is the purpose of life: to be an expression of God— pure love— the highest in me— I am.**

I can be on our the other each moment. It I am not feeling aligned I can rechoose now.

Discovering Alignment with Truth

One day many years ago I went for a walk, following a path from my neighborhood into some vacant land that ran up into the mountains near my home in the Western United States. I had seen this land for several years, but on that particular day I decided to keep walking through it to see where it led. Exploring there also soothed the emotions of my troubled heart, which was overwhelmed with confusion at the time.

As I walked and walked through woods and by some ponds, seeing some wild animals and climbing through some webs of tangled vines and shrubs, eventually I came upon a clearing — a sacred little cove of land that I did not previously know existed. It was a secret garden, and simply discovering it filled my spiritually starving soul with awe.

As I stood there, I felt like it was mine — the exact manifestation of something my soul had longed for since leaving the luxurious woods of my beloved home in East Tennessee years before. I didn't covet the place; I just instantly felt *at one* with it, as if I recognized its familiarity to my soul. I drank in the love I felt just being alone in such a woods.

I noticed the deer lazily sunning in the grasses, barely making an effort to notice me, as if I had been there all along. I noticed the orientation of the sun and the view and how perfectly aligned they were with where I stood. I noticed the little spring flowing through the fields and into a natural pond a hundred yards beyond. I fell in love with those woods — the wildlife, the fields and waters.

I breathed in the joy of discovering such a place of perfectly natural creation existing right over the hill from my suburban neighborhood. I expressed a simple prayer of gratitude that such a place could be found so close to where I then lived, like the woods I enjoyed as a child and wished someday to live in again. I took all of this in, feeling my heart full of joy for my secret find, then I turned and walked home, spiritually satisfied.

So what exactly happened there from a perspective of spirit? That day on that spot of land was the moment when a spark of truth within me aligned with the *abundance of all truth and love in the universe*. Add to that spark the fact that I asked, and God agreed with my request. My prayer was in alignment with my path, which aligned with my inner knowing. That spark of truth aligned with the abundance of heaven, which caused *a creation to manifest* in that moment, and all doors began to open for its fulfillment.

This energetic alignment with truth allowed me to buy the land, develop it in perfect balance with its natural energetic flow, then design and build my own home there. The beautiful front porch is now exactly where I stood on the day I discovered my secret garden and ignited the first spark of this creation. A few years after my spiritual connection occurred, that sacred and secret garden became one of the prettiest places to live in that region.

Always in Perfect Timing

Spiritual creations happen at the right time — God's time. I did not take a walk that day looking for a new place to live. I had not been trained in land development. While I had quite a bit of experience in design and sub-contracting and was fully capable of making my creation a reality from a professional standpoint, it did not begin from such a plan. **It began from a spiritual ah-ha, and that was all that was required of me.** The rest came all on its own, as if a delivery man pulled up and brought it to me, completely ready and packaged with a bow. Everything I needed to make this creation happen lined up to offer its services. I must have had a lot of passion in that first moment of creation, and it must have been totally aligned with my purpose!

I honor the goddess of creation within me. I know and love my own perfection in the eyes of God. My creations come from deep within. My babies — my creations — depend on me to live in spiritual integrity, honoring the truth that is. *I will manifest what I know about life, love, and light, by being the truth about life, love, and light,* and I invite all others to do the same.

Thoughts for Processing *The Energy of Creation*:

- As you analyze what it is you are *experiencing,* you can get in touch with what is going on in your subconscious belief system.
- You can have power over your experience by correcting your thoughts and beliefs. We are the creators of our own life experience!
- God gave us the gift to make personal choices so that we can learn to act from spiritual inspiration. Do you honor your feelings?
- Feelings of the heart come from the spirit. Get to know your heart. Don't argue with the spirit speaking to you through feelings of the heart!
- Exercising the power of choice allows us to grow spiritually. When you feel like you are hitting a wall yet spirit is speaking, push through the wall!
- 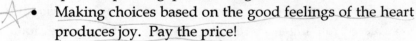 Making choices based on the good feelings of the heart produces joy. Pay the price!
- Choice is an integral part of our life on this planet. Our power to create was planned from the beginning. This is the name of the game. Pay attention to your choices!
- As a parent, it is even more important that we get these concepts figured out so that we teach only truth to our children, to allow their experience to be blessed. Don't ignore your promptings!

- How do we get in touch with our creator-self and not let it run wild on its own? Start by noticing what you are experiencing right now. Is it perfectly aligned with spirit or would you like to change the direction of your experience?
- To change your life you must recognize and release old and false patterns of beliefs.
- You must establish beliefs that match the spirit of love deep within your heart—your *inner knowing*.
- Check your instruments. Is your guidance in line with known principles of truth?
- Get in touch with what you know about yourself. What are your natural gifts? What can you do without even knowing how you do it?
- Practice being consistent and true to the natural gifts you possess. Honor yourself. How much time do you spend everyday doing what you love? What feeds your soul?
- What are you passionate about changing in the world?
- Feast on the feelings of joy that come when you allow your real self to manifest. This is your goal—to stay in this joy. **The presence of joy is the signal that you are there!**

Chapter 2

The Energy of Nature

The masculine and the feminine,
The square and the circle,
The walls and the movement within the walls,
Like mountain and river.
Heaven comes to earth,
And the power of creation lies within this energy.

A few years ago, I spent a week in what is known locally as *the womb of Mother Earth* — Havasupai — a remote Indian village deep in the heart of the Grand Canyon. It had rained just before my arrival, and the brilliant turquoise spring waters that usually flow through this magical land were gushing down the canyon, taking with them a lot of earth. But the muddiness of the water that day did not keep me from indulging in my personal spiritual ritual of skinny-dipping. Finding myself alone, I buried myself in the orange-colored river and allowed the cleansing of earth and water to take me to the center of my being, wherever and however that might manifest in the moment.

Water has always provided a powerful connection to my peaceful center, and on that day, I felt starved for healing. As the earth and river flowed over me, all that was not the *real me* seemed to wash away, taking the burdens of my life downstream. I felt completely original, perfectly clean — the feelings as real as if I had actually just been birthed.

Somehow energetically I had the feeling of starting over as a brand new baby, in the arms of my mother for the very first time. Those feelings were as real as the water and mountains all around me, and I stayed in that space, honoring them, allowing the amazing joy of being an adult and yet feeling brand new to linger for a very long time.

I followed this ritual with spontaneous dancing on the sandy shore, celebrating in gratitude the goodness of being alive and feeling new again. My spirit yearned for a return to God, to know myself as the beauty of the loving peace that is — the real me.

Again from a sense of inner knowing, I continued by lying on a boulder-sized red rock in the sunshine, offering myself to heaven that it might give me whatever was mine to receive. Feelings of peace swelled through my whole being, and in that moment, I realized my own baptism: physically from the earth and water, then spiritually as I reconnected to the Source of Light. It was a holy retreat.

While others in the area were connecting to spirit through shamans and mind-altering drugs, I found my private sanctuary and floated freely into the space of spiritual enlightenment through my soul's connections with my beloved Mother Earth. Being one with the spirit of the earth in nature has always healed my soul and felt like home.

Finding Home in Nature

This sensitivity to the spirit in nature became obvious very early in my life. For as long as I can remember, I have spent my free time retreating to the woods. As a child, I found peaceful safety from an unpredictable world as I wandered about in nature, exploring for hours every day. With my siblings I built all kinds of huts: little girl cabins on the ground and spy lookouts in the trees.

I found joy in discovering the textures, patterns, colors, and smells of the earth, as well as all the amazing life spreading through the woods: violets, mosses and vines. I loved the way that nature freely spread itself over anything in its way, like the honeysuckle that covered the fences and the tiny wild strawberries blooming through the grass. It all seemed so relaxed, without any boundaries — the ultimate example of living in the moment, with complete freedom to *just be*.

As I felt the spirit of life radiating throughout, I enjoyed talking to trees and vines as if they were my personal playmates. I created images of make-believe to bring to life even the giant trunks of fallen trees whose long limbs gave endless summer days of bouncing *pony rides.*

My small corner of Tennessee countryside became the whole world to my delighted, creative, and intuitive mind. A hidden pond where cows watered and giant turtles swam graced this magical land. I imagined councils of wise men and fairies coming there to meet, meditate, and relax, and I believed they were as joyfully alive and real as I felt in creating them.

When it rained, the ditches filled with water and ran into the woods, creating a fresh stream flowing through my private sanctuary and into the secluded pond. That little stream was all mine. I was the only one who knew of its existence, which made it all the more sacred. I ran along side of it, splashed my feet in it, and floated anything I could find down its current: sticks, leaves, and majestic make-believe boats carrying grand and important characters into my fantasy world.

The blackberries grew wild and random through the fields and woods. Eating Mother's pies made from my own berry pickings brought me a sense of the delicious abundance of nature, which returns taking me back to my childhood every time I connect with their smells or tastes.

I have spent much of my life rejoicing in nature. Anywhere the earth appears untouched since creation, I feel at home. I go alone in the woods to reconnect with God's energy: the rocks and waterfalls, the bears and honeybees, the wild plants, the stone foundations left from some pioneer dwelling. I wonder how long the trees have been standing there, and what they must have seen in all that time. I sense what that would have been like to have been there observing for myself.

Time stands still in nature. Its energy is vibrating, alive and radiant, with just as many variations as people, all different, unique. Exquisite in beauty, everything in nature has its own crown of majesty, purpose, glory and joyous abundance. Nature was created by God, and it speaks His love.

Gratitude Energy in Nature

There is vibrant life in even the tiniest part of nature, freely giving the energy of love, peace, and generosity, which I connect to, becoming one with any part of these elements. In this process, I know my own reality, my own perfection. There is magic in all these creations, and I know in my deepest self that it was all created for me and for all of humanity—a gift freely given to bless, to heal, to delight, to entertain, to allow us to become as nature—*full in the expression of creation, peace, satisfaction, even joy.* To be inspired by any part of nature—to take it within myself and re-unite with spirit—is to become one with God's abundant offerings, in gratitude.

It's a gift to receive the energy of gratitude while being in nature. All that is love and all that makes me happy is forever vibrating there, and such energy makes my heart very thankful. The very essence of this thankful energy—gratitude—is to shift into the state where one can then *receive* God's gifts. Think about it: Gratitude usually comes when a gift has *already* been given, when a thankful heart responds to the gift by sending out *gratitude energy.* If the energy of gratitude actually allows gifts to magnetically come to you, *feeling gratitude in nature is a powerful tool.*

This is why it is so essential to spend time in nature, where I can immediately feel this gratitude energy and resonate my desires on the spirit channel that will announce those desires to like particles throughout the universe. These likenesses are then attracted to me, providing from God's abundance all that I desire to create. So being in nature is the catalyst that actually allows my gifts to be manifest through God's grace. Becoming one with nature allows me to powerfully connect with the energy of gratitude—the essence of love, light, abundance, peace, safety, joy, even perfection. Nature brings gratitude, which opens me to love. In love, I am one with spirit—the

50

ultimate enlightenment—turning on all the lights of my soul.

Union of Man and Nature

In every spot on earth there is majestic beauty, as if God had quite the party creating it, expressing love in every possible way. I imagine how much passion He must have enjoyed as creation exploded in exquisite variations in life forms, temperatures, colors; life force put into the tiniest seed that became a whole forest. Drops of water that over time carved dramatic canyons. There is nothing but passion in the making of this world, with all its life forms, including the crowning jewel of God's creation: mankind.

Man was created as an integral part of the earth's purpose. Body and spirit join to allow the soul's unique growth in experiencing mortal life. Spirit lives in all the earth, especially in man, who has been given dominion over this world of energy.

With birth comes the spiritual cord to God, a connection which some call our *conscience*. Connection to this *central system of inner knowing* comes from a place of *stillness*. It is the process of becoming aware of all truth that is within me now—always has been, always will be. It is all truth from God and from the many expressions of God in the universe. When I am in tune with the vibrations of the earth, in balance and harmony, I find my *knowing* place—the center of my soul—the point from which I create my own life's expressions.

It is not complicated: when I melt into nature, I hear its voice and watch its dance, then my answers are always right in front of me or in my heart. All of nature is alive and speaking to me, connecting to my place of inner knowing, from *spirit.*

In the mountains, nature is as God made it, vibrating according to divine laws. In that energy, all truth is alive and radiant with a higher frequency than anywhere else—a place where I connect to truth and know my path. Mountains, seashores, forests, and deserts—all intense natural energy fields, abundant with spirit that can raise man's limited view of life to God's omniscience.

What am I creating? What am I doing with this majesty freely offered me? I enjoy being still in the quiet radiance of nature. I dissolve myself into oneness with all of it, as if to allow my body to melt into the earth's beauty. There is only peace and balance and perfection in nature. Messages in nature are complete truth. Listening and allowing them to serve me—as if they are healing me—makes everything right with the world. *Who am I to think I know anything until I too become one with God in nature's peace and balance and perfection?*

Could it be possible that the elements of creativity and truth found in nature are the same essence as God's love that fills our very souls and the entire universe? This *love energy* is what we must become familiar with. **As we become connected to this energy of love—spirit—we can channel it to bless life in every way.**

How do we connect to and become acquainted with love energy in nature? From my experience with spirit (love energy), I notice feeling *whole and divinely connected* when I am by a flowing creek breathing the fresh clean herbal air. As I watch the water washing over rocks, in and out of roots of trees, I feel that same freedom and purity in myself, bringing loving energy—spirit. A river is always moving, with no stops, going on and on, around and over and through, *just like spirit!*

The constant movement of water suggests to my spirit to do the same, moving through everything in my way, allowing my inner knowings to continually flow toward their creation. As I allow myself to freely flow, I become one with the energy of love. A river is doing what it came here to do. The rocks and sticks and trees and air are doing what they came to do—in magnificence. **If I likewise allow myself to flow with the spirit, being and loving who I am created to be, I may**

experience such peace in my every moment of life.

The constant movement of ocean waters is also symbolic. With every wave energy comes towards me as powerful as the whole earth, bringing me fresh energy and new life. As each wave returns to the sea, I imagine it takes with it all my sorrows, my confusions, and my emptiness.

Ocean waves cleanse me with their tangible rhythms — the *heartbeat of the earth*. Being near the ocean waves or the mountain rivers, Mother Earth's rhythms re-train the patterns of my own body's rhythms, returning me to my natural, peaceful, truthful flow.

The Nurturing Spirit of Nature

Mother Earth is the beautiful feminine energy of nature — an energy that is as real as anything of spirit. As I study the energy of the earth and find my connections, I notice everything about Mother is alive and constantly moving: gravity, water, the changing seasons, growth in animals and plants, shifting of mountains, life and death. It's the energy of reproducing itself over and over and over. Nature is giving and giving, infinitely nurturing.

A reflection in a mirror is simply the movement of seeing back and forth: here a body, there an image, in and out, over and over, like the ocean tides and migrating birds and spawning fish, always celebrating and bringing forth new life, the very life that nourishes our souls.

Perhaps what we seek in dancing and love-making and swimming and even breathing is a return to our natural existence of oneness with truth, being a part of the rising and falling, the washing away and birthing anew of all living things, like Mother Earth from which we are a part — reproducing and birthing and creating, infinitely multiplying life through each form of life — such beautiful, nurturing

energy!

Things of Mother's nature give energy and attract energy like a magnet. I am attracted to nature and happiest there because I am a part of earth and creation and perfection — one with all. This is the spirit of Mother Earth — always nurturing, and perhaps another reason I connect — being full of the nurturing, motherly-energy myself.

There is something glorious about being in the quiet majesty of an untouched piece of living world, nothing changed by man; all is as it was created. I am safe in the womb of creation. My soul can create in such a peaceful existence. It speaks to me and raises my own vibrations *because it is alive with truth*, because it was *created from love* and because it holds *no judgment of right and wrong*.

All of nature is trusting and satisfied. All runs its own course and has a part to play, a part of a whole. Science calls it the food chain; I call it *manifesting one's destiny*. It is *being*. *Does any of nature not do and be what it was created to do and be?* Water flows and seeps into the ground, always wet. Mountains stand, hard and firm. Animals feed and reproduce. Trees blossom. Flowers send beautiful fragrances. Bees buzz. It's a bit refreshing — something I can count on — so real, something that never changes, but will remain forever, *always giving!*

I imagine the strong connections to *spirit* that our ancestors must have felt. They lived so close to nature, spending much of their days outside working in the fields with the plants and animals and many times living in the wilderness. Nature provided for their lives in every way: their food, clothing, housing, fuel, and even transportation in the form of some animals and on foot, allowing them the experience of connecting to the spirit of the earth on a constant basis. By spending their lives in nature, their own energetic vibrations were raised consistently, creating connections to spirit which would naturally guide them to live more peacefully and more honest and true, with each other and to their own inner knowing.

I have often wondered what literally happens to lift my energy when I am in nature. I feel better almost immediately upon entering such spaces. Nature is God's magnificent creation, radiating His loving essence — *spirit*. Somehow, being in that energy of spirit, the light shining through the elements of nature seems to absorb my own darkness.

Could it be possible that *spirit*, also known as *light*, literally changes all my darkness to light, healing me instantly? Being in the presence of creation is like being in the presence of God. It is the energy of love — spirit — that is felt there, and *spirit* heals me, body and soul. It's no wonder I love to live deep in nature's bosom, returning to my natural state of existence, being one with God in His garden — my first and happiest home.

Thoughts for Processing *The Energy of Nature:*

- What evidence do you have that you are connected to the spiritual energy and strength of Mother Earth? How much time do you typically spend in nature?
- What of nature have you collected, loved, and placed in your home that feeds your soul?
- Signs of life are also evidenced in your own heart. What feelings of being alive are you noticing right now from within?
- What messages does your heart speak when you stop and listen?
- Where do you go to feel most connected to the spirit? Have you created your own sanctuary in nature?
- When did you last spend time there?
- How much time in nature does your soul deserve, and when can you schedule it?
- If you had to let go of something less important in

order to keep the balance, what would you be willing to postpone or eliminate from your schedule?

- Within the next week, schedule a time and a place where you can stay in your own sacred garden long enough to allow your heart's vibrations to rise to a level of pure joy!
- When in your sanctuary, ask spirit to explain answers to all the questions weighing on your heart.
- Take a journal and write all the impressions you get, especially the answers to your questions.
- Commit to staying in nature as long as it takes to get a satisfying answer to your most pressing concerns.
- When in your sacred garden, focus on one thing you know from within that you get to create. Send gratitude energy into that creation and allow that energy to carry your creation to the universe on the wings of love. Keep those grateful heart vibes radiating until you absolutely know that your desire has been energetically created.
- Look around in your sacred space and notice a gift from nature—something alive that speaks to you, reminding you of your experience there. Ask your heart if it would be okay to take it home with you as a reminder—a trigger allowing you to return to this gratitude energy anytime you see it.
- Allow the energy of love in nature to heal you in its presence. Stay as long as it takes to feel perfectly whole and happy as the light radiating in nature literally absorbs your *not-love-energy*.

Chapter 3

The Energy of Elemental Design

I sit on a rock in the midst of a flowing mountain creek
with my face upstream.
I am alone and yet amidst ten million years of creation,
The same essence as my own body.
These are my friends.
This earth is my body.
I am born from Mother Earth,
And she will always nurture and calm my soul.

Now we come to the part that inspired the creation of this book in the first place. In this chapter, I take more artistic license as I write from my spirit about interior design. During my solo month in the lush Appalachian nature, I celebrated self-expression as I put into words what I have always known in my soul about design, and the feelings created a dance of excitement within me as I began to even *think* of orchestrating the placement of artistic things in rooms.

But this is an **art** that is less about *things* and more about the *balancing of energy with those things*, within the walls of any space. My **brushes** are my connection with and gratitude for the *earth's elements*. My **medium** is *spirit*, and my **canvas** is the home and family. For the next several pages as I describe the *energy* of design, I invite you to open your inner child heart and enjoy my soulful **paintings**, becoming more aware of how to empower your own spaces with higher energy in the process!

To understand this energy, begin by picturing this scene: While hiking in the forest far from civilization, I come upon a rugged log cabin. Like a character in a fairy tale story, I approach to see if people might be living there and if I am safe to enter. I am looking for *signs of life*. I touch the fireplace. Are the coals hot? How long has it been since someone tended the fire? I notice the smells. Has anyone been cooking recently? Is the air warm? Is the fragrance fresh? I notice the linens at the windows, made from earth's fibers, woven by man's loving hands, drawn open, letting in light. I notice the handmade, carved pieces of furniture, the leather drawn over the bench. I sense the man who might have made such pieces. Not only do I sense the man, I sense the land, the plants, the woods, the animals, the life that expresses from each. I sense the presence of *life happening here*.

Looking further, I see the pot on the stove as the handiwork of creation, the elements of beauty taken from the earth. Are there life forms nearby to be eaten, fresh plucked from the ground, alive and growing moments ago, ready to be recycled into the human life force? These are all *signs of life*. The rocks on the fireplace were put there by an action of a human hand. I can see the movement from the fields outside, the sweat and brawn of the muscles that carried them here, the design of the rocks showing lines of earth from years of shifting and forcing and merging. All *signs of life – life happened here*.

The design of the wood on the mantel and the bowls on the table, cut from the hands of man—some man who actually perceived a pattern and created this shape from a slice of a tree. Such a tree. Such a man. Such a heart. Such giving. Such caring. Such expression of being. All *signs of life*.

The heat that formed the metal pans, the fire that made the heat, the years of heat in the earth that turned a piece of earth into layers of iron, the touch of the hands that melted the ore and tended the fire and shaped the pans, all with love and his own creation, his own life happening all the while. A man's life, real life, was offered, and millions of years of earth existing and moving and living, all to give a piece of iron for a pot. That is life. Who do I think I am? I am nothing without this pot!

But not just the pot! It's the earth's work and offerings and the hands of men that worked the earth and the connection I have to the life existence of all of these, all of which express as signs of life! When I connect to the signs of life in earth's energy and in all truth, I am ready to create a home that radiates a powerful expression of my own humanity.

So that's how it works: get in touch with the earth, its elements and our human connections to these elements, the patterns and purposes and quality of all of this energy, and how to align it within spaces. To explain these concepts further, I have divided this chapter into four sections: *getting* the elemental earth energy, *holding* the energy, *circulating* the energy, and *balancing* the energy.

Getting the Elemental Earth Energy into Your Home

The first step is to find the energy outside of the home and then open the home up to receive it. Nature is my constant—the tangible source of energy—vibrating all around me, ready and waiting to bless me. To bless me, we first have to connect, to become one, so that I can feel her light.

I go to nature and find her, just as we have done for the past chapter getting in touch with these energies. But I want more: I want her to live with me so that I can continue to enjoy the high vibrations of spirit in nature while in my home. I make choices to design from nature, to bring beautifully created elements of the earth into the home.

I imagine Mother Earth is spirit, like a beautiful angel, the spiritual presence of all that is good and loving. Energy of Mother Earth is obviously abundant in the out of doors, but I want to allow her to move into my home. To do this, I have to create gardens around the house with open channels to flow so that the plants, art pieces, and walkways allow this Queen Mother (nature energy) to know she is honored, welcomed, and invited to come and abide with me. This kind of designing will invite good energy into the home and into its resident's lives, so I make the outside as strong a statement of artistic creation as possible. The doorways must be inviting and clear of anything but beauty. I place fountains and planters, seating and art sculptures, signs of life, carvings—places for spirit to be attracted, to attach, and to stay.

The energy of Mother Earth is the breath of life I channel into my homes. I invite spirit in and allow it to move around my spaces, nurturing and blessing me. I imagine Mother Earth's energy completely filling every space of my room and how perfectly divine that feels. She is like the air, the wind—a real spirit—my own Mother Earth, and a grand, natural setting is waiting. So all pieces must be made from earth. Originals from the hands of the artist are best.

I am speaking of products made from of all kinds of earth's elements. I notice this design style in many foreign countries: fresh, simple and natural—styles we Americans are always trying to copy. These divinely natural looks don't come from large manufacturers stamping out counterfeit designs being sold on the cheap by the boatloads. These natural looks are always a collection of originals, usually made by local artists.

I love traveling and seeing how close to the earth people choose to live, and where even meager possessions look and feel so nicely balanced in the home. They use stone and large beams for construction. They have natural gardens and live close to nature, even in urban settings. Colors and styles and textures from the elements of nature surrounding are used freely. We can copy the Europeans and many other cultures that are so close to perfection in design because they draw everything from the elements of Mother Earth, and from those whose hands carve their hearts in it.

Holding the Energy in the Spaces

Next, I place things of elemental materials in the home so they can attract this elemental energy and *keep Mother Nature's energy alive and vibrating in the home.* The point is to channel this energy into the home, keeping as much as possible circulating within. The energy of Mother Earth brings balance to the energy of the occupants, holding them in perfect harmony.

Personally, I *need* this creative energy in my life—a generous amount of it—in order to feel all is right in my world. Being in tune with Mother Earth energy provides the joyful balance, the point where my creative processes begin. It grounds me, centers me, calms me. This connection empowers me intuitive: I know the amount of energy needed to enter my spaces as well as ways for that balancing Mother Earth energy to stay, constantly feeding my soul. My arrangement of *all things natural* must be peaceful, calming, balanced, as well as *creatively original*, and it will be when the creation process begins from spirit.

Energy is like a magnet, attracted to itself. If I invite earth energy into my home, it has to find a likeness of itself in order to attach, admire, hang out, and stay. Energetically speaking, it has to find an energy that is equal to or greater than itself. Remember that *itself* is Mother Earth, a connection to our Source of all light, truth, radiance, perfection, and joyful energy. Can you imagine the intensity of the vibrations we are talking about here?

Mother radiates the most wonderful, playful, happy energy ever created. She flits around like the birds. She flows with grace like the rivers. She reaches heavenward like the trees. She smells divine like the flowers. She serves humanity like Mothers everywhere who care for and love their babies. This is my *life source*, and I want to get as much of it as possible to feed my soul and to raise the vibrations of loving energy for myself, my family and my friends who share these spaces!

Not only do I want to get as much of this powerful energy in my spaces and my life as I can, I want to *keep it* for as long as I can. I want her to live with me always, bringing life force to raise my vibrations forever!

So how do I do this? I make Mother Earth happy! I give her the magnets. This is how it works: Mother Earth energy moves around and around, growing bigger as she attaches to things of her own energy form. With each gift of life she discovers in the spaces, she becomes happier, breathing more and more life force into this circle.

I show her what she recognizes as familiar to her: rocks and water and plants and fabrics made of fibers grown from the earth, pieces of wood and glass and metal, forms of earth matter, art forms filled with passion from someone's heart— someone in touch with Mother. I show her my collections with pride. I display what I love: the collections I bring home from the abundance of life.

I place these things as her *path to travel*. As she passes by each, she becomes a part of each, blessing each and then enjoying the next, around and around, as she proudly observes my abundance of creation, connecting with objects made of *earth elements, with positive attachments*, which is real love and pure truth.

I see every element as a life form, a natural essence, an actual power regenerating itself by its contact with other forms of earth's energy. This is the elemental energy that feeds me:

- Rock—floors and stone fireplaces, geodes, whole & crushed like gemstones
- Wood—on floors, natural finishes, beams, carvings
- Glass—windows, tables, bowls, crystals hanging, fused glass art
- Plants—all growing things, fresh flowers everywhere
- Water—fountains, pools, bubbling and still
- Metal, leather, fur, linen, wool
- Any moving thing—clocks and wind-up toys, fire, candles, logs burning
- Earth—pottery, moss
- Carved animals, statues—birds, turtles, dolphins, bears, frogs
- Personal symbols of life—my life—totems, memories of places and times past
- Gifts with endearing attachments that flow with loving

energy — always continuing to give life.

For each room, I am drawn to a focal point. All lines energetically flow to and from the focal point. This item feeds my soul with the greatest amount of energy. It has the highest amount of vibrations in the room and the most visual weight and strength. It has the greatest amount of earth's natural products, vibrating as the most majestic, most glorious, most obvious piece. All the pieces in this energetic circular space must balance with and lead to this focal point, so all is placed in such a way that allows this energy to flow in the peaceful rhythm of the circle, always in continuum.

Circulating the Earth Energy in the Spaces

The third step is to place things in such a way that *the energy moves between the things with just enough space to allow the vibrations to radiate comfortably.* For inspiration, I always refer to nature, where even vast open spaces are dissected with *things.* In the wild, these things are trees, rivers, rock formations, many small plants and animals, all interesting diversions to the vastness of the whole, yet all living together in perfect harmony as a whole.

Each of these parts is a creation of its own, but all of them are connected in sharing — like one grand extended family. As these elements work together in nature, I see a network of circulating energy on any part of this earth. Each part has a role to play, always in perfect balance with the others.

This is how I design any space: many different elements take the eye into and out of spaces, bringing interest and surprise everywhere. And like the great outdoors, every element brings fascination and healing energy within this perfect rhythm, balance, and movement of energy, to bless and heal the souls who call it home.

Observing the perfection of nature, I notice that nothing is made in straight lines. While trees *appear* to grow straight, on closer observation, the shapes of trunks and branches move in and out with many curves as they make their way upward and outward. Stems seem to be straight lines, but they always hold a curved feminine angle. The only thing in nature that may be a straight line is the surface of still water, and even that creates circles of ripples when something moves or lands on it. Everything of Mother Earth is feminine, has curves, and moves in circular motions, as is the earth itself.

I learned about the energy of the circle by years of observing my connection with the earth's energy. Imagine the earth as a globe—a circular body—with an energy form around it holding that circle or globe together. It's like a body of itself with many moving parts but still one aura: one big energy field, majestic and powerful and complete.

Within that aura are many complex and moving, reproducing parts. All of these parts are moving within the whole, and that is what makes it so incredible: this whole of an energetic space is like a *skin* keeping all the energy within its orbit, so that it doesn't scatter all over the universe.

The same idea defines the atmosphere around the earth, holding us in orbit so that we don't fly off into outer space. We remain in rhythms and patterns, with enough energy vibrating within to provide for the whole. A circle is holding all the vibrations moving within it. It feels like the corral around horses, allowing them movement but creating a safe haven where they will live and learn and be cared for and feel safe, and where we can enjoy watching and learn to work together.

The energy of the circle is everywhere. I live in the West now, with majestic mountains in every view, creating areas between them called valleys. These valleys are surrounded with high mountains as boundaries, holding the earth's powerful energy in a stable corral (skin). The energy

66

in such a valley surrounded by powerful elements of nature is exquisite. I notice even sweeter energy when such valleys are fed by streams of water flowing into the space, even rivers, and forming lakes, bringing much more powerful energy towards the area, which again is held in place by the guardian, skin, atmosphere, mountains.

There is a vortex of energy feeding the souls who live or stay in such a valley. The energy is powerfully alive, moving around and within that circle, giving life as it revisits each spot over and over and over, going around and around in its orbit, never ending.

Spirit feeds on spirit. When there is the living energy of nature in such a valley, with grasses and trees and animals, rocks and formations, waters and clean air, the energy of spirit feeds off its likenesses in nature and continues its dance, building and growing, moving and flowing, around and around, forever blessing the land with its dance.

I notice this energy when I am by a lake, when I see the whole body of water before me. The sounds and moods of that body of water are most feminine and graceful. The morning mists are elegant, and the evening sunsets across the water are radiant. The face of such a refreshing, nurturing presence smiles the grace of God to me.

I feel the energy held in such a whole (circle) by the shores of earth's solid, constant, hard, fixed elements of rock and soil. The space for this feminine dance is kept sacred by the boundaries of this masculine presence, creating a whole — a circle — allowing this lady of the lake to do what she came here to do. I sense this masculine presence is greatly blessed for his guard duties as he watches these lovely expressions of grand feminine beauty!

Our bodies are made of the same elements as every part of the earth. We are all of the same chemical components and feed off of each other's energy (love). Since each part of anything has the same energy as the whole, imagine that this circular rotation of energy in nature is even symbolized in the auras or energy fields of our human bodies!

There are halos of energy rotating the vibrating life force in and around the earth, holding it in orbit. And there are halos of energy rotating in every possible direction in our bodies, holding each cell and each organ in unified working relationship with each other cell and organ, and yet as one body.

As much as I need the energy of the river, which is constantly moving my old energy downstream, taking with it all that needs to go and bringing me fresh new life from upstream, this is not the rhythm of my home. The river may be my *retreat for renewal*, but I don't live in such a constant mode of cleansing.

Everyday life is meant to be more still, like the pond, as a constant. Constant energy — stillness — is found as the energy of earth's vibrations are held in a circle. So energy moving within a circle is what I imagine as I place things in a room.

To go deeper with this concept, think of indigenous peoples, who by nature are spiritually connected to the reality of the divine parentage of Mother Earth and Father Sky. These communities built homes of igloos and teepees, allowing the natural flow of energy in a circle. Their homes, perfectly designed in circular shapes of earth's elements — open on the bottom to earth and on the top to sky — allow the energy of nature in perfect harmony with daily living.

In the modern world, notice that perfectly circular spaces are not economically feasible or intrinsically beautiful without some contrasting straight lines, and the opposite must also be weighted and balanced. Many of today's structures are built with all straight lines — something to do with being chic and modern. But notice which of such spaces feel good, and which feel uninviting and cold.

To make these straight lines work, circles of living energy in radiating design must be used to soften and allow the peaceful flow required to nurture life. Circular shapes from the gardens to the porches to the hallways must reach out to take you into its flow, *as if the welcoming arms of Mother herself are open to receiving her guests.*

Circles of Energy in Design

Since the *circle* is the perfect way for the energy to move and channel, I translate these principles into the designing of our homes. I create circles of energy moving within the walls of the usually square spaces of the buildings we live in. This energy I am working with is the energy moving in a circle within even an *imaginary* square.

The circle is the feminine movement, filled with life-giving nurturing energy, while the square is the masculine strength—the guardian angel—keeping the space sacred and safe. **The combination of the square and the circle within it represent perfect balance in creation: there is movement, and there is something to contain that movement, which creates balance.** *Recognizing this circular dance is the most important observation I have learned which guides me in harmonious creation and balance of design.*

Like a volcano, a tidal wave, an earthquake, an avalanche—*energy gathers strength as it moves.* As the energy moves somewhere laterally through the room, a *flow* of energy is created. I think of it similar to a *connect-the-dots* picture: Energy enters like a beam of light, like an angelic spirit. As it moves in a window or doorway or generates from a natural element within, it must find the next place to go to, and the next and the next and so on, in order to remain there alive and active, creating the wonderful tangible feel-good vibrations that bless our souls.

I know when there is too much space between my things—too much for the energy to easily float from one thing to the next. There can be no question how spirit is to arrive at each point. *Something must send or guide her there*. This is how I know where to place things—assessing the energy of these things, how much energy is radiating from each, and making sure there is a measure sufficient to fill the spaces.

Everything in creation gives off energy equal to its elements and power of expression. Each piece deserves an area of space around it to honor it properly. To know how much space is required, I pause and concentrate on feeling the energy of any given item. I ask, ponder, notice, measure, weigh it, and sense it as if it were a physical presence. I visualize its aura. How far out does its energy reach?

I can usually assess the size of the energetic field by the effect a piece has on me. I honor each by allowing space around it to radiate energy and to breathe freely. I never push any item up into walls and corners or too close to other pieces, where its energy field—aura—would be diminished or blocked from flowing with ease.

Sometimes a piece should snuggle up with another piece, like my potted vines growing down and flowing over a stone fountain: a shared energy, friendship, partnership, each blending and serving the other's need for balance. At other times, as with a statue or a tree, I feel its purpose suggests that it stand alone, *basking in its own glory*, with enough space around it to honor its powerful and unique message.

When I visualize the actual size of any piece *and* its aura, I consider that whole energetic area as the *true size* of the piece. Then I have a better visual on its proper placement. When something is placed on a ledge or shelf close to the edge, without consideration for its *energetic* size, it may appear to be falling off. When the energetic size and purpose is considered and it is placed accordingly, it will always look perfectly in place.

Finally and most importantly, **the total energetic size**

of an item should connect close enough to another item's total energetic size to allow the energy to flow from one to the other, (*but never so close that they bump into each other's space unless invited!*) Mother Nature needs the pieces to be placed in such an order that guides her travel through the room. Placement of items in such a way allows the necessary flow of the natural healing vibrations of these creations from earth's elements.

As you look around your room right now, notice what your eye is drawn to. That is the actual path on which energy will flow. If there is a big red pot sitting all alone up on a ledge, you better believe the eye is going to shoot right up there, and that may not be a nice path for spirit to travel unless it allows a gentle, circular motion around the area.

Practice doing this exercise: Pretend you are the spirit, the energetic guest. What are you drawn to? What is calling for your attention as you go from wall to wall, corner to corner, all through the room? This is the line that should be circular — not perfectly round, just *flowing* around, like a random pond-shape. The placement of some of these things may need to be adjusted to define the flow.

Now, what keeps your attention? What has good energy? Are the things you see in balance with each other and with the whole? Go to work now and correct the energy as you balance the placement of all your furnishings!

Balancing the Energy Between the Spaces

The fourth consideration is to arrange the use of the spaces so that the balance between them is consistent with the flow of energy that you intend to create. There may be several circles generating energy within a given space. If a room is rectangular, I find the area in that rectangle in which I choose to create the circle or multiple circles. I create these by the areas of purpose: sitting areas, eating areas, study areas, play areas, areas for

71

meditation, beauty, gardens, display. There will be different energetic spiritual *visitors* for each of these different spaces— the guardian angels of such expressions of life in each of these different ways.

As I label all the spaces of the home, I see that I have focal points for each activity, and then I balance them with each other, creating a flow that always makes sense energetically and brings the most peace. As the owner, I get to decide what energy is in each space according to my needs and lifestyle. Quiet places are kept still, while busy places are open to more people and conversation. One home will have spaces for several different *feelings,* different energies: several different guardians of the different energies I decide to create, all from an inner knowing of who I am and what I must have in my spaces.

How do I live? What are the different feelings I enjoy experiencing? I make a little sketch of my home, drawing the circles of energy, describing and labeling them, rating them, balancing them. Does each energy-area complement, enhance, and respect the others?

As I ponder my drawing, I ask questions to myself, to the spirit of truth within myself. Which energy fits best next to which other energy? Ponder and consider all impressions. I remain open and willing to look at things differently. Everything is a possibility when you are studying energies. What are all my options? I wait until the answers come. I write them down. I move things around. I consider any and all options. Spending quality time with spirit in this way, I always find the perfect answers.

I want my bedroom to have restful, even romantic energy, so I am not going to put my office in there or anywhere nearby. I am not going to put my playroom or my laundry next to my bedroom either, if I can help it—or anything else that is noisy. If possible, I want to open the bedroom to the gardens to allow nature in day and night, and to allow me to slip into nature in privacy if I choose.

In the kitchen I want access to the outdoors, allowing in the energy of the vegetable and herb gardens as well as outdoor cooking and entertaining. I want my kitchen to have open areas where the family may socialize while cooking and eating. These areas should be open to easy access to the front and back entrances to allow visitors to be included easily, because serving others in the kitchen is very important to me.

Offices have the energy of organization and business (and busy-ness), so being near the kitchen would be a good choice. Doors to close them for privacy would be useful.

Bathrooms suggest personal cleansing which requires privacy, so remove them from public areas. Make them as remote as possible while still offering realistic access. Their focus is minimal; so do not give them the honor of being the center of the home or anywhere near those areas. Keep the center for the most important and most celebrated lifestyle activities.

For me, children want a little privacy from the parents. Near but not so near is a good idea: near enough to find me in the night when they are small, but far enough to give them independence and to give me quiet retreat.

To create a private sanctuary in the home is my dream: a place to go and meditate and pray, knowing I will not be disturbed. Being close to gardens for such a space would be exceptionally perfect.

Considering the nature of my lifestyle and the feelings I want to create in any given space, I arrange my rooms and furnishings accordingly. I am creating a flow that is natural to the ways I live my life. Creation is a maze, but a joyful one. I just keep moving circles and uses of room around on the drawing board, balancing the flow of all my needs, knowing there is always perfection in the end. I create the circles of lovely flowing earth energy, honoring the elements and the creations

73

of those who made them. Thus I create a *living* home, alive with the energy of love — *spirit*.

Thoughts for Processing *The Energy of Elemental Design*:

- Spend an hour and study the items in your surroundings, inside and out, looking for products or pieces that are made from the natural elements of the earth.
- Notice the energy of these items and your reactions to that energy as you focus.
- Open as many draperies, shutters, windows, and doors as possible, allowing maximum light energy to flow into your spaces.
- Clean windows and clear outside spaces, allowing earth energy to channel a pathway to your doors and windows, and then into your home. Create a *spirit-filled* entrance.
- Observe what is the first piece that Mother Earth energy will attach to as she enters, and determine if that piece is a grand enough welcome for your very special guest.
- Notice the lines created from the movement of energy between your things. Which way does your eye travel around your room? Does the line make a comfortable, random circular shape? Can you move a few things to allow the lines to flow through the area gathering energy into the circle?
- Is there an obvious focal point, and are you happy with it and its placement?
- Are your high-energy pieces placed in a balanced arrangement in your room?
- Is there enough natural energy moving in the room?
- Is there an obvious black hole where something needs to be placed to create better flow of energy around the space? Can you get a feeling for what that item's shape

might be, as well as materials and design?

- Is there something in your possession that can be moved into this space to assist in the balancing of higher energy? Bring in pieces from other areas, using as needed in your main areas.
- Spend a few moments with some of your favorite pieces, focusing on the aura of each. Can you get a feeling for the energetic size of those pieces? Does it surprise you to know these pieces are vibrating such an aura of energy? Enjoy being aware of this energy of spirit in your things, feasting on the good vibes!
- Be sure to place your pieces with consideration for the space required to honor the total energetic size of each.
- What design styles have always made you smile? What country's designs are you attracted to, including colors and patterns? What do you suppose caused you to have such connections in the first place? What of such pleasures have you actually used in your home?
- Are there any areas of your home that make you feel confused or like things just aren't working for you? In what spaces do you feel the energy needs to be corrected?
- Draw a sketch of your home and write the *energy* of each space, (not the *name* of the room). Are the energies compatible? Do they flow nicely? How can spaces be traded in order to create a better balance?
- On a scale of one to ten, how busy is your daily life? Does your décor give you the perfect balance to bring either the rest or the excitement needed when at home? Are your things as powerful as you are? Is there a balancing energy with your things?
- Does everyone who lives in your home have his own sacred space? Are all the artistic needs being met?

Chapter 4
The Energy of Art

Ask each piece to tell you its story: does it delight you?
Does it match the power in your deepest soul?
Honor the treasures, but toss the rest.
Does it come from the earth? Can I feel it?
Do I live with the giver and the gift? The giver is my gift
if I love her.
Does it make me feel beautiful to share my space, my energy, my
sacred home? Does it match my power and beauty and make me feel
like reaching higher still?
I buy some blessings for my soul, but only the ones
that belong to me:
The ones that I can hear singing.

I bought a new house as a new single mom, and started over creating a new life in those spaces with my newly reorganized family. That house had a large master bedroom with high ceilings and many windows, allowing great natural light that filled my soul with powerful, healing energy. I bought a cushy purple *chair and a half* with a matching ottoman and made a sitting area in one corner, joining a bookshelf full of healing and children's books, artistic collections, a modern slate waterfall fountain, and a large healthy ficus tree nicely planted in a stone pot.

My two little girls and I could all fit in that chair at once, and we did, as I read to them for hours each evening, and sometimes just cuddling up talking about their days. Often they begged to sleep on the big purple chair, spreading blankets across the seat and ottoman, making a nice little child's bed, sleeping in the loving comfort of the energy we had created in that space.

We also had a very large jetted tub in an adjacent area, where we would take relaxing bubble baths together with our wonderful essential oils, laughing as we celebrated just being girls and being free. Over the days and months and years we lived there, that purple chair and that nurturing space were alive with the energy of warm, healing, happy love.

There were similar stories for each room of the house, so much so that after we moved away and now years later, we still feel it is *our* house. The energy of what we created during our years there is still vibrating with love when we drive by. And both little girls, now grown, still adore that purple chair like it is sacred. When one of them wanted to recover it and take it to her college apartment, the other one gasped in horror that she would even think of touching *the* purple chair. *The* chair, while an inanimate object, has become as real as any person. It didn't come that way when I bought it. *We gave it this energy through our experience with it.*

The same thing happened with our car: a Suburban we affectionately named *The Tank*. *The Tank* took us everywhere for many years: safely along steep mountain trails, through deep fields of snow, and across the whole United States and back. If we were running low on gas, we would just give her a little *talking to* and tell her to help us out until we could get to the next station, to which she always obliged. The seats folded down to make a full-sized bed for sleeping comfortably while camping out in the middle of nowhere, and the tailgate opened out to allow a dozen cub scouts an adventure while discovering and exploring nature. My kids delivered hundreds of dozens of donuts out of *The Tank* to raise money for our summer vacation, and most of them learned to drive behind the wheel of this trusty family protector: more like a cherished family guard dog than simply a car. Nothing could stop us or nothing could hurt us when we were in *The Tank*. Because she seemed to know she was loved, she never had any need to break down mechanically; she just kept on going and going for many years.

Everything that exists has energy, and everything is radiating energy. Sometimes it has loving energy from your connections to it that bless you like the chair and the car did for us, *but sometimes it's just the opposite, and you don't even know it*. The *message* in each element's energy and how that message affects you is what is so important when creating spaces. **Your own personal energy is in a constant state of reaction to everything around you.** In many ways, these reactions can control your life force, so it is important to learn more about this and to make the necessary adjustments.

Managing the Energy of Your Things

I consider everything in my possession as some form of art. It was created somewhere, sometime, as something, and at some point I bought it, received it, or allowed it into my spaces. So I am the *manager* of every bit of it, and I can take control over how these energies are affecting me, beginning with an analysis of each piece.

With this exercise I get to decide what is happening to me with the energy of each element I possess. I do this from within, from my inner knowing place, which I trust completely. I examine one room at a time and all the *things* in it. I check every single piece to decide exactly how the energy affects me. I enter the realm of spiritual connection to my own real self. When I feel those satisfying loving vibrations, I consider if any piece is a match to those vibrations, or if it bothers me, taking my loving energy away from me.

These exercises are empowering to me as an intuitive, and a method that should work for anyone. I could simply take any item in my home and consider what it feels like instantly, but that is not a reliable test. Because there are so many complexities to our emotions, *this process must go deeper.* I find it useful to relax into a state of peaceful clarity first, to remove any chance that my analysis is being misconstrued in any way by my stresses or present needs. You have to be stabilized by aligning with peaceful truth within yourself, then you can know how you are aligned with the energy of any of your things.

To do this, relax into a peaceful, happy, restful state. Breathe in and out, releasing any fear or judgment or preconceptions of right and wrong, which could cause separation from truth. You want to become connected to the *peaceful flow of truth within yourself* before beginning this process. Allow yourself to float into a field of loving energy, a high vibrational meditative state, above and beyond where you normally exist,

81

where nothing matters and everything is love. In such a space of oneness, you will feel incredible peace. To relax, you may connect with some things that raise your vibrations. Try some good music with power to move you intensely, or flowers with all their intricacies and fragrances—anything to stimulate your artistic senses and state of contentment. When you find yourself centered in this blissful state, speak an empowering clear intention such as:

I am the creator of my life, my home, and everything in it. I have the gift of knowing who I am and what I am about. I am the only one who knows what is best for me. I am perfectly capable of making choices based on true feelings from my heart. I trust my heart to tell me only truth. When my heart is happy, it is truth. When my heart is empty, this thing has to go. (I never question my heart!) *I am creating a powerful, loving, nurturing connectedness to myself and to Mother Earth through the elements of my life and my home, now.* (Breathe in the love!)

Next, in this space of alignment with truth, begin the process of examining the elements in your home or space. Your goal is to discover the energy in each of your things. You *test* each piece by asking this simple question: *Does this item give me energy when I see it or think about it?*

If your heart vibrations raise, tingle, vibrate, sing, or just mildly lighten, the item gets to stay, if you wish. *Spirit is speaking,* so listen carefully without forcing or questioning its reply. The first reaction is the correct answer. *Does this piece serve me? Is it connected to me in a positive way?* Highly intuitive people will be able to test the energy of their pieces using other spiritual gifts too, such as seeing or feeling the vibrations emitted. (I can place my opened hands over any piece and feel a cool vibration radiating when the energy of a piece is good for me.)

If a positive reaction is *not* felt, consider that the item is *taking* energy from you. If your heart does not react in a lightening, happy way, but instead feels empty, dark, fearful, unfulfilled and without happy vibrations, it could be labeled as having *negative* energy. Keeping anything that sends negative vibes will adversely affect you, repelling love energy and sucking the life — little bits at a time — out of the room and out of you! If this is the response, toss the item. The process is usually very easy to determine.

Things that give me energy may fit into these categories:

- **Beautifully made of natural products:** a real work of art, giving off natural energy. I feel this whenever I notice the finishes in my glass, granite and stainless kitchen, or my custom-made natural African mahogany furniture.
- **A keepsake:** an heirloom, with generations of family energy attached. I couldn't dare part with it, like the mantel clock on the shelf that has been handed down parent to child in my direct patriarchal line since 1810, or the Tiffany lamp that sat on my grandmother's desk and now mine. Since childhood every time I pass by, I like to give it a flip with my finger to enjoy its surprisingly deep sounding ring. And every time I do it makes me smile.
- **A purchase or piece that reminds me of the place I went:** something which touches my soul in a generous way, taking me back to that place every time I see it, like my replica of the bronze bell from the wall of Suwon, reminding me of that day together with my daughter and all it meant to her. Whenever I look at my mother's watercolor painting of the misty river by my house in winter, I remember those few short years and the few places we sat together memorizing nature.
- **Made or given by someone I adore:** the thoughtfulness touches me, and I want to bring that person's energy or that memory into my life, like the massive depth

of regenerating energy expressed in the most artistic doodlings of my son, then framed behind glass to forever give me his loving energy. The same thing happens with the Lladro on my desk that doesn't match anything else in my house, but was given to me by a dear friend who bought it because it spoke my spirit to him.

- **Very precious:** expensive, bringing the energy of being RARE, special, honored, or come by at some sacrifice, which touches me just to think about, such as my six foot grand piano for which I saved and waited many years, the money for which was often depleted with the unexpected costs of raising children. The joy of its long-awaited arrival returns every day of my life as I play it or see it sitting stately in my home.
- **When I look at it, for whatever reason, it just makes me feel good all over:** my bronze of the naked woman with arms spread ready to leap into water, or flight, or her new life, reminding me of the time when that was me!
- **It is connecting me to my passions:** what I love, what excites me every time I see it, like my paintings of boats sailing in the sea, connecting me to water and sailing and traveling to beautiful places, and all the warmth and thrill those feelings bring me.
- **It reminds me of happy times:** from photos of people and places with all the grace those memories include, to remembering the loving service from my son as he replaced all the lighting in my house, which makes me smile every time I flip a switch.

Everything that I possess, everything in my presence is radiating the energy of all the memories associated with it, *in as much detail as my heart chooses to hold.* I examine everything and keep only what brings these good vibes.

Reasons that things take away my energy, and which suggest that such things should be remodeled, cleaned up, or tossed include:

- **Poor quality:** cheap materials, dead substance, like plastic pots and artificial trees.
- **Trendy:** style or color dated, like whitewashed oak with shiny brass handles, 70's mauves in abstract patterns, and thick varnished finishes on wood.
- **Reminds me of someone with negative energy:** either the person who gave the piece or a person's bad attitude in giving the piece, or the negative energy of the person or place from which the piece traveled before arriving to live with me!
- **Reminds me of something negative:** incites my dark side.
- **Makes me feel inferior.**
- **All of the above:** is it too small and insignificant?
- **Not needed or too much:** is my design just as well without this?
- **Out of balance:** too little power, as if an uninvited guest. Not a match for the room or me.

This may take a while, but it feels so refreshing! It is my own personal *house cleansing*, which is quite energizing, as all that is *taking* my energy is removed, leaving only high-energy pieces. Even if very few of my things remain from the cleansing, it will feel wonderful, and that is what I am seeking: feelings of clarity, love, and energy, all to *serve* me and mine; not just busy-ness from rooms filled to the max with *stuff*. Everything that is left will make me happy when I see it. There will be nothing remaining in my spaces to cause me to feel *less-than* in

85

any way. I continue to cleanse my house of all *energy-suckers*, and I continue to adorn it with *energy-generators* from living and loving sources.

Soon I am going to remove the paint that was added to the base of my grandmother's Tiffany lamp. I don't care that it is the way she left it: the paint is not original, and I am longing to free those beautiful raw metal forms of art deco! It's just a feeling, repeatedly calling to me, which I have to honor. I am sure my grandmother would approve, as she was very much a naturalist too.

Saying Goodbye to the Rejects

Sometimes people can't let go of their stuff. Sometimes that's because they don't know what to do with it. So where do we send all the rejects?

There are natural choices for these groups that will evolve, such as one for family members living elsewhere who may have a connection to a certain piece—one pile for each person. Perhaps it would be best to return some items to the person who gave it, who may want it back—they get a stack labeled with their name. Every town has a place where donations are taken and shared with the less fortunate, or young people, or smart shoppers—a box that goes to charity. Then lastly, and I feel really good doing this one, toss it in the trash—let it go. **Unless it serves you, *let it all go.***

This is a most empowering experience, one that frees your spaces and your soul, and I know you can hardly wait to get started checking out your own rooms! Take a look at how far this energy exchange process can take you and go the distance. Toss unless you absolutely *can't* let it go, then you know it gets to stay.

I love to keep *life* in all my things. **Everything in my home requires my energy to manage it, to have it in my possession** and on my premises. All of it must feed my soul with joy and serve me well.

Energetic Cords from Things

I imagine that everything I own or have in my possession is somehow connected with *cords* to my body. This includes everything in all the obvious areas of the house plus closets, attics, garages, under the bed, in the car — everywhere. I accept that I am the master of my life, and I am in charge of maintaining everything in it. I brought or allowed all these things into my home. I *own* them, thus my energy is required to *maintain* them. They have to wait for me for whatever they do or whatever happens with them. They have no ability, direction, or will of their own.

Energy is flowing through these ethereal, energetic cords. An item that is on the giving-me-energy list will cause energy to flow *into* me. An item that is on the list of that which *takes* my energy will cause energy to flow *out* of me. There is a balancing process going on wherein the low or negative energy in pieces requires some of *my energy* in order to raise their vibrations, to make them acceptable. The same is true in reverse: if a piece is flowing with good vibes, it will send those vibes through its cord to me as its owner, raising my own vibrations in the balance with such — another form of the natural high of spirit.

Everything is either taking my energy to maintain its existence or giving me energy from its presence. This is how energy flows. It is vitally important to find out which way the energy of each piece is flowing! If something gets to be in my home, it will require an imaginary cord to me to give it a blood supply, so it better be serving me by feeding my energy and not taking my precious energy away!

I want to have every single thing in my home of such a

quality and life-giving energy. Remember, Mother Earth feeds on things of like-matter to herself. She is made of pure love. If something speaks to my heart, it must have good energy in it that my heart likes.

This process is something every single person can and should do. This must be done before anything else is decided about the life and design of all your spaces. Get the energy cleansing done first, and then we will go on to talk about what we are going to do with the spaces. This activity is easy and free, exciting and fun! *It is personal — one's own knowing experience using empowered intuition in the creation of their home!*

There is no one who can do this for you. There is no one else who has any idea how these pieces affect you! You know your own history and your connections with the messages in every piece. You are the steward. *You get to play this game.*

If afterwards there are only a little bit of things remaining, you know that the *little* will make you so much happier than the *volumes* that just filled spaces and sucked your life-force away. Notice how free and full of energy you feel as you clear out the clutter with its negative energetic attachments. Notice the loving energy emitted from the remaining things that bring only happy, positive, love-generating energy!

When your spaces are finished, you will feel very nurtured living there, and it will always be so, never changing — never. You will have created spaces that are a part of you, in truth to your natural being, which truth never changes.

Choosing New Things

Next you may want to add to or replace some of your things. Where do you go from here? How do you keep the virgin spaces pure? How do you choose?

Here is a great tool, and so easy: simply ask, and *let the house speak.* I love reading energies, so I focus on any given area, taking a *spiritual* inventory, looking for the placement of good energy. I notice what would be the perfect shape, color, weight, and style that would work in that area to complete the flow of energy in that space. What direction does energy need to flow to keep things fluid here? What materials would make a good balance with others around? What color, if any, and what about the volume and intensity?

Soon I get a general idea of space, shape, color and materials. After I know what that piece might be like, I visualize it. I hold that truthful visual of what is needed within myself, spiritually allowing its creation. It seems to become real in my imagination as I keep my focus. I have made an attachment, spiritually, to that piece. It will find me or I will find it, and usually very soon. I will be guided to a certain place, following a nudge, a gut feeling, without even knowing what I am out to find. Even while shopping for something else, I come upon this thing that I know immediately will work to fill the need.

I buy it and take it home, and it actually does always work for that space, because it was created *from spirit first* and then it manifest into creation! I take as much time as I need for this *gestation period*, even if it's months. Perfection in expression of energy cannot be rushed: it has its own natural course, so trust it.

If this process is reversed, and instead of *pre-designing* from spirit, I simply find and buy a wonderful piece while out shopping, it never works! I am always sorry later, for as I attempt to place the piece, it doesn't really fit in my home, or I really did not need it; it is not a match. Only when I *let the house speak first* can I know it will be perfect. A powerful house is a house full of originals — created from your own inner spirit's knowing of your own needs and your own desires of what blesses your own unique soul.

The Energy of Art and Artists

You have to know, does it match your soul? Did the creator feel the love you hold so deep? Was she there with you as you watched the sun rise, to see how to lighten your world with truth? Such a creator becomes part of your family, yours forever, heart and soul, a gift to bless your life, so bring her home to live with you.

A house full of original art is magical. There is exponentially more energy in original art than replicas; just notice that. There is no rule about what kind of art may be displayed in combinations with other art forms. All art is just that: an original expression of *life happened here.* Paintings may be collected from every medium and used throughout a room. Oils and watercolors and acrylics, metal arts and wood sculptures, glass and clay, all existing side by side because of their beauty and the interest you have in their individual presentations.

While the medium and presentation have an intense gift to share, the real gift is in the deeper message of the art itself. What does it *do* to or for me? Where does it *take* me? I choose art for its ability to move me, that by gazing into a painting it may *take me somewhere that I cannot go right now physically by myself.* It may take me to a beautiful place to enjoy a wonderful view just by mere observation; I don't have to travel far away. As I invest my spirit into a connection with a work of art, it brings that far away energy to me.

I would not choose a painting that depicts something that I *could* bring into my room, such as a vase of flowers. I will bring the vase of flowers instead of the painting of the vase of flowers. If I could not bring a vase of flowers into a certain room for some reason, I would then enjoy a painting of a vase of flowers.

Sometimes this is not applicable, such as when someone special to me is the artist and it is a gift, or when such a painting celebrates some botanical piece that I adore. In this case, it is not about the vase of flowers at all, but the love that created and brought the painting to me, or the intimate connection I have to such a creation, which is the highest order of priority.

When you bring a work of art into your home, you bring the artist home; the energy that the artist shares with the world is in that piece of art. The artist put a part of his very soul into the piece. You cannot even begin to imagine all the experiences and all the inspiration the artist grasped and endured to cause the creation of that work of his hands.

It's a great gift to own original art. You take the art and the artist's energy and his life full of living, all home with you in that piece of art. He is not just selling or giving you a piece of art, but a piece of his *life*. It's always amazing to me that he can even dare part with it, but that again, is the deeper beauty: he does, because he wants to give it to you. He wants it to bring you joy. *He wants to serve you with his love.* This generosity is what keeps him motivated to create.

How do you feel about this artist's spirit or energy in your home? These are people who can reach into their depths and discover the creator — the god within — and use that depth of love to make life more beautiful for the rest of us. This is why I adore attending art shows and museums. The creative energy of time and place and expression of the larger perspective of life is there, free for the taking. *Breathe in the love!* Always honor the artist.

The same applies to all other forms of art as well: music, literature, dance, film. It is *life* in every conceivable form of expression from the heart — the source — as the artist connects to a place of knowing and shows us another original glorious sign of life.

The Energy of Things with a History as Art

It may have happened long ago and far away. The creation from a different time and place, like an old movie re-running over and over, bringing the story to share with you. And if you've been there, in this memory or another, it serves to remind you of years spent living another life. See life evolving as the creator creates, the past moving eternally on, an hour, once spent, then no more, carving this stone, but oh how I knew you were here.

Sometimes we collect things that somebody has used: heirlooms, antiques, or collectible hand me downs. The mantle clock my father gave me was restored before it arrived as a Christmas gift a few years before his death. But as a little girl, when I first saw it in his storage room I remember it having its genealogy penned on the back panel: every person who had cared for it and passed it down for about 200 years. That impressed me deeply, as I felt those ancestors with me, as if I was caring for *them* in addition to their clock.

If something has been owned before, whether a house or a vase, it vibrates that person's energy. It has a history — a story. It has observed life from the other side of time. Yes, *life happened here!* History as art is a beautiful sign of life.

Imagine having some authentic piece that has already lived a hundred years, or a couple of hundred years, or even a few thousand years, like a piece of ancient jewelry or a book. If you allow yourself to shift into a connection with the spiritual energy of that piece, just noticing such brings to you the energy of all those years between then and now. Imagine all the things that have happened in all those years. *Time is a powerful sign of life,* magically connecting you to the energy of spirit.

But these pieces could also carry negative energy from those times and people. I once had a necklace made from a piece of sea-glass which was several thousand years old — very gorgeous and rare, but which sent me some intense and mysterious vibrations that bothered me, though I loved the colors and textures and design of the necklace as a piece of art.

Soon after noticing this phenomenon, I accidentally lost the piece, or maybe it was no accident. Even though I had spent a lot of money on that necklace, I was sort of relieved to discover that it was gone. The lesson here is to pay attention: notice the energy. Enjoy its good vibrations or choose to let it go.

On the other hand, with a glass piece like that with no obvious cause for the bad energy, I could have simply asked for those negative vibrations to be released, but at that time, I did not know how to clear the energy of things. Any item that holds negative vibes can be washed clean, laid in the sun for a day or two, soaked in salt water, prayed over, or a myriad of other ways of clearing energy. Calling upon angels to do this for you also works. Many old things *and even old houses* need clearing of negative energies, or you may choose to leave them behind.

As you collect historical pieces, you may decide to restore them to good shape and repair. Doing so creates the energy of *I care for this piece. It was valuable once to someone else who has now entrusted it to me, and I will honor that trust by keeping it as close to its original form as possible.*

If you are going to maintain some piece in its old, broken, or poor condition, it may speak the energy of being *discarded and devalued.* I don't suppose that you would intentionally choose such a form of energy to be a part of your spaces. But if perhaps an old, broken piece is in fact used in its deteriorated state, it could be stating that it is being kept exactly as a beloved ancestor last touched it, or some other positive message.

Thus **it is only the energy that you attach to or feel from any piece that matters.** But you do absolutely have to notice the energy that it speaks to you and assess whether or not it pleases you in order to create your spaces with intense, living, happy energy.

A Work in Progress

Things left in the *process of creation* have their own suspenseful energy and power to share. Sometimes for no particular reason, I might have a piece of something that is unfinished. I call it *a work in progress*. It might be a chair that is draped with a fabric that is being considered for the new upholstery, or a painting that was sketched but no paints added yet.

In these cases, notice the energy of *expectation*, like the presence of someone who is coming back, or still there, deciding, or pondering the next move. It's the energy of people and creation evolving, and you are a witness—a part of this changing energy—as if the vision of what has happened and what will happen is already in progress, busying the spaces before you.

A little boy lines up his collection of balls on the floor all in order, smallest to largest, an array of many colors and sizes and materials, all in a perfectly straight line. I wouldn't want to put that away in the toy box for days, as its very presence reminds me of the thinking mind of such a toddler and the concentration involved, as well as the joy and pride in his perfect creation. All that *innocence and concentration, joy and pride*, is the lovely energy that remains to bless me.

An opened book marked where I read it last seems to bring the energy of *me in that moment:* time past but coming back to finish, *anticipation*, feeling the energy of coming and going, reading and stopping, up and down, here and there. Time: an intriguing sign of life. Even in the stillness, life is happening here.

The Energy of Sounds and Music as Art

What is that I hear? The rhythms of life, knowing she is there, just in case we felt alone.

The train tracks ran near my home as a child. I grew to find solace in the whistling and rattling that sang out every night as I went to sleep. It was and remains a loving sign of life to me, while to someone else this same sound might be quite disturbing. Every sound is relative to what it means to you by how it relates to your experience.

My connection to the healing rhythms of flowing water has caused me to place water features in every available area of my house. Heighten your senses further by noticing the sounds in your home, knowing that Mother is there. Will you add the dimensions of music? What sounds bring peace to your soul?

Music is the *voice* of art and passion. Music fills my soul when I am craving the passions of self-expression. For instance the exquisite music of a soundtrack is written to depict and accompany the journey of the characters of a movie in rich emotion, and it does the same for my soul. Music can be life's pacemaker: keeping you going in the state of the place and the feelings from which you want to express. With music I can channel my own emotions, expressing with satisfaction what I feel and who I am.

When my children were small, I put loud music on to do the housework. It served to pump me up to get the work done in joyful-playing-mode. Those children now grown still do housework to the sounds of Neil Diamond and Barry Manilow, perhaps unaware of why but knowing it works so well! The energetic attachments create the return of the original energy associated with it.

I have found a connection to what is known as *New Age Music*. There is a new freedom of expression of sounds accepted in any form, from waves upon the sands to the haunting but healing ring of Tibetan bowls. The creations in this kind of music are more ethereal, as if reflecting the voice of the earth, a match for my heart. New Age music typically holds me in my center, where I can mediate and focus on truths.

These are sounds that are constant, like the ocean shores that repeat over and over and over, holding a certain space. Being at the coast, standing in that space, I become hypnotized by these rhythms. They are *grounding* me.

Music can also *take me somewhere*. It is another vehicle for traveling through time and space. There are sounds that actually *move me far away*, like those movie soundtracks. They hold me where I am now with calm and basic central tones, then rise and fall and move all over the octaves, taking my energy with it.

Music has the power to connect all of my body with all of my spirit being. It is a process of scanning all the voices that are sounding within: connecting with each, honoring each. Then as the music ends, all the grand sounds return to the beginning, to the center notes again, bringing with it the orchestra that is *my own energy*, and holding all parts together as one. For me, soundtracks and classics are a spiritual workout.

The earth itself with its voice does the same. Nothing of this earth or the many creations living on it is without voice. Every element is singing its own song.

Do all the parts of me have voices: individual sounds speaking? I believe we must recognize the theory that we have been created in God's image. We are a representation of His wholeness. Each of God's creations has the same basic parts, created with His loving energy. We each have a body with a need to be fed, a need to speak, and feelings with a purpose to serve. Some people have developed spiritual sensitivities to listen with their spiritual ears, to communicate with animals and plants and waters and all that is alive with spirit.

I have learned from my own eternal glimpses and from

those who have visited beyond this mortality of the magnificent music of the spirit realms. I have heard it described as *exquisite beyond anything we have ever heard or created or even imagined on earth*. Such a reality of sounds has within it the power to move one to the deepest depths and the highest heights. It has the power of creation within its chords.

If the earth had a voice, or as many voices as all the creations in existence, it would truly be the most ethereal, majestic, passionate choir and orchestra. Such a soundtrack would be grand and godly: the expression of the different sounds of all the parts of the whole universe. It too can move me everywhere as I listen and follow the rhythms. Tuning into the sounds that are vibrating throughout all creation, I can discover feelings of life in completely new dimensions. Life is a gorgeously radiant, living *hologram*, with as many different possibilities and dimensions as we are willing to explore.

Possession and placement of musical instruments creates magnificent energy. These beautiful creations represent grand possibilities for art, all of which share good vibes with me: the music, the musician, the audience, the creator of the instrument, its value and quality in financial terms, and the generations of all the varieties of music played on that instrument, as well as all memories associated with such. It represents intention and desire to play the instrument, all of which are positive applications of sounds as signs of life.

Years ago my mother reminded me that as a child, I would sit at the piano and sing whenever I felt stressed. I do feel better when I let my own voice connect with spirit by singing the songs that are in my heart—the music that brings me joy.

When my babies were born, I took them into my arms and sang while rocking them. I had wonderfully happy and healthy babies; a happy mother makes a happy home. The state of the mother affects everyone in the house. I make myself happy by singing what I love, wearing what I love, doing what I love, and my loving energy will bless my home; being one with spirit is the origin of my joy.

The Energy of Fragrance in Creating Life Force

I have grown fond of certain smells in my life and recognize their powerful affects on my sense of well-being. A home has its own unique scents: from the people who live there to the aromas of foods that are cooked and to the activities that create smells such as wood burning in the fireplace.

My pleasure for smells takes me back many years to the herbal fragrances lofting in the humid air on warm summer evenings at the lake surrounded by those Tennessee woods. Honeysuckle vines grew on every fence, filling my senses with a sweetness that always serves to return me to my roots. I delight in the musky pine tones of the old forests and streams in the Smoky Mountains, and the pungent cottonwoods along mountain streams in the Rockies, giving comfort and reminding that all is well in the world. My grandmother's sheets, hung out on the line to dry, brought the smell of *clean and spring* to my bedtimes. I feast on such smells, which bring signs of life with them — the life that is *mine*. I am!

In more recent years, I have discovered the power of essential oils, straight from the abundance of nature's garden, bringing life and healing in powerful ways. The vibrating frequencies of pure essential oils from earth's organic plants are extremely high — much higher than the frequency at which my body resonates on a daily basis. These oils may be applied to the body or distilled into the air to raise the energy levels. The frequency of each oil represents a certain type of energy: some relaxing, some invigorating, some healing, some sensual and romantic, some for connection to every form of energy.

As with all other applications of Mother Earth's gifts,

inner knowing can assist greatly in choosing oils. Everyone can feel the frequencies. When in the presence of essential oils, just ask: *which of these is good for me, or for my friend, or for this ailment?* Pass your middle finger over the oils. The middle finger is the receiving and giving point that connects with earth energy. Believe in the process. You will feel a slight breeze — vibrations — coming from the particular oil that will serve you best as per your request. You can also sense which part of your body to apply the oil to: the feet, toes, shins, belly, heart, throat, temples, top of the head. You can also sense which oil to use in a particular setting, depending on the need.

Due to their innocence, teachability, and connection to Mother Earth, children are especially good at these processes. My youngest daughter was barely five when I discovered essential oils and learned to test energy in this way. As I showed her how I did it, she wanted to do it too, making selections easily and very accurately. It is precious to witness a child using this trusting connection to spirit, which most people lose as they grow older.

A house has a fragrance that tells the world you are there, creating life in ways that match your soul. Find spirit in the smells of cleanliness, fresh air from open windows, blooming flowers and trees, essential oils in diffusers, personal perfumes, air spritzers, foods baking, woods burning.

The Energy of Plants as Art

Have you noticed how flowers display themselves in nature? They are not a mixed and complex arrangement. They are light and free, flowing gently from long stems, remaining mainly within their own species and in different stages of blooming: from new buds to fully opened flowers to dried remains of buds, usually with a few bees visiting! I create my interior arrangements from this example of nature's simplicity.

In the wilds there are not multiple arrangements of differing types of flowers growing together as from the same stem. Flowers grow in nature in a group of their own kind, and for the most part, should be displayed in the home that same way. They look most natural when they stand alone, just as they grow, with buds and full blooms and the remains of blooms fallen away, giving the most pleasure and the most spirit-power. On the other hand, the contrast between a few different flowers can make each one radiate even more beauty — different species working together to serve one another's higher purpose, like teamwork, with purpose and simplicity. Just notice the energy of blossoming plants and your relationship to them, and be open to receiving the many lovely gifts they offer.

Live trees are essential in my designs. I want to feel the energy of earth vibrating in my spaces in abundance, and nothing serves this need better than indoor trees. I have always had good luck with keeping them alive and blooming. I treat them with respect as I would any person, talking to them while I water them, praising their elegance and energy, thanking them for gracing my spaces, and then leaving them to do their work of growing, blooming, and shining as they do. I actually have a spiritual experience being with my plants for a few minutes every few days.

When I hear people say they can't keep plants alive, I assume that means they need to connect to their own loving, powerful energy first, and then awaken to the vibrations of love in every living thing. With respect for self and all of life, I believe anyone can enjoy the gifts of nature indoors.

If you must have man-made flowers and trees, be sure to choose ones that are so similar to real that no one will believe they are not! Place them in containers that would be used if they were indeed real. Do not crowd flowers and vines, overloading containers unnaturally. Even in a formal setting, the minimal touches of nature are perfect, and especially when the energy of the design is very pleasing to you, replacing the fact that by being man-made they give no natural energy of their own.

The Energy of Contrasts

Notice the energy existing between contrasts: the masculine and the feminine, the square and the circle, the walls and the movement within the walls, earth and water, darkness and light, rough and smooth. *Contrast* is to design today what eclectic was in the 70's. It's the energy created by the surprising elements of *opposites* that we use to bring more elemental spirit energy into spaces.

When I moved to the Southwest, I noticed most people were decorating with heavy, dark, warm colors, textures, and elements. We are talking about an environment that is already intensely hot in many months. In this desert setting, I wanted to give my rooms a splash of cool light. So instead of browns, I chose to use *whites*. I wanted my interior colors to *balance* with the exterior views of red sandstone mountains, so I used the cool, clear tones of aquamarine, like the deepest tones of sagebrush growing everywhere in the surrounding areas. Know that the more contrast you add, the higher energetic vibrations you will create.

I feel perfectly joyful having my extraordinarily fragrant paper whites blooming amidst the holiday evergreens every Christmas. Similarly, the use of crystals with natural elements makes a great statement in any season. There are endless possibilities for using earth elements to create delightful contrasting energy:

- Shiny bright, colorful dishes on a heavily textured cloth
- Warm glowing candles next to fresh cut spring limbs blossoming with buds
- Linen draperies hanging around covered outdoor

sitting areas
- Traditional fabrics on modern frames, modern fabrics on antiques
- Outdoor vines growing on iron frames above indoor windows
- Upholstery in the bathroom
- Elegant mirrors above the stove
- My best china and cloth napkins on the patio table for dinner
- Metal wall art next to ornate oil paintings
- The good silverware with the casual dishes
- One gorgeous leggy antique chair next to the sophisticated leather sofa
- Shiny purple pillows on that tan corduroy couch
- Big picture windows by the bathtub allowing the full view of the gardens outside
- A rough stone sink gracing a sleek granite countertop
- Crystal chandeliers over old stone dining tables
- Velvet cushions on the metal benches
- One painted piece of furniture amongst all the natural finishes; balance of painted and stained cabinets in the kitchen

It's using something in a way that isn't usually done, and making the decision to do it anyway. That's what makes it exciting, and that's what makes it work. It's like opening the front door to an old historic house and seeing it completely renovated in modern finishes: a very nice surprise, bringing those good vibes you breathe into your soul in the process of enjoying such a display of creativity. Who told you it has to match? Wake up to what's new: if it brings a smile and you like it, use anything to bring spirit with the creativity of playful contrasts in your decor!

How the Energy of People Affects the Design

If I have a very busy career, and if I am in charge of many people or some very important work, I have a lot going on—a lot of extra *busy-ness energy*. When I come home, I want that energy to be *balanced* within my spaces. Busy with issues and personnel all day long at work, such people may not want to see or have much in the way of *things* when they come home at the end of the day. They may need *simplicity* to balance the day's *complexities*. Additionally, if such people are connected to a lot of power in their professions, symbolically their home must reflect pieces that are also equally empowered, exquisite, rare, and usually with strong colors and bigger statements— perhaps even using *less is more* principles.

One who is more withdrawn in personal nature, or whose life is quieter or less busy in the way of interactions and accountabilities, may feel a need to allow his home to bring balance with *more* busy-ness, even cozy-ness. He may choose to have *more things, smaller details, mixing of patterns, more fussiness, more happening.* Just notice the energy of people and their things and spaces, and how intimately *right* the balance can make them feel.

Animation as Signs of Life in Design

Your space may be filled with the most amazing collection of *things,* but if there is no *life* happening in those things, the space will have *no power;* the energy of *life* radiates in your spaces when you consider that you have an energetic or spiritual guest, and that you are placing things to please that guest, especially if that guest is you or your family! Adding elements of animation suggests you are ready to let the show begin; energy is turned on in this very moment; the lights, action, sound are running; the entertainment begins, and you

103

get to enjoy it!

This could be done by turning on music, displaying fountains of water falling, seeing pets curled up by the fireplace or chirping away in a cage, the smell of something good being created in the kitchen, or a game set out to play. There is *life* energy—someone, something is happening, right in the very moment—and *you are a part of that activity* as you enter the space. No, you are not alone without life all around you. You can bring your spaces to life with the energy of *something good is happening*, right in the here and now!

This concept allows you to decorate things with the delight and surprise of animation, as you would if you were decorating for a birthday party. Look around your spaces and see if there is any suggestion that *life is happening here,* and if it's the kind of life that makes you happy, that makes you want to stay and enjoy yourself!

I recently visited my friend's back yard to help her create some *life* there. She had helped me plan, place, and plant trees in my yard—lots of them. She had watched me add the *signs of life* to that setting: water fountains, bird feeders, art pieces, open seating, light reflection balls, sculptures. We both love nature, and she loves to come over and see the things I have added that make my landscape *come to life*.

My artistic additions serve to draw me into the setting, taking me from piece to piece, creating an energetic reaction with each display. Each art form has an energy all its own, and each plays a part in the whole. For example, many interesting and colorful birds are drawn to the feeder and then to the fountain where they splash and drink. The cats drink there too, and then chase the birds, creating playfulness; life is definitely happening here. The round sea-glass colored light reflection balls bring my travels back around and around, in and out, creating the circle and making me feel like I belong in this space, like it was created for my personal entertainment, which of course, it was.

In contrast as we visited my friend's backyard, I pointed out that it showed no elements of surprise. It had no pieces other than the natural plantings. It had nothing to invite me to stay and study the setting. *It needed animation!* What could she add that would show some activity, that people actually had a life there? What could she create that would invite me to come and stay a while? That is the question you ask to inspire you to create some of the spirit of animation. Artistic additions show the human hand has blessed the space. Has the party been prepared? Is the surprise planned? What will bring delight when you enter? What elements of the good life will you immediately see and enjoy?

Animation must be added indoors as well as out. Sometimes this can be as simple as the trail of little stone sea turtles placed in a random line across a table, showing movement and symbolism of life happening somewhere on this planet, brought home to entertain. I have four such turtles, reminding me of the four of us that stayed a week on that catamaran in the BVI where my daughter bought the turtles: it was our all-time favorite vacation, the sweet memories returning every time I notice that trail of stone turtles creeping across my desk.

Living energy may be created with a simple collection of unique sea shells on the buffet by the window, shining in the sun, reminding that a hand (mine) actually picked them up on some foreign seashores over the years and brought them all the way here; they represent some wonderful moments in time and a connection to my own great life. In that display, I bring the energy of the shells, the places where they were collected, the memories of the trips, and any desires or anticipations or residual feelings lying within. In this case, animation makes a wonderful gratitude generator!

These signs of life can be a table set with beautiful dinnerware, suggesting that people are invited to sit and be

105

honored with such beauty while eating there. In my anticipation for what is to come, I can sense the energy as if the party has already begun!

Thoughtful personal touches create loving signs of life. When I am a guest at a certain sister-in-law's house, she will do something special in preparation for my stay, such as placing a photograph of my family by the bed where I will be sleeping, always with a vase of fresh cut flowers from her garden. Another dusts my pillow with my favorite lavender sachet, insuring a wonderful night's sleep. Such an act of kindness shows that she was there and thought of me being there, with love: all signs of life.

Likewise, a chair may be placed in a bathroom by the tub, showing that the way has been provided for someone to lay a towel there or perhaps sit before she soaks — again, showing honor for *the person*. It's that spiritual butler, showing that someone has thought of *the one*, the needs and comfort of real, living people. It's the inevitable mark that someone has been here and prepared the way to make life a little more pleasant. Above and beyond all the *things* we bring, it's all for the love of people — *real people — real life* — that we do what we do in design.

Integrity with Elemental Design Energy

Sometimes, the answers you need for design perfection lie in questioning the *integrity of things*. For example, have you ever seen fake stone placed on a single face of a house? The fake material itself doesn't bother me as much as the fact that it shows no regard for the obvious: *stone is supposed to be structural*, and had it been *real*, it would have faced the sides as well as the front! I have seen the same application on fireplace façades, completely ignoring the small bit of stone required to wrap the side returns which would at least have given some integrity to the possibility of what it was supposed to be: a stack of rocks surrounding a firebox, making it a *real fireplace*! I have also seen rocks placed on exterior façades that don't go all the way to the ground, even hanging cantilevered, again out of alignment with integrity, exposing the fact that if it were real rock, it would have to sit on a foundation, which is what rock is supposed to do — not hang in the air some inches or feet off the ground!

I wonder about the sanity of people including developers and consumers who design and buy homes with freeways in the back yard, or sanitary dumps, or huge buildings, or cinder block walls hiding such. Is there no respect for the need for peaceful energy and personal space in nature? Who cares so little for humanity to build so close to industry and who buys with no attachment to the energy of cars and gases and factories in their faces all the time? Energy vibrates and moves as do the things in the spaces, so there is constant movement from cars and trash and business in places that are supposed to be our *retreat* from all of that.

The energy of *honoring self* is what I am talking about here! I want to awaken people to notice the energy in life all around them, and to make choices that honor the very real need to align with the energies that *bless and heal with spirit* in our own personal sanctuaries.

Learn to notice energy everywhere and what happens to you with the movement of those energies. All elements: electrical devices, machines, schools, buildings, shopping centers, roads, geography, all places and things have an energy form that affects you. Additionally, there is always energy remaining in places from previous *events* that happened there. Do you ever wonder why a business fails in a location where another business previously failed? The first business left the energy of *failing business happening here,* and the second business did not know how to clear it or create a better one. If the energy of happiness and love is created by those who live in a certain house, others will feel those powerful lifting vibrations simply when approaching the borders of the real estate. Just notice the energy and ask what is happening there, past or present, and make decisions accordingly.

The energy of your home will be as the energy of your things, your rooms, your landscape and views, the amount of quiet, the kids on the block—you name it—it all affects you more than you know. Get in touch with and honor all *energy*.

Conclusion

By now I expect that the concept and reality of *energy and spirit alive and well in all of life* has grown in perspective for my readers. The only message I offer is to ask you to *honor spirit*, and to *use it* to make life work in every aspect of your life in perfect divine order.

I ask everyone to honor all living things. I ask all to not only be *in touch* with the idea that there is energy in all living things, but to go further—to the level of *respect*. Whatever purposes were created with each living thing, that purpose must be allowed, even honored, with gratitude. Becoming so in tune with all living things creates a greater sense of knowing within self.

If everyone followed these principles of design, there would be no two spaces alike; we would not be copying others creations. We would all be living in original works of artistic expression of one's life and *loving every minute of it.*

I love my life of studying energies in everything, especially in design applications where our creative attentions can bless our family's lives more than we will ever know. Remember: everything merely has the energy that we give it, whatever makes sense and happiness to you as the creator— from spirit, from inner knowing. And that's **the whole message of my theories: to become aware that spirit is always speaking**

in and through all creation, and in and to you.

With spirit there is only truth—no judgment. Spirit speaks the language of love, which is the literal *element* through which energy is always transferred. With this clarity, you can study feng shui and any other interpretation of the use of energy, understand its power, and use the principles in your own applications, as they feel right. **Connect to the energy of life all around you, clean it up, and allow it to serve you well.**

Thoughts for Processing *The Energy of Art*:

- What inanimate objects do you own which you have animated by your loving connections to them? Do you recognize how things have the energy we give them?
- Take one room at a time and analyze the energy of your things. Rate them one to ten—one being little to no energy or bad vibes, while ten is serving you with great energy.
- Make a box for each of the different places your rejects will be going. If anything has energy less than a rating of six, it might have to go in one of those boxes. You decide; have courage!
- Do the overhaul, then ask if all of your pieces now *giving* you energy?
- Are there places that will need replacements, and can you energetically visualize the size, shape, color, and material that such pieces should be? Keep these in mind, and soon you will find them!
- Do your art pieces take you somewhere you want to go? Pay attention to the kinds of art that please you, and make it a priority to purchase such.
- Notice the messages of any historical pieces you possess. What energy are they giving you? How does this feed your soul?

- What music or sounds bring your energies higher? Do you have some of this available? Make plans to enjoy the energy of sounds more often.
- Notice where music takes you, and note that when you want to feel certain ways, music can take you there—a mode of travel that is free and easy!
- What fragrances delight you? Raise your vibes by finding ways to get some of your favorites in front of you regularly.
- How are you with live plants? If your circumstances allow, become a nurturer of the abundant energy of nature indoors. As you check out your local nursery, practice noticing which plants speak to you, raising your energies by merely being in their presence.
- Determine a schedule for having some fresh flowers always near. Spend time studying their intricate beauties and how this makes you feel.
- If your décor is a little boring, find ways to add some *contrast* for excitement.
- How busy and involved with others is your daily schedule? Does your home bring the requisite amount of balance and relaxation? What could you change to accommodate these needs?
- Your home and all the things in and around it are speaking to you. How do you like the relationship, and what are you going to do about it?
- Becoming more aware of *all things alive with energy* is the most important and first step to enjoying this primary sanctuary for your soul.

Chapter 5

The Energy of Divine Order

Everything I have is speaking to me — sounds so loud
I cannot find my way,
And sounds of comfort for a brilliant day.
The noise dear God, it has to go — I must have simplicity,
Where only loving friends and servants stay.

There is perfect divine order in every part of the universe, except for one place: people. Born with the gift of choice, and easily disconnected from spirit, mankind can create a lot of chaos. I wrote this chapter to show the simple math on the importance of aligning our lives with spirit, starting with something as simple and obvious as the order in our own physical spaces. To maintain good energy *within*, we have to take charge of the order of things *without:* a reflection of our honest intention to live in harmony with spirit in every way.

Our connection to such beliefs may be vague, as most of us did not grow up choosing to be *clean-freaks*. In fact, based on the conditions found in the rooms of most young people, just the opposite is probably true! For most of us, the relationship of the *physical* to the *spiritual* is not intuitively discovered; reluctantly, we have to be taught; and it does matter, as I will explain.

I grew up in a fifties bungalow, a modern one with seven people in the house. Mother had five children in six and a half years. There was a lot of laundry; I know because I was always folding it! Mother would bring it up from the basement laundry room and drop it on the long brown friezé sectional in the living room, where it would wait until I folded it—not fun, especially when my friends came over and piles of laundry were still there waiting for me to do my job.

Saturdays were cleaning days, except for summers when we finished on Fridays and spent weekends at the lake. My sister and I somehow got the assignment to polish the furniture, vacuum the floors, clean the bathrooms, and shake the rugs. We also had to do the dishes every night after dinner. (Where were my three brothers?)

All grown up now, I still feel those good vibes, knowing that everything is clean and in its proper place. Maybe it's that high I got as a child, knowing that once the work was done, I could go out and play. There are great blessings from living in a house of order. The effort allows one's energy to stay focused on *personal creation* without distraction from other messages such as what is *not* done, what does *not* fit, what does *not* work. A house of order allows the focus to stay in places of what *is*: what I *can* do, what I *want* to do, what gifts *are* mine, and what I can do with them—all very positive and enlightened forms of energy. I will explain further.

For much of my life, whenever I went into my closet I would stand and stare, forever wondering what to wear. I realized that much of what was there was the wrong fit, the wrong season, out of style, or just plain didn't work for me anymore. People change, but we don't always tell our closets! It always made me feel confused trying to sort through all the clothes that *didn't* work, searching to find something that *would* work. That's a lot of *wasted energy* knocking me off balance every day, at least once for each piece that didn't feel right—a lot of *effort* keeping my good positive energy from constantly being derailed.

The same thing happened in the living room: the color of the sofa worked in the last house, but it seemed to take on a different hue in this one, clashing with what I thought were *neutral* wall colors when we bought the house. *When did they turn pink?* I lost energy by becoming sickened just thinking about it every time I went in that room. It was challenging to keep my good-feeling vibes going for very long at all; I wanted to run away. There is enough negative in the world without facing it at every turn in our homes!

Every year or so I overhaul all of my things, reevaluating my ownership. Recently, I gave away seventy-five percent of my closet to charity. I choose not to think of the money. I

114

realize the value is not in what I paid, but in *what it is doing to my soul to keep it*! I decided that everything—even my tray of earrings—must be of such good energy that it makes me happy just seeing it there, or else off it goes!

As I examine anything, I am noticing its energy—how it makes me feel. What might be the energy of dirt, clutter and trash? Perhaps dust could have the energetic message of *neglect*, of *being too busy*, or just *not caring* for one's things. Clutter could be saying that you have too much on your plate, *too busy to do the basics*, and you *need to make some changes*. Trash could have the energetic message of *confusion, wastefulness*, or maybe *ignorance*. Unmade beds may have the energetic message of *laziness* or *lack of pride*. Clothes on the floor may speak the energy of being *unaware of self, leaving a trail*. Being unaware of the effect we have on others by leaving a trail of our messes is possibly selfish, disconnected to others, or disrespectful to self and others. Simply said, clutter and dirt and trash send messages that can *take* from our energy.

Honoring Connections

Of course I may choose to put off cleaning or making my bed for a while at times, such as when inspiration comes and I have to act on it immediately, (the higher order of allowing spirit to flow). But later I honor myself by making my house a house of cleanliness and order. The place we live while on Mother Earth is our connection to her energy—God's energy—the highest of all forms of life. With this connection established, we take it literally and begin implementing awareness of this energy into all parts of our lives. As I keep things clean and in order, I am honoring God, all of the loving positive energy of the earth, and myself. Remember, man is the only part of earth life that is *creating chaos by his choice*!

Since I am writing about energy and especially your

own personal energy, know that you just feel better when the work is done! Allow me to remind that you feel less stress when you can quickly find everything you need. Life just goes smoother when you are not distracted by anything that creates negative energy in any way.

The state of our rooms is a reflection of how we see ourselves and how we view our lives; it's also a reminder of the *state of mind* we may be in. For example, whenever I am super disorganized for more than a day, I notice how frustrated I am, how depressed I may be feeling, how lost in *mental* garbage I have become — definitely verifying this principle. Lack of order represents a loss of personal power. Just look around at your house and see if the shape it's in is a reflection of how you are feeling right now!

I ask, *how can I reclaim my power? Who have I given it to? What thoughts and beliefs am I buying into that are keeping me from my joy?* There is always a connection that I may choose to change. *Mental* garbage shows up as *physical* garbage. It is a truth — a law: **spiritual and emotional thoughts and beliefs manifest physically, in your rooms and in your body.** *Take your cues from the condition of your house or office: it's a mirror of the state of your mind!*

Facelift for the Home

Now that I have overhauled my closet, everything that I see there *brings* me energy. I don't have as many choices, but the ones I do have always make me smile. No more wasted time and wasted personal power by having to wade through the *nots* for the things that work to bring me good satisfying energy! I keep only the things that I like, that fit, that are in season, and that are aligned with my personal style; everything reminds me that my life is working just fine in that department.

I also remodeled parts of my house, doing what

116

absolutely had to be done to keep me from having experiences with negative energy greeting me in the face. As I looked at each thing—each wall and space—I noticed if it blessed me or if it irritated me in some way. Anything that did not bless had to go or be overhauled.

Now everywhere I look in my home, I feel gratitude. Everything feels right. Everything *is* right: just what I need and like, all of which brings me happy, satisfying energy. Whenever I think of the costs of our remodeling and what else we could have done with that money, I just remember how uplifted my energy is in every vista I see now, and you can't put a price on that kind of inner satisfaction.

Following inner guidance and matching my personal energy with the choices, I made my home flow perfectly. I filled it with pieces that work for our family's lifestyle, as well as what continues to interest me. All of my things now radiate powerful energy that pleases me, and the gratitude connects me to my source of light and joy. Since the overhaul, very satisfying and creative energy is constantly feeding my soul while in my house.

Organizing for Sanity

In the remodeling process, I made sure to find or built a place for everything. If there was no place to put it, I had to consider that I might be unnecessary. Sometimes I had to put things farther away from their use. The things I use more often, I put at my fingertips. If I couldn't find a place for something, I had to assume I didn't need it. Now whenever I want something, I know exactly where it is, and I can access it quickly. I avoid a lot of negative energy by being able to find everything on the spot.

Don't put it down: put it away! One effort is required either way, so I may as well put it where it goes when it leaves my hand. I pick it up, I put it down; my only consideration is probably a few more steps and some mindfulness to put it where it belongs. If I always put it where it goes, it's always there when I need it—no extra energy required.

Cleanliness and order don't take much time. Fumbling in the disorder takes time: time to work around the mess, and time to get my sanity back as I have to shift my focus in and around and away from the mess, trying to figure where something might be. Cleaning and organizing takes a lot less time overall than *all the moments of frustration that creep up from the lack of it.*

How often I have fretted over a messy garage for months, tripping over boxes and bikes and bags, and then finally cleaning it up in a mere thirty minutes! Good grief, all that precious energy that could have been used for something blessed and happy! All that sighing and being overwhelmed, draining my reservoirs of goodness, taking with it my peace of mind! I work hard to fill myself with good energy, and I can do better to *keep it!*

Rules for Shopping

I have learned a few tricks for limiting the stuff I bring into the house. Some people say that for every new thing you add to your perfect spaces, you must give away one old thing, as there is only so much room. Bring in new energy; send out old energy. Maybe so, but in the least, if you bring home something new, it must add to the power of all the good vibes already radiating throughout your home or office, making the new addition a very good fit with the rest.

I am one of those people who *loves* to go shopping. I am fascinated with creativity in every form. I get excited when I see new design ideas. The more I shop, the more new, creative, artistic expression I see. The more creativity I see, the more excited I get. The more excited I get, the more I buy. The more I buy when I am in this emotional state, the more I later realize I don't need it! So I have learned never to shop for the sake of *entertainment*. Educating myself in creative arts is necessary, but mindless wondering and wandering in stores is not.

My mother taught me this rule: if I am out shopping and I think I must buy something, especially if it's expensive, I put it on hold and go home and sleep on it. If I can't get it out of my mind and wanting of it, then it is mine. I am *missing* it. I get to buy it and bring it home.

If I do not use this test for choices, my home and closet will be filled with lots of *stuff*: just clothes and things — nothing special. I want to have empowered pieces that serve and lift and love me back. *Everything either brings me power or takes my power to possess it.* That *ethereal cord* is attached and real, so I must be careful to pay attention.

My second rule of shopping is the same as my rule for making choices in design: let the person and their closet speak and tell me what it needs. This is how it works: when I get in touch with something I think I need to wear. I keep it in mind, just like getting in touch with what the space in the house needs. I imagine the approximate shape, color, materials needed in any article, and then I look for it while I am out shopping. When I find it, I buy it, and it always works. That's all: a simple idea that saves a lot of returning and regrets.

I have clients who do the opposite: buying something because they like it but have no earthly idea where to put it. While I can help to find a place for it, it is unnecessary, and does not serve to add to the higher energy we are creating. Create from a space of spiritual knowing. Let the house speak, let the closet speak, let the pantry speak, and *then go shopping*.

The Hiding Places

I get a high from cleaning out all the unnecessary items anywhere in my life, from my pantry to my purse, my wallet, my cell phone, and my computer. I remove all that is old or unattended to, un-liked, or better kept somewhere else. I feel good when deleting names from my cell phone directories and unsubscribing from unwanted email lists. Cleaning up these spaces and directories gives me less to be keeping up with, and less calling out my name to attend to it. It's the same *umbilical cord to my energy* thing. All the old and out of date can be deleted, leaving more room for fresh new opportunities. I notice *every place my energy is being used,* and do what I must to always keep it in the positive! I know there is a need to keep some extra supplies in storage for emergencies, which is just plain common sense wisdom. But to all people who keep stacks and stacks of their old stuff, hoarding things just in case they might need them someday, here is the truth: **Everything you need at any given time is always given to you when you ask spirit,** so you can stop stock-piling right now! The energy of your stored *stuff* will stagnate and do you no good anyway. By releasing all into the flow of abundance, you let go of all that does not serve, allowing another to enjoy it instead. Living by faith, you allow spirit to bring everything fresh and new always flowing towards you; in your hour of need, all will be provided.

My home is the sanctuary for my soul — my sacred space, and clearing its energy to serve me in every way is the dutiful gift I must continue to offer to the goddess I am, indirectly blessing all in my circle of influence.

Thoughts for Processing *The Energy of Divine Order:*

- Notice your feelings when your home is clean and organized.

120

- What routines for organization have you or are you planning to establish?
- Notice the similarities of the state of your rooms to the state of your mind, right now.
- What bugs you every time you look at it, like a messy jewelry box or workbench maybe? The car? Your make-up drawers? Your desk? Your piles of filing?
- Make a list of all the places in your home that need some organization. Prioritize, with what is most affecting your sanity at the top of the list. Schedule a thirty-minute organizing session once a week and start marking off that list.
- Check out your closet and remove everything that is out of style, old, rarely worn, or doesn't fit; give it away. Notice the powerful opening to new energy that fills you in return, and the awesome vibes of empowerment that come from the pieces that remain.
- Do the same with your pantry, cupboards, linen closet, attic, basement, back room, purse, wallet, cell phone and email directories—all the places you stuff things, having ownership but never using—all the places that take your energy. Make them work to bless you with life-*giving* energy.
- Notice the energy of your stores of old stuff (just in case you might need them someday). Does the energy represent security or fear? Be honest. Let it go and trust in the system of abundant supply on demand!
- Simplify your collections and re-energize your life!

Chapter 6

The Energy of the Physical Body

Mother Earth,
Thank you for sharing your beautiful babies with me.
You are most creative and wise,
And I care for them as my own.

I believe we are innately *spiritual* beings here on this planet to have a *physical* experience. Looking around we must admit: things of this world *appear* to be all about the physical elements, which is where most of our attention is required. But I believe we can continue using spirit as a guide to live in alignment with more empowering truths when it comes to choices about our physical bodies, which feed on *spirit* much more than you might think. This chapter is about the relationship of *spirit over body*, including many ways such an idea might be applied: food, water, plant medicines, emotions, exercise, and sex.

My children are adults now, and still show surprise as they reminisce the reality of their childhood food supply. Somehow they can't wrap their minds around the fact that as the rest of the neighbor children were enjoying cold cereal every morning, I fed mine such healthy things as homemade granola over homemade yogurt flavored with homemade jam, berries picked from Grandma's garden, hot nine-grain cereal, (limiting the brown sugar to two spoons), or whole wheat pancakes topped with real maple syrup and homemade applesauce which we bottled ourselves, (without sugar), from the local produce we picked. For some years, we drank raw milk from the local dairy, and sometimes I whipped my own butter from the un-pasteurized cream on top.

I guess it's obvious: I have a love affair with the produce of Mother Earth! I feel a greater sense of serving and nurturing others when I am able to share my healthy and gourmet cooking using all good things from the earth, which are filled with the energy of *spirit!*

It wasn't very hard for me to do the math on cold cereal: if I reduced it to its origin of raw materials, I got a few spoonfuls of *powder* consisting of sugar, flour, and artificial additives, which certainly did not seem very healthy or look very satisfying. Hyperactivity would be the least of the reactions, and I doubt my children's bodies even knew how to process it, much less be nourished by it in the least.

Compare that to the ingredients in my pancake breakfast: a cup of fresh ground whole wheat, some buttermilk just off the dairy, as were the eggs, a whole apple in each serving of applesauce; sorry kids, the choice was clear. They thank me now, though they grew up swearing they would give their own kids sugar-cereals every day of their lives.

I gave them cold cereal on their birthdays, and it was a really big deal. They got two boxes each, (since all the children in our family also got to eat the cereal that the birthday child had). The birthday child got all the leftovers, and each of my children can tell you the exact cereal and the exact birthday when someone *stole* their leftover cereal. Yes it was a treat, but nobody had cavities, and we had healthy, happy, peaceful children in the house.

There is no doubt about this truth: *there is vibrant living energy—spirit—in the elements of the earth.* It is also my firm belief that God put it all here to feed our physical bodies from this fountain of abundance—spirit—living within the elements of plants. Spiritual beings need to be fed *spirit!*

Choosing Natural

Back in the eighties, spring water was mostly available in 5-gallon dispensers used in offices, but I had one in my kitchen. The refills were delivered in glass bottles right to my door. Heavy as they were, I managed to lug them to storage and lift replacements onto the dispenser as needed. I have a scar on my right hand where one of those bottles didn't quite make it once. But I cured that cut very quickly with *miracle water*.

I got my *miracle water* from a local herbalist at the suggestion of my eighty-year-old friends who said it quickly cured someone of a badly burned body when he bathed in it; nearly one hundred dollars for that gallon of what looked like rusty water, but it cured my deeply cut palm in two days. I have always trusted in the *old-time-cures*.

Spring water has been in my kitchen all these years. It makes me happy just thinking of all that virgin sweet moisture right out of the mountains, blessing my babies and my own need for clean energy to flow in and through me. So close to its natural state, such water has life generating within it, which passes into my body and onto my cells as I drink it. (I can smell and taste chlorine a mile away, which seems to not only kill the germs but also the life-giving spirit in water.)

As a young mother my education in natural cures increased as I read a book that suggests you can *own your own body*, and not give that power to others. The messages convinced me to stop running to the doctor with every little achy, touchy issue. I found simple remedies using natural products available to me at herb shops nearby. At first I was scared that I might cause further pain to my babies, but when a few drops of some tinctures of healing plants stopped their crying instantly and the pain never returned, my confidence grew. Soon I was teaching other mothers this simple, natural wisdom.

I learned all I could and even invested in an herbal company of my own for a while. I learned which herbs work for what ails, and I kept plenty on hand. I learned that if the right herbs are used early when symptoms first appear, we avoid sickness. It was nice to know what to do, and to not spend half my life in a doctor's office.

127

Using plants from the earth has always seemed the right thing to do. I have an innate belief that God put us here with everything we need to successfully experience life. It's fascinating to me every time I discover a new product or flavor that is grown in the earth. I sense there is life in all of it—more of that *life-giving energy*. As a mother and homemaker, I was so focused on enjoying these gifts that I made almost everything we ate from scratch.

If someone wanted mac and cheese, I boiled some noodles, made a roux with butter and flour, stirred in fresh milk until it made a creamy sauce, added lots of real shredded cheese, maybe a few spices, drained the noodles, stirred it all together, and voila—mac and cheese—maybe ten minutes start to finish. In my innocence I didn't know there was another way.

One day I was visiting a sister-in-law when she served me some of her mac and cheese. It had intense cheese flavor. I asked for her recipe, and she laughed as she showed me the box. That was in the early nineties. I don't know why I was so out of touch with what everyone else was doing. Perhaps it was because I had a big family, bought in bulk, and never gave myself the option of buying pre-packaged foods; or perhaps it was because I didn't consider those mixes to be *real food*.

Fresh Food

I followed wisdom's guidance in my younger years and started gardening. I learned to till and fertilize the soil, when and what to plant, and how to weed by pushing and pulling the earth between the rows with a triangle hoe. The best garden ever grew the year we had a load of manure delivered. It smelled like there was more manure than dirt but it worked. It put Jack's beanstalk to shame: the darkest green colors, the tallest stalks of everything, practically overnight—I couldn't even find the weeds amidst the large, vibrant vegetable plants.

The favorite garden was the one that grew in planter boxes all around the landscape of our second home. The children would pick and eat peas and strawberries straight from the vines to keep from having to come in to eat lunch on summer days, (which I later learned was their plot to save them from being accountable for their chores).

I remember the fascination I felt when I was in the garden—delight that things grow like that, that we could eat them, and that they taste so much better than store bought. I remember the very day that I realized that I was connected to the earth in gardening, and that by noticing the energy of life growing there—spirit—it fed my soul, (which is also made of spirit). This revelation added to my love of self as I realized another strong bond to my beloved Mother Earth.

There wasn't enough room in our smaller homes to grow everything we wanted to eat, so my favorite stop was a roadside market nearby, where fruits and vegetables had just been picked from the fields that day. The flavors were intense, unlike anything available in the stores. I felt the powerful energy of plants being *alive*, of just being picked, which I knew would supply the same power to our bodies by dinnertime that night. I compared that intense *living* energy to the *low if any* energy of foods which have been sprayed with chemicals to withstand days and weeks of shipping, storage, and display, with little life left by the time it got to our table! Whenever possible, *buying local is the way to go*. It makes me feel good all over.

In the growing season, I always make dinners of just fruits and vegetables. The contrasts of the colors are so beautiful that sometimes I have to take a picture before we eat. Radiant living food versus dead food (animals and plants cooked to death)—again, I know eating living plants brings the same radiance to our own faces.

For much of my children's early years I fed them vegetarian. Again this was a very long time ago, before it was popular. I could feel the energy from the living foods, and I knew that same living energy was doing good things to our bodies. I had heard the example of how meat smells when left out at room temp for a few days, and could only imagine it would be even worse for all those days it took to digest in our bodies at even warmer temps! I compared this to how fruits and veggies smell in the same time. It just seemed natural to eat what was sweet and fresh, even after being left for days in the sun.

I also began comparing the energy fresh foods *give* to my body, versus the energy *required* of my body to process meats and dairy. I saw it all as an *energy exchange*, and I wanted to live as close as possible to the *spirit*.

Spiritual Connections to Foods

My sensitivity to the energies of foods expands to *flavors*. With my love of fresh foods and their energies, I have noticed that I can taste anything and figure out what it's made of. With this same awareness, I pay attention to what my body is craving and figure out how to make it. Bless my family for always being subjected to eating the foods *my* body is craving — the privilege of being the cook!

I have always wanted to try everything I heard of — every new fruit or spice or method, so my children were exposed early to international cuisine. We had a Vietnamese neighbor — a dear family friend — who loved to cook for and with us, showing us how to make really tasty food without a lot of sugars and oils. It is *clean* food, as is Japanese and Korean, prepared with vegetables and fresh sauces with unusual and intense flavors, which along with my roadside-market-dinners, I found more acceptable than the traditional American diet.

I fed my children with everything as alive with energy as I could find and learn and make. I am sure our grocery budget was way more than others who ate a lot of hot dogs and casseroles, but mealtimes were a great adventure and education in what is *real with spirit!*

I have read books that compare the shapes of fruits and veggies to the human body parts, suggesting that each plant was miraculously created to give the nutrition needed for the part of the body that is its physical match — walnuts for the brain, avocadoes for the uterus, tomatoes for the heart. This amazing theory once again shows the magnificent divine order in the creation of our universe.

Eating these *first generation foods*, (Adam and Eve's menu), I never have to diet. If it is from the earth, I eat it in whatever quantities I desire. With this plan, I never put on weight or have to watch calories. I eat often and until I am full. The fresh flavors and textures not only fill me physically, but also spiritually, as I stay tuned to the high vibrations of Mother Earth's abundance. Yes, there is a grand design for our time on earth, and if I am observant, everything about food is very obvious and perfectly divine.

Natural Beginnings

As a child, I learned to cook while playing in my mother's kitchen. Her only rule was that I had to clean up after myself. I honor my mother for allowing me the joy of experimenting with anything I wanted, spawning my desire for cooking and my love for all that grows from the earth. (I also honor her for paying for all my groceries while, according to her, I fed the whole campus in college.)

My mother also taught me simple plant-based remedies, such as vinegar rinses for my hair conditioning to restore the PH balance, warm salt water through my sinuses to kill infection, and enemas to release toxins at the first sign of sickness, (which I hated, but they worked). That was life in the fifties — the beginning of the revolution towards new-age thinking, building the groundwork for our present-day enthusiasm for living so completely *au natural.*

I gave my children a similar awareness of the energy of natural living and the same freedom in the kitchen, and we have lots of funny pictures to prove it: buckets of spilled flour and quarts of spilled juice, singing as they enjoyed slopping through the messes. Fond memories remain of digging through the rice, making our own custom gingerbread houses, filling and rolling up gyozas on the bar, and churning the homemade orange ice cream—all of which express the true meaning of *the good life*, which makes me very happy.

Spirit Energy in the Art of Food

It's an honor to eat beautiful living things, so I believe in showing this respect by the elements included in its presentation. I use real glass, real porcelain, real sterling or stainless, real napkins—everything real. It just seems right to me to use natural elements and creations of artistic hands to serve and honor the natural elements of our food—again, recognizing *spirit* in all these things.

Asian people are known for the energy they put into their food through its preparation. As they finely and evenly chop the ingredients and as they artistically arrange the elements of their meals, they imbue them with love to be passed on to those who partake of that food. *Connection to spirit through food* is found in every culture in vastly interesting varieties, always delighting my inquisitive mind and providing inspiration for creative cooks everywhere.

Nowadays throughout the world, food is becoming a celebrated *art form.* No longer is a burger just a meat patty and a bun with the usual condiments of mayo, mustard, ketchup and a slice of pickle, but may include a grilled portabella

132

mushroom, aioli sauce, some artisan veggies, rare herbs, and on and on—you name it: if it's from the earth and the artist's hands, it brings new life served on a plate.

Fascination and love for all things natural from the earth's elements has allowed artistically connected chefs to rise to unlimited possibilities. Everywhere I go, the food industry is offering the energy of love through their spiritual connections to organic produce, celebrating joy with others as they share from that fullness of love. These *food artists* are some of my most admired friends!

Prayer and Gratitude

I know the body houses my spirit and that I am connected to spirit in foods that nourish my cells and keep my body alive. As you can see by now, I am absolutely in heaven eating fresh, organic, heirloom produce in season, and high quality exquisite flavors from the purest sources for everything in my recipes—fresh and homemade. I might choose to go hungry rather than eat low quality and poorly prepared foods. I literally *feel* and absorb the life-giving energy in fresh produce, and I am very blessed when such is available to me.

But when that is not an option, it is just as important that I don't send the energy of *fear* into my foods by my *beliefs* that something will actually hurt me, give me cancer, or otherwise cause my demise! People do that all the time, worrying about being perfectly in tune following certain food beliefs and regimes. Which is worse: worrying or eating poorly? With loving *intention*, I give everything a prayer of gratitude and allow everything to serve me perfectly.

There are no rules to food; there is only *spirit*. There is nothing to fear or panic about. Some people smoke like a chimney and live on fried foods every day of their lives yet live happily to a hundred years old. So it's definitely more about the *attitudes and beliefs* than the actual foods we eat. I have been healed by macrobiotics, which is mostly pressure cooked, and also by raw vegan diets. There is scientific evidence that many forms and combinations heal the body, yet they may be vastly different. Food is here to nourish our cells, fill our tummies and please our palettes, and serves with whatever connections *we* give it. I happen to feast on *spirit in live foods*, so spirit from live foods is my reward. When live foods are not an option, there is still a way to bring *spirit* to my plate.

Using gratitude instead of fear, I choose to pray over and bless my food. We have power from on high to create good energy in what we eat, no matter what's in it. It may simply be in the act of showing gratitude, but a prayer of sincere desire will bring spirit to align the food's energy with my intention that it nourish me. Spirit is here, ready and waiting to bless the food, to change the elements, to improve the flavors, to imbue healing when there was none innately. When given with innocent intention, a prayer is a form of instant scientific rearranging, so to say. I imagine all that might have been *less than pure energy* actually changing upon my desire and gratitude into a form of matter that actually *brings* energy, healing, and perfection to my body!

Before I eat, I innately feel like holding my hands out with open palms facing up while I focus on the heavens pouring down spirit. I imagine God is filling my hands, my heart, and my food with all that is good, and I feel abundant gratitude blessing it all. A prayer with desired intention will open the way for the creation of that intention, which is technically the higher order of anything to do with the quality of our food supply.

Personal Awareness

I have also learned that it is important to create a pleasant environment while eating. I believe that the *energy* around you is actually being *swallowed* along with the food. If people are angry or trying to rush through dinner, they might feel ill afterwards, indicating the unsettling effects from taking in the vibes of that discontent along with the foods ingested. Conversely, I have noticed that humor and fun during mealtimes allows foods to digest better. Notice what you are thinking about or feeling when you eat, and create the most pleasant, peaceful, happy, and healthy environment possible.

Connecting even deeper, I often ask myself while eating, *what is the purpose of this food?* Am I merely pleasing my oral fixations, tastes, and chewing needs, or am I inviting healing into my body? Am I eating for my mouth or for my cells? I may ask and notice what my physical body needs on a cellular level and if my choices will give me enough of the right things to satisfy those needs.

Sometimes this kind of awareness makes me stop eating sooner, getting in tune with my cellular situation, realizing my body is already satisfied. Sometimes my mouth could go on eating forever celebrating the wonderful tastes of many good things, usually in ignorance of what my body actually *needs*. Sometimes the reverse is my choice: I keep chewing even when my taste buds are uninterested, simply because my body needs the elements of nutrition included.

I may have never created the same meal twice. My body sends out the signals telling me what it wants, and that's what I make. If I don't know how, I figure it out by trial and error. That's the way I learned to cook—starting meal prep with an *inner inquisition* of my body's wants and needs.

I ask if this food *gives* me energy or if this food *takes* my energy to process it through my digestive system. I have heard it said if you feel like a nap after dinner, you ate the wrong foods. Eat to receive energy!

The body will speak what it wants and needs if we stop

to ask and wait for an answer. It only takes a few seconds, and the perfect items are actually *felt,* maybe tasted, or the effects are noticed as to how I will feel if I eat them. Without this awareness, my mind or my mouth may send a signal that it wants something, but it may not be what my *body* wants or needs. When I ask my body what it wants and needs at any given time, I get a good suggestion, which is usually a better choice, leaving feelings of satisfaction all the way down to my cells. For the higher good of all concerned, the relationship between my body and its fuel of choice should always be centered in spirit.

Emotions and Food

The scale of hunger to fullness is an interesting place from which to explain overeating, dieting, and the energy of foods. Technically, we eat because we are hungry; then we eat certain foods that satisfy that hunger. But we have to ask, are we eating the foods themselves to satisfy the craving, or are we eating the *energy* that those foods represent to us—our emotional connection? If we eat cookies because as a child we were given cookies as a treat, reward, or message of love, eating cookies as an adult is not just about having a sweet tooth! It's about a literal, energetic craving for the *love* you received as a child, and the cookie will never give you that. You could eat cookies all day long for the rest of your life and never be satisfied, perhaps adversely affecting your healthy body in the process of trying to find the *energy* of love.

I propose that most of our mindless eating is an effort to seek some form of emotional energy, and has nothing to do with the reality of the physical requirements of the body. As I see it, food cravings fall into two categories: 1) The cells are calling for what they need for their perfect healthy well being, or 2) The subconscious mind is calling for something that it believes will fill an emotional need. The body is complex and intelligent and certainly will send out signals for what foods are needed at any given time. If we become sensitive to this system of inner *messaging,* we will eat perfectly well and be very healthy.

The second category of food cravings comes from an entirely different form of energy — emotional needs. We attempt and always fail to satisfy these needs with food. Emotional eating comes not from your body's needs for nourishment but from your *history.* When you feel an emotional need, the brain scans its memory for another time in your life when such a need seemed to be satisfied. Acting on what seemed to work before, the brain will make a suggestion accordingly, while you are usually consciously unaware.

I tested this theory on my brother. He was on a diet but was craving brownies, *especially the crunchy corner pieces* — cute. I asked him to tell me his earliest memory of having those crunchy corners of brownies. He said he remembered having them all the time when he was little. I reflected on my childhood which was in the same household during most of the same years, and I had no such memories of brownies — none.

As I thought of this, I asked him if it was possible that Mother made the brownies just for him, or if it perhaps meant a whole lot more to him than it did to me. Maybe I was used to making my own brownies so it was no big deal to me when Mother made them. My brother agreed it was possible that Mother may have made them only for him as a special gift. I further asked if it was possible that those brownies were more a sign of Mother's love and attention for him than actually being a desired food in particular. Then the *ah-ha* came.

My brother admitted that he had been feeling very lonely the past few days and such *mother-love* would be the exact energy he was craving. If so, such an energy form (desire) was translated into a subconscious physical craving of something tangible that the brain (stored intelligence) knew would take him (his body) back to that time and place of *mother-love energy actually being present.* Supposedly, this would make everything all better!

Following food cravings for emotional satisfaction will repeatedly fail. Guilt follows self-doubt and creates frustration, and nothing good comes from such ignorance to our choices. On the other hand, (since I don't do guilt), *once I am aware of the source of my cravings,* I can make a conscious choice to celebrate my favorite *comfort* foods as a fond memory of happy days gone by, choosing portions intelligently!

Choosing to be clear and wise about our cravings, we will notice the energy of the foods we crave — what those cravings represent energetically. Seek to discover the truthful desires behind your cravings. Once enlightened, as you become attached to the actual physical energy of any given food item, you will make choices to feed your *body* from the abundance of Mother Earth, and feed your *emotional needs* in more realistically helpful, spiritual ways. The word *diet* would then become history.

Spirit Over Body

As we become more sensitive to our bodies, we learn that *we* as our higher spirit selves are to be the masters to our physical presence. Look at the issue of addictions to foods and drinks and other cravings of the body; we all have been there. Like most everyone, I become hypnotized with certain smells and tastes, which cause me to desire them. Over the years as I have sought to get in touch with my power of spirit over body, I have realized that some of those foods and drinks were controlling *me*, telling *me* that I wanted some. That's when I had to admit my *affections* were actually *addictions.*

Choices should always come from inner knowing — from spirit — according to what the body really wants. I remember the exact time when I choose to master some of my *affections*. I noticed the power these foods and drinks had over my body. In these cases and at that time, I was not the one in charge of my body. I was not making choices from inner wisdom. It seemed these affections ordered *me* to choose *them*, almost unconsciously, so I consciously (deliberately) took control back from these *dictators*. It is possible this is how all addictions are overcome.

My *spirit* always knows what is truth for my *physical* needs, while the body knows pleasure and uses its senses to seek for satisfying *emotional* needs. I am grateful to know there is a way to please and care for both the body and the spirit, if I take time to pay attention and make choices according to my highest good—from spirit.

Fasting is a way of commanding the body to obey. A body can survive on liquids without foods for days. Christ taught this purification process by His example of a forty-day fast. It shows discipline and creates personal mastery, after which spiritual enlightenment cannot be withheld. It doesn't have to take us forty days, but to become the ruler over your own life, you have to teach the body who is in charge and become a heart-centered person in every way. With a little practice, regular fasting allows the spirit to reach a *high* that creates a very special experience with truth.

Other physical cravings and addictions include the misuse of sexual relations—an otherwise most powerful, healing, and enlightening energy. Such lack of understanding of this magnificent spiritual power is seen in rampant participation in pornography and illicit sexual relations. Is the body really craving the feelings of physically experiencing the act of sex, or is it craving the truthful meaning of what that same experience can produce energetically? I propose that **the body is always craving the energy of real love.** We physically *need* to have *spirit present in the body*—alive, awake, and participating—and sex is a powerful way to short cut that process.

The Body and the Spirit

Spirit moves through the body when the body is in motion, so the body *needs* to move. We have been taught that work and exercise feel good because such movement releases *endorphins* — naturally occurring feel-good chemicals, but it's so much more than that.

Each of us has a *spirit* body that lives in our *physical* body. Somehow this is a very important element of our design from the beginning. Perhaps the purpose is to strengthen the spirit by giving it something to manage, to act *through*. At first as a child, the body does not immediately obey the spirit-you. But with time and determination, your spirit learns to *will* the body to do many wonderful things, and the body learns to trust and obey the will of the spirit. The body becomes home to the spirit. Sometimes, the body thinks *it* is all you are, but you know better: spirit is always meant to be in charge.

The spirit is actually much larger in energetic size than the body. Spirit generates through and out of the body, into what we call auric fields. This aura expands when clear and active, radiating several feet outward from the skin in every direction. The more enlightened one is, the larger is the aura's radiance.

The purpose of moving the body is to allow the spirit to generate that radiance of enlightenment into all parts of the body in perfect balance. As you move, stretch, breathe, work, and dance, *spirit* moves into those areas. It feels like the body is *making room* for the light of your spirit to be felt in these areas as you move, co-creating a feeling of joy.

Additionally, the spirit knows nothing of age. Spirit is timeless and eternally youthful. Think about it: the more *age-less spirit* you have within your body, the younger and more vital you will feel!

Sometimes this spirit-body connection is difficult to access. Many have suffered forms of physical and emotion abuse, causing them to feel a need to hide to protect their spirits. This is not just an idea; it literally causes the spirit to retreat from running the body — a body that then seems to run on some sort of autopilot. Do you ever see someone who you don't think is really there, who seems to be physically operating almost mechanically, with little joy? Since the soul of a person is made up of both body and spirit, which must work together to *create* that good life, these forms of abuse are sometimes referred to as *soul murder*.

When I was emotionally troubled for years of my life in abusive relationships, I had little energy to exercise. My spirit was not there to run my body — to move like it would *have* to if I exercised. My spirit was *in hiding* — avoiding, due to trauma and extreme stress.

After I removed myself from those relationships and began learning to love myself again, I could feel my spirit returning to run my body, as if it felt safe to again be there. As anxiety and resistance caused by fear were no longer blocking the way, I felt my body move with so much more ease and freedom through the same physical workouts that had been previously blocked by a body with an absentee spirit.

Yoga, Tai Chi and other spirit-based forms of exercise are designed with movements to open the body to feel spirit. As you stretch, reach, breathe and hold these perfectly aligned poses, you are opening the exact areas of the body where the energy fields are centered. Opening these fields (we have hundreds of them in us), spirit can be re-balanced, lightened, strengthened, connected to the healing powers of heaven and earth. It's like charging the batteries of all your energies, and they must be — regularly and routinely.

There are energy fields in every general area, organ, and

even every cell of the body—in constant communication with each other, like a network of competent business associates all working together for your ultimate good! Imagine that such communication and joint effort creates a very happy community. When spirit and body are one, you feel really good.

Chakra is a word used to describe each of the main energy centers of the body. From the base of the spine all the way up to the area above the head, the centerline of the body holds the energies of all of your connections to the physical and spiritual realities. The lower ones are connected to the physical (things of the earth and other people), while the ones from the heart up are connected to matters of spirit. The right side of the body is considered male, with the energy of giving, while the left side is female and the energy of receiving. Each function of the body has its own energy. For instance, the throat area is all about speaking your truth, while the belly button area (where our umbilical cord connected us to our mother) is all about how we see ourselves in relation to others.

Understanding all the energies allows one to identify what's going on in your life at any given time. By noticing where in your body you feel any resistance to light, you can relate that place with the associated meanings of that particular energy center, and then ask yourself how those particular issues are controlling you at the moment. You may then choose to forgive and shift your thoughts and beliefs to more truthful, empowering ones, thus opening yourself to again being one with spirit. There are volumes written on this fascinating subject.

Spirit and Sexuality

When one climaxes in sex, all of the chakras are super-charged with energy, opening up the whole center channel of the body with light. This process spiritually connects you to earth and heaven, as well as to the spirit of the other body participating. Sex is a process of spirit connecting to spirit. Since spirit is the energy of love, and when through sex you enter the energy of love — from which we all are made and where we all are one — sex creates a very powerful spiritual bond.

Sex as a form of *awakening-your-spirit-within-your-body* is completely healthy, wise, glorious and necessary, when done in the right circumstances. It literally sends spirit-energy throughout the body. The more climax is repeated, the more *spirit* is sent to super-charge even more of the energy centers throughout the body, filling you with the *energy of love*. Thus the name used for *love-making* is very literally chosen.

When spirit and body are participating together in sex, spirit fills the whole body, and *spirit* (what you really are and eternally will remain) is the energy of *the physical element of love*. This is the closest to God we can achieve in the physical body, and probably the reason sexuality has become so corrupted. With something so powerful as **becoming physically encapsulated in the energy of love,** *impostors* appear, wanting a share of your love energy. But know that real love doesn't come in those jaded ways, which are counterfeits to the truth. The true powerful meanings of this magnificent gift we are born to use is to procreate more of what we in truth are — *love* — and this can only happen when we are acting from complete integrity, following the guidance of spirit.

Thoughts for Processing *The Energy of the Physical Body*:

- Notice the energetic connections you naturally have to favorite foods. What emotional connections do you feel to these foods? Are there good body-mind connections, or do they cause you to deal with messages of guilt, shame, and fear?
- Do you feel gratitude for what you eat? Do you speak

or feel those messages of thanks before you begin to consume, allowing the foods to bless you?

- Make sure you release all negative connections to the foods before you eat them.
- Ask your body what it wants to eat. Pay attention. Notice the cravings.
- Before you eat anything, determine how you would feel *after* eating those suggestions. Does it still feel good to make that choice? Honor your inner knowing about foods. Let your spirit, not your stomach, be the master of your choices.
- What do you put in your body that you know always makes you feel worse afterwards, but you do it anyway? Ask what are your emotional connections to those foods, and then let those negative beliefs go.
- Choose healthy connections to all foods, based on gratitude and your own body's signals.
- What kinds of things go into your mouth without you even choosing them, like they are on autopilot—a habit? These are your addictions. What emotional needs are they meeting?
- Which of these would you like to exchange for something with better vibes?
- Do you get your energy from healthy foods or from products with stimulants? As much as possible, get your energy from the higher vibrations of live foods, then go to the spirit for all the extra help you need to complete your tasks.
- Spirit over body. Do a one-day fast once a month to allow your body to remember *spirit is in charge*.
- Contemplate and imagine the size of your spirit body. Allow your spirit to fill your body from heaven into the top of your head all the way down to your toes. Then do it in reverse and let spirit rise from the earth upward

all the way to the top of your head and outward. Can you feel these energy fields vibrating?

- Is all of your spirit in residence in your body? How much exercise can you participate in? Examine what you would like to do better with your physical body (that is aligned with truth), and make a plan and assert your will to do it!

- Spend some time awakening love within yourself, receiving spirit, then share that *love-making* with your beloved partner. Notice the enlightenment throughout your body, and the bonding of your two spirits as *love* — in you, your beloved, God and the oneness that wholeness of love represents. This is your spirit's home.

- Be kind to your body. It is your best friend. Learn to communicate well — spirit to body as one.

Chapter 7

The Energy of Relationships

I celebrate the innocence and perfection of each child of God.
I honor such sweetness – our true identity – pure and transparent,
Knowing our infinite worth.

147

In the summer of 1987, our family took a five-week, eight thousand mile cross-country road trip, from West to South to Northeast to West again. Four children, two parents, one grandfather, one 4-wheel drive Suburban—camping, staying with friends and family, checking into hotel rooms when it was stormy, eating from roadside stands of summer produce, seeing the history and landscape of our country first-hand.

Prior to this trip, my opinion of my nation's peoples came from the media, which caused me to have little hope in the good of mankind. But what I learned about humanity that summer warms my heart to repeat. Everywhere we went, people were just like us: folks who love and are loyal to their families, their homes, and their country, and who would do anything they could to help. People were friendly and caring, deeply patriotic, and just plain *good to the core.*

Maybe I had been sheltered, but I really did not know how much everybody is the same and how connected I could feel to my brothers and sisters across the land. It was a powerful experience for our family to bond to each other and to all of America—the history, the places, and the peoples.

What I have learned about life is simple: *you get what you give.* When I share love, love is what is returned to me. When I share wonder and amazement and gratitude for the smallest things, more of such goodness is freely offered to me.

In the spring of 2007, I learned this lesson again. Out of nowhere in a cherry blossom park in Suwon, Korea, a lone photographer was arranging his tripod to capture the morning's beauty. Three amazed women were also taking photos with our simple equipment, taking in the pleasures of spring that

149

had just *popped*, as the Koreans called it. As we approached the same area, we asked if this man might take our picture using our camera. How he happened to be there at that exact moment, and how we happened to ask him in such a way that touched him I will never know, except that it was divinely perfect and the memories indelibly printed in my heart.

This man was instantly amazed at us, searching to fathom the joy we ladies were sharing as we traveled in this foreign country, and my daughter, one of the three, speaking perfectly fluent Korean. As the two of them spoke, the photographer shared his impressions of us, including his observations of the joy he saw in my countenance. Americans are rare in Korea, and a blonde one (my daughter), speaking the language, laughing and linking arms with natives was unheard of. These images impressed him beyond words.

As this man learned of my design background and my interest in his art, he wanted to share more, so he took us to his car nearby to see printed copies of his work. He even felt impressed to give us two of his most beautiful prints — rare views of the exquisite mountain areas of North Korea and China, which we treasure both for their beauty and for the sweetness of humanity that it represents. Later we learned that he was quite famous in that part of the Orient, but it was his gentle, loving and generous goodness and connection to the beauties of nature and our happy spirits that I will always remember him for. He had a sincere and peaceful radiance all about his whole being, and especially glowing through his eyes — the window to his soul. *Loving spirit* was in him, vibrantly alive, and allowed him to recognize the same in us.

I was amazed at the gifts of love that came to me in Korea. Love and honor are its innate culture, which touched me deeply. As I left America, I spiritually asked for Korea to give me her gifts. I *felt* to ask this. I had given my daughter to that country for two of the hardest years of my life, and I felt it was time for me to know why such a price of service was required, and to experience the blessings for myself. Surprisingly dear relationships developed with precious friends there in a very short time, which remain and grow through the years since. I can recognize Koreans anywhere, and when they begin to speak, sharing their gentle natures, my heart swells with tenderness and sometimes tears of gratitude for the love they gave to me.

It is my desire to intentionally see the best in everyone, holding them in their highest self, and I choose to send out love wherever I go. I sent clear intention to feel the gifts there, as my daughter had, and they rolled before me like a red carpet from the time we boarded the Korean airline bound there.

With my innocent childlike heart, I *felt* to ask for love. I *believed* I would find love, and love in the form of endearing relationships was my reward. Following spirit, asking, believing, everything is manifest. The quality of love in our relationships has everything to do with *the conditions we find in our own hearts*.

Becoming Like a Little Child

My favorite spirit is that of a child. The heart of a child is perfection. Jesus taught that unless we *become like a little child, we cannot enter the kingdom of heaven*. If the *kingdom* is where the king reigns, and if that *king* is the Master of Love, I want to live in that place! Like all children, I bask in love.

I compare that desire to the heart of a child, whose innocence and perfection express as a presence of love; always ready for smiles, hugs and kisses, joyfully open with time and attention to the constant sharing of love. Children are always open to giving and receiving love, which is perhaps why they are Jesus' example of the *perfection of love*.

A child is the master teacher of forgiveness, always willing to let things go and give others another chance. To a child, there is no time, only the *present* — the perfect place to feel love. To become as a child means to be teachable, to listen from the heart, and to be willing to believe. It means having *faith that someone is out there who is going to take care of everything!*

Having an innocent childlike heart, I have found myself being taken advantage of, left behind, and misunderstood. I have lost money to scams and believed just about everything I have ever been taught along the way. Yet I have grown in wisdom through each lesson, and now know that *wisdom does not have to leave innocence behind.*

The very good news is that being this way has allowed me to consider every possible belief system about who we are, as well as how and why life works. Because of my childlike heart, I accepted the concept of forgiveness quickly when it was taught, and now have the tools to choose to always be in joy. Though because of this childlike faith I have found myself lost a few times, taking a few turns off the higher road, I have always been protected, provided for, safe, and I wake up every day to a new world of choice from a buffet of abundance.

I feel deeply connected to children. In my heart I feel I am still a child myself. I want to give *children of all ages* — that means everyone who lives by faith — the knowledge of their own perfect worth and power. **I want all to know they can keep the heart they were born with — the heart of their inner child spirit.**

Whenever I am in a public place and notice little ones, I speak from my heart to theirs, without any verbal words or physical movements. I tell them with mental and emotional communication that I know they can hear me, and that I know *they know* I am speaking to them. I tell them that they are perfect, and that they are wonderfully loved. I send them this message from the voice in my heart. I feel it leave me like a movement of energy, a literal physical exercise generated from my heart muscle — my spirit. I watch as the faces of the little ones light

152

up, look with a question at me, become still, listen, smile back, then watch me the whole time we are in the same local, with a look of surprise that I can speak their language.

I did the same thing with my own children, never leaving them without a heart-full of love generated their way. Every day of their lives as I left them at school for the day, I asked for protection to be given by God and the angels. I kissed them and held them until I felt a giant burst of love exploding within my heart, passing that energy to my child, and then I knew they would be okay, wrapped in the *energy of love*.

I know little ones are connected to spirit; it is my greatest wish that adults would respect and honor the perfection of these little ones. It is also my wish that adults get in touch with their own inner voice of spirit; ask, listen, and live by that spirit. I know how powerful and yet how simple spiritual communication is, and how quickly it responds — *thought speed, love speed, spirit speed.*

Whenever I hear a crying child in my presence, I feel compelled to send my non-verbal love messages, and it always works to soothe the little one. It helps if I am facing the child, as if sending loving attention directly into their soul-beings. Children *are* love, and need a constant supply of peaceful, loving attention.

Most of the time when I see children crying, they are in a shopping cart. The parent is focused on the task at hand, oblivious to the child. Usually these children don't want to be out shopping with parents; they want to be home in familiar, comfortable simplicity. But when they can't be home, they want the same comfort by being acknowledged with peaceful love, and that is not where the parent's attention lies when out shopping.

In these cases, the child feels neglected, and he is being neglected, even though it is temporary. It makes the parent just as unhappy as the child to have to divide his attention from his focus on getting the groceries. Most of the time when I see a crying child, the parent is just about as unhappy too, wanting to help, but needing to get the job done. If we could all just learn to relax and multi-task with love, always staying connected in love, remembering to continue to let the child know you are there in peaceful love, then everyone would feel a whole lot calmer.

What is it about our culture that keeps us on such a fast-paced schedule? Little ones, recently arrived from the trusting peace of heaven, need us to slow down and enjoy life; no one or nothing could be a better teacher of truth than a child.

The Spirit of Parenting

The first relationship we each have is within a family, and the family setting is the basis for all further relationships in life. For this reason, I use my own family life experiences as examples to share the values I have learned on this subject. The spirit of parenting has been the focus of much of my life's work. Raising six children who showed themselves to me spiritually as a group before they incarnated, telling me I was their mother, was the joy and much of the purpose of my life. My belief is that we are a team: we work together. We teach each other. I believe in the sanctity of each of their souls. Each came with divine and individual purposes.

I believe it is my job to keep my children safe and to guide them to manifest their purposes. From the time my newborn babies were laid in my arms, I looked beyond their beautiful faces into the depth of their souls. As I gazed I asked, *who are you, really*. I knew that the body in my arms held within it a soul of a mature and wise spirit who chose to be born at this time and place and with this chosen family. I am humbled seeing my children from the eternal perspective. I am honored to be the mother — the *chosen* mother — of these spiritual beings.

154

Such feelings opened my mind to a relationship of reciprocal respect and trust, even mutual connections of knowing that we both signed up to be in such a relationship at such a time and place. I was not his or her superior. I was not more spiritual or of a higher rank in the body of humanity. Actually, probably the opposite is true.

But I had been here longer and knew enough to show this newborn spirit what I had learned so far in my exploration. Over the years, my child would take what I had learned and comprehend it based on his own inner knowing, shed his own light on matters, and increase the clarity of truth in many of life's perspectives more perfectly for and with me. As I received my newborns into my arms, one by one, I saw these children as *partners in life, learning, and love.*

I am teachable, knowing that these little ones have just come from the presence of God, and that they are closer to truth than any living being. Why would I not honor such a truth, and be still about my opinions, encouraging their infinite worth, and listening first to their spirits to learn fresher perspectives?

My job is to hold these spirits in the space of truth. As they are born into their bodies and are faced with emotions and choices foreign to them, I know they will question what is truth. **My job is to remind them of who they are as children of a generously loving God, and that *love* is their constant.** My role is to hold them in such love. I listen. I feel. I reflect. I teach them and remind them about forgiveness. I assist them in recognizing negatives for what they are—someone else's creation, not truth. I guide them to release the negatives with forgiveness, after which they can return to their original and intended state of living as the embodiment of the innocence of love.

We give power to anything with our beliefs, so I disregard any possibility of truth in the negative words and experiences of others. Sometimes parents want to become the

155

warrior to fight their child's battles, but I do not accept the negativity of others as reality. Anything negative is not true; only love is true. So why would I engage such an illusion of reality by taking on such a battle?

I remind my child that the negative is *someone else's* illusion of reality—their stuff—generated from that person buying into a false belief. These beliefs come from forces of opposition, such as fears and pressures of failure from within, based on something outside of them—outside of their love— nothing to do with my child.

When it comes right down to it, nothing outside of love is real. So what is this other reality? I see it all as if actors on a stage, performing so that we can practice staying in love. As they *choose* to accept false beliefs as truths, these other realities show up, performing for our learning,

But fear is never truth. Anger is never truth. Ridiculing or shaming or guilting is never truth. So I teach my children to separate the truth from the illusions, and to release the illusions to God via the tool of forgiveness.

If I accept these illusions as truth I give them my power. Then I become the *servant of the false energy*. A child is quick to accept this concept and to shift the perspective. I assist by separating the energy form: for example: *control*. I ask, where did this *control energy* first begin? Perhaps an older brother is being controlling to his little sister, and such behavior is causing a lot of contention. How do we look at this controlling energy in a way that allows us to heal the negative effects of it?

Seeing everything from the perspective of energy, I think of all possibilities, such as this young man may have chosen long ago to be born first in order to prepare the way for his younger siblings, to be there as a guide and protector of sorts. Focusing on that more positive *shifted perspective*, an older brother is now a hero. Maybe he was using his original intended energy of *guide and protector* incorrectly, showing up

156

instead as a controller. But with the shift in perspective, he can laugh, the sister can laugh, even love, and maybe she will choose to feel and radiate gratitude for her previously perceived controlling older brother!

I learned long ago that a child's bad dreams are the manifestation of negative energy endured during the day. Once I discovered this, whenever a child would awake crying in the night, I would ask him to tell me about his dream, which always included a monster. I would then tell him that the monster was wearing a mask, and ask my child in his half-awakened half-still-in-the-dream state to imagine removing the mask.

Each teachable child did as I suggested, and in every single case, saw the person behind the mask — the offender. It would be a teacher, a family member, a bully — someone who had shown up to a child as a *monster* that day. Realizing such made it simple for my child to release the negative energy, to sleep better, and to be less affected if the offense reoccurred.

Using this and other techniques taught my children to separate negative energy (caused from sources outside of themselves) from the truthful reality of love, which they innately knew was their true self. In the presence of love, truth becomes very obvious. Being taught about spirit is the right of every innocent child, allowing them to know the realities of life and to choose accordingly.

Disciplining from Love

I remember so many times when my children were small and I wanted them to do chores; I could ask and remind them a dozen times, and still if they did not want to do the work, they would find a way to avoid it. In my earlier years, I used force, anger, and other forms of control, but soon I learned such a mode of reaction was not consistent with the loving beings that they are. To act with meanness, loud voice, dragging them to it—all forms of control—serves only to demean them, reinforcing what they are *not*: their nothing-ness. I wanted to teach them their *intrinsic value as beings of the perfection of love*, and nothing less than perfection, so I learned from spirit better ways to be a parent.

I appreciate the wisdom shared in books teaching discipline with natural consequences, putting rewards on behaviors that when done are received, or if not done, are simply a missed blessing. Child suffers: child learns. This works, but it also takes a lot of discipline from the parent to organize the plan and to be precise on the follow through. This method puts the responsibility onto the child and off of the parent, keeping the spirit of the relationship healthy.

Being the mother of six and with my very strong need for simplicity, peace, and loving energy to abide, such master planning was sometimes unrealistic. Being of a more spiritual nature, (meaning more like a fairy-goddess than a human), sometimes instead of all these methods, I chose to *sing and dance*. I would make up little ditties, like Mary Poppins—singing as we washed toilets as if it was a game. As we danced, we picked up clothes and toys, depositing them in their proper place—getting the work done while keeping our happy hearts full of love.

Such a choice is absolutely consistent with my spirit, thus it is the *right* choice for me and my family. I honor the light within myself as well as the path these souls came to experience from *this mother. All right relationship will be guided by inspiration from spirit and will always involve honoring one's own nature.*

Negatives of any kind are intolerable to me, as they are inconsistent with the perspective of the holy nature of each of God's children. I feel such intensity about this—it is as if my whole purpose is to protect them and others in my circle from the destructive energy of darkness. So intent am I to live by spirit, contention of any kind sends me into a strong desire to stop it, giving me opportunities to find creative ways out of it.

As a young mother, if two of my babies cried at the same time, *so did I.* My threshold for suffering, unkindness, anger, hurtful comments, doubting, shaming, criticizing of any kind, is *zero!* When any negative comments are directed at a child, it's as if a passion wells up within me that wants to fight such untruth, for *the only reality in my world is of our intrinsic individual worth and perfection as God's sons and daughters,* and you don't treat *royalty* like that!

I live in a world of childlike faith and innocence, and I intend to continue creating such a vision for all, with all my energies. It took me a lifetime to know myself as beloved of God, and I must honor this truth for everyone.

Children live what they learn from the adults in their lives. I can always tell why a child acts a certain way. Children don't invent negative behaviors. Children may act out to get attention; it seems so much lovelier to just give them their rightful due in the first place! If the adult is peaceful, so will the child be. If the adult is losing it, handling things with intense stress, there will be no peace from the child. *Energy is bred: w*hatever I am displaying is what I will create to manifest in others, starting with my children.

Sometimes I notice that adopted children carry an attitude that they are not loved as much as a birth child. In most of these cases, it is not the actual truth of the conditions of the love they are getting, but beliefs the child acquired at the time of loss. The best solution to this confusion is in the science of inner child work — the process of realizing you are no longer a child, but may be seeing with the same eyes as when a small child. Operating from such a place — stuck in the past — of course we cannot possibly understand very much about those apparently painful circumstances, and some continue to live from that loss throughout their lives, creating a lot of misery in the process. Energetically (therapeutically) returning to rescue

159

ourselves from those traumatic times, we can find wholeness in the love we can choose to accept in the present.

Effects of Spiritual Communication

An unwed mother came to live with our family for six months back in the eighties. Her home was in South Africa where at the time, her mixed race baby would have no chance of being accepted in the culture or to receive a proper education. With great inner will and deep unselfish love, she determined to find a good Christian home in the States, and to give her baby up for adoption. Through some combination of miracles, which blessed all of us, she found our family to stay with during her process. During those months together, I cared for our expectant friend and taught her the principles of *spiritual communication*.

For the rest of her pregnancy after learning these principles, this young woman talked lovingly to the spirit of her baby, explaining the deep love that precipitated her choice to find this soul another home. She asked the spirit within her womb to forgive her, and to know that the perfect family would be raising him, that her love would always be with him too. After she gave birth, she bid adieu until the next life, giving him to a wonderful new family, and then returned to her native homeland. Everyone who knows this young man, now adult, knows that there is nothing but love in him. He has never shown any energy of being rejected, orphaned, or misplaced in any way. He is a fine example of humanity at its best.

Could the difference with this story and many others where the child struggles with self worth issues throughout life, simply be the attitude of the birth mother in communicating the truth with loving energy, explaining the situation to the baby, as if he understands completely? Because of course, he does.

This technique of spiritual communication also works

to resolve conflicts with others. The practice includes choosing a peaceful place to go, alone, and then focusing on the energy and the image of someone you wish to talk with. Visualize the person standing or sitting there across from you. Focus on the reality of their being for a few minutes, until you have a connection, until you believe some representation of their spirit is there. You can fake it until you practice enough to know the results validate the process.

Next, say what you want to say to them, as if they were really there. Ask for what you want—whatever needs to be clarified or understood. When speaking to another's spirit, the message will be received. You will feel better immediately, and things will change accordingly between you, very soon.

A spiritual parent in touch with truth can spiritually communicate anything to her child at any age. Spiritual communication is as real as verbal, and maybe more real. Anybody can communicate on a spiritual level to anyone, anywhere, and it will be felt and heard intuitively. People know what you are thinking about them even if you don't say it. The energetic message of your feelings is always sent, and you cannot hide your vibes, *especially from an intuitive!* Learn to trust your spiritual impressions and act on them.

When I was away from home, feeling intensely homesick, I always got a call from my father or mother. They knew I was missing them because they always thought of me about the same time and then began feeling my energy—missing me too. We lived this way for our entire adult lives, talking to each other's *spirits* from across the continent.

A spiritually centered parent listens from the heart and weighs everything. There must be constant flexibility to follow spirit and feel some happiness. Homework and dishes can be done after dark, but playing in the sunshine can only be done when there is daylight; a child can't get enough of sunshine and love. When I was a young mother, I found this verse on a wooden plaque, and hung it in my kitchen: *There will be years for cooking and cleaning, but children grow up when we are not looking, so hush a bye laundry, work go to sleep, I am rocking my babies, and babies don't keep.* The joy of nursing and rocking babies, giving and receiving love, is my greatest mortal happiness.

Parental Love Creates Spiritual Awareness

I must have had some of this kind of love myself as a child, for I remember one particular lazy summer day in my youth while I was meditating on my bed, somehow the vastness of life opened up to my mind. *At that moment I awakened to the clear understanding that there was nothing in this world I could not do if I set my mind to it.*

To the best of my memory, this was my first epiphany, and so delighted was I in its discovery that I raced to find my mother (in the laundry room again.) Announcing my newfound truth, my sweet mother confirmed my belief with a comment of assurance that I was absolutely on the right course. My father did the same. They believed in me. They seemed to know my soul. They loved me unconditionally, which gave me wings. They trusted and had great faith in my potential and destiny, which confidence and encouragement gave me the energy to soar. Such unconditional love is validating, building confidence, and is what every child deserves and *must have* in order to find and live their joyful purpose.

In previous generations, such genteel and spiritual parenting was thought to only spoil the child or be the cause of a grand ego. But results have shown that these children — raised mostly on strict discipline and little display of love — grow up to look in all the wrong places for the love that *should have been their birthright and their constant!* When children know they are loved, they can move on to share that love with others in their own unique and creative ways. *This is the world I am creating!*

162

With a desire to enable them to live from their own spirits, I chose long ago to never say no to my children, unless their lives were in danger. If they have a wish, I will guide them within parameters for achieving their wish. I always say yes to their requests. Yes but. . . yes after . . . yes if . . . yes sometime in eternity, but the rest is up to them, and sometimes requires more effort or consequences than they are willing to expend. But then it is *their* choice, not mine as some kind of controller, squashing their dreams. And when they reach their goals, *they* gain the rewards. They don't live for approval from me, because I am investing my unconditional efforts in making sure they already have it! God's gift of the free agency in man is this very same principle. God created a universe around this truth because He absolutely knows it is the only way we can grow — empowering ourselves — living our own lives by choice.

I believe creativity comes from within a child; it is my job to simply nourish those gifts and keep them safe while they learn. I honor the spirit of each child. I am not here to make them into something I design. **I am here to give them wings to be who they already are, and to do and be what they came here to do and be!**

This is delicate work being a parent — to not deny their dreams or crush their creativity. I live to show the way of all possibilities of how they can make their dreams come true. This style of parenting allows the child freedom *to create his own life*, and not to simply be an attempt at an improved reproduction of mine.

Each soul is incarnated to experience the power of choice with a physical body. Why would I want to take the responsibility of making choices for another? What a burden this would become, to not only be responsible for my own choices, but for those of others! **It is vitally important to use every method to teach the child accountability for noticing and following the spirit of truth within him.**

I teach them correct principles — to listen to spirit — and they govern themselves, following their *own* inner knowing. We can only truly learn from our own choices and our own experiences, and the *feelings* those bring. We gain little from information spoken or read. We learn when we *challenge* that information in our own lives, having our own experience, or sometimes from watching others go through it.

I have enough to handle owning my life without feeling responsible for every decision my children make. That's a lot of burden to carry, and what have I taught them in the end? To only trust me? I want them to develop their *own* heart muscles, to *know when spirit is speaking*! They know the feeling intuitively when they are small. I want to kindle its development and recognition, so that they have their own *personal guidance system*, (PGS), which is always there and always dependable. The earlier this starts, the easier it is to apply, and the more personally empowered *with spirit* the child becomes.

I honor my mother for teaching me this principle in my teen years. When I was a high school freshman, my older brother was a senior. He and his friends were great mentors to me, giving me many opportunities to feel accepted and important as I was acknowledged and valued in their circle. In the spring of that year, I was invited by one of my brother's friends to be his date to the May Queen Dance. Overjoyed and feeling very grown up, I determined that I would like to go out with this very good-looking senior. Most of my friends and associates were not in that league yet, as only the most *popular* younger girls were dating. I had not been planning on joining that group so young, but the opportunity was irresistible. To a teenager, it seems normal to experience the energy of receiving self-worth from the approval of others, and this invitation made a big impression on me.

I asked my mother for permission. Knowing the reality of every part of the dynamics of this situation, and in perfect motherly wisdom, she said *yes . . . but. But know that you will be put into situations that you are not prepared for, such as drinking and sex. Yes, you can go, but you will be responsible for the consequences.*

It was the first time in my life that I remember feeling the weight of my own choices. Did I feel so connected to my parents before this time that I saw myself only as an appendage to them, without power over my own life? Probably. Nevertheless, I felt the weight of this responsibility, and I knew that I did not want to have to temper my joyful perception of fun with a good looking guy by being immersed in a world that I did not desire to partake of, so I declined the offer, and never blamed anyone for my apparent loss.

So when is the umbilical cord really cut? Educators say that it is several years after birth before a child realizes that he is not a part of his mother. Several years! How many exactly? And these are the years that children are constantly being separated from half of their *perceived whole self* by so many mothers who have to work and be away from them? The wholeness of love that is nurtured through that *several years* of spiritual umbilical cord connection, unfortunately in many cases may never happen.

The nurturing love of an enlightened mother and father is the divine right of every child. The energy and spirit of parenting means *being there* as much as possible, with dependable buckets of unconditional love. Then the peaceful child will understand when absences are required.

Relationships founded on these principles are relationships that last eternally. Knowing I am loved and knowing I love another person, knowing that each in that partnership is listening to that heart space of inner spiritual guidance, everything will always be perfect. Inner spiritual guidance speaks the truth; and anyone listening to it will know, intuitively, what another is feeling, needing, going through, and respond according to the feeling that speaks from within.

This is fascinating to me, and I believe it is absolutely true, and that there is a great and masterful director of this universal stage of connections between us. All who listen to the guidance from within find themselves abundantly blessed with healthy, loving relationships.

Parents have a natural intuition as stewards of their children, which must be honored. Those feelings are real; let them guide you.

Being Open to Loving Relationships

The depth of a relationship—the amount of love it provides—is up to *me*. How much do I notice, receive, and let in? When I moved to the West, I missed my home in Tennessee, as well as many of the customs of Southern living. One of the jokes I would tell people in the West is that in the South, you know the whole family history of the grocery checker and she knows yours before you finish scanning the groceries! Southerners are well known for their innate gift of hospitality. People in the West may be just as friendly, but they don't seem to reach out quite as quickly or easily. Perhaps they just haven't experienced how comfortable it can be.

To heal my feelings of loss, I decided to practice befriending others as if they were Southerners. I opened myself to people at restaurants, in grocery lines, standing next to me in various public places. I found many people are very happy to talk, to open up their hearts, and to share every bit as much as Southerners. *Everyone is open to love.*

No matter where we are, whenever anyone is serving my older brother, he expresses sincere appreciation, complimenting with gratitude for the service. He makes some personal comment to let the person know of his respect and honor as an equal. In so doing, they become instant friends and open up the sharing on a much more giving level. He may get driving directions, tips on local attractions, and other friendly insider news. Somehow, to my Southern soul, I feel more loved when I too make an effort to have these connections with others as real people, and not just as workers in my space.

Being open to love is up to me. I may have a blank moment with a person where no energy is exchanged, or I may open the door to let in a bit of deeper spirit. I made a comment to the guy at the market the other day, someone I had seen there every day this week—something about him working 24/7. He smiled, and said, *yes, it seems like it.* He seemed to light up, to be more energized and present after my comments. I had honored him by acknowledging he even exists. In that moment, our spirits connected because there was a bit of love given in the form of caring.

I walked into a cafe yesterday. The food was gorgeous and healthy—just my style. I ordered a sweet veggie wrap for lunch and a take-out dinner for later on: a salad with every possible fresh green, fruit, and nuts. I told the gal there how much I appreciate finding this kind of good food, that I would be back, and I left. Today I am wondering, what is her name? She seemed quiet, maybe a bit lonely, or at least overworked.

What would happen if I go back again and this time, I introduce myself and ask a little bit about her, not just her food? I would then create a *love connection.* I would have shared my heart, and I would be a little richer for it. My love supplies would be fuller today. I did that the next time I went in, and she remembered me. We talked a bit more personally, and I felt a deeper connection to her. Every time I make such a choice, I connect more deeply to all of humanity, which then increases my own spiritual energy as I connect to the whole. I know many people and I adore many people, but the people I *remember* are the ones with whom I have had an actual *energetic exchange* – giving and receiving love, leaving a tangible imprint on each of our souls.

When there is an exchange of communication on a spiritual (love) level one person to another, or even to and from the plants I put in my garden, I have formed an *energetic bond* that is real, which can nourish and bless us both. I still remember an Indian man wrapped in his white sarong who blessed me with his presence in a Japanese garden in San Jose years ago. The gardens wrapped around some walkways that allowed me to pass this man multiple times, and at each passing, he bowed to me. It was his way of acknowledging that my spirit is real, and that he honors my spirit.

Southerners lift their forefinger or simply nod when passing one another. In the old days, men tipped their hats — all traditions to honor one another with a bit of humanity. Some eastern cultures believe we should give a gift to everyone we meet, even if it's just a smile or a prayer for their good fortune, or a bow, as was the case in the Japanese gardens. I agree with this loving tradition.

If we are going to have a *relationship* with someone, it must be centered first in love. We must find a place of love — spirit — where we can connect, then relate. Everyone is different in where that place is. Some feel cared for when someone touches them, while others feel love when verbally affirmed with words of validation and encouragement; they crave love in the form of meaningful conversation. Some feel loved when sharing undivided time, while others get the message from gifts or acts of service. It is important to know what feels like love to the people who share your life, and give love in the style they receive it best. From a *fullness of the good within and feeling our own connections to love,* we cannot help but share that abundance with others.

The Value of a Relationship

So how do I know when and where I should share my

love? I was pondering the concept of friends one day when this scriptural verse came to mind: *You are they who my Father has given me — You are my friends.* If all the people who are in my life are sent from God, he wants me to treat them as I would my friends.

Also, I consider that even though a relationship may be difficult, that person is my friend on a higher level, here for whatever lesson we came to teach each other; and all of these were sent from Father. If I connect the dots, I see every soul who enters my life as a gift. I have a lot of friends indeed, and when I see all the people in my life as heaven-sent, I should never be lonely!

Just like our art pieces and other possessions, relationships require my energy to allow and maintain them. Some are givers while others are takers, or somewhere along the scale of that energy of giving and taking. Some give me loving energy just thinking of them, while others can suck the life right out of me. I ask, *what does this person do for me? Why is she in my life? What can I learn from her? What has she got that I want? What is our purpose together? Have I learned the lesson yet?* Just noticing the possibilities gives the relationship value, but also allows me to consider that people are not possessions. They are not here for my use. They are here to be recognized simply as the love that they are.

I turn around my question and ask myself, *why am I in her life? What do I have to offer her? Am I giving this? Enough? Can I do more? How does it feel to me to know I might have a contract to show up with this person in such a way?* Again, the value of the relationship begins to be clear. With these considerations, this person may shift up or down on the giver-taker scale from where I imagined she was before I counseled with my inner knowing to know the higher purposes.

I imagine that when I consider the nature and energy of a certain relationship — why we are together — then I have the choice to pump the volume up on that number and make the relationship as powerful as possible. By being the person I committed to be for that partner, the value of the relationship will change for the better. *By being aware of the spirit of the contracts I have with another person, I have the power to allow deeper gratitude for each of these relationships.*

Using spirit as my guide, I can heal and enjoy even the most difficult problems in relationships. To do this, I might use a simple technique: I think of somebody who seems to be showing up really low on that giver-taker scale, maybe even kind of scary to me, and then shift into a different paradigm, considering another possibility. I have learned that when a relationship is negative to me, I get to ask what is it about this person that I don't like. It is obvious that this person is buying into false beliefs, living in fear, forgetting the truth about self, and not being loving. I can observe and figure out what about the energy is negative.

Then I get to look at myself and ask, how am I like that? On what level do I have this same false belief or irritating behavior? The answer always comes. I get to make a change, and then I get to be in gratitude to the negative one, who usually doesn't appear negative anymore — once I learn the lesson he provided.

Thankfully I know that we humans made contracts with each other before incarnating — promises to show up at certain times, places and ways to teach and guide one another to our perfection. My job is to *be the love* and to remind others that *they are the love. How another person acts towards me is never really about me,* and recognizing this, I can release any control over how that relationship manifests. **Focusing on my own behaviors in any relationship gives purpose to it and releases all expectation and need to control the choices others make.**

Integrity with Self

As a middle child, I often find myself in the mediator-peacemaker role. From early years, I saw everything that was contentious on one side of a judge's scale. I saw *living in loving peacefulness* on the other side of that scale. I made decisions to react to others based on this scale. Winning arguments, having possessions, being right, being first—being anything that took away peace—was never worth it to me. To me, nothing ever weighs in heavier than *love*.

Using this pattern in raising children, it is my belief that I will do nothing that would detract from the energy of love. When we are about to be late and a child is disobeying, do I start shouting and pulling that child into the car to get there on time? What kind of energy would that create? Fear? Anger? Being on time—what is that about? Is someone going to hurt me if I am late? Is someone going to speak ill of my name, ruin my reputation? It's not as if it happens every day, after all. Weighing what I am getting when I am willing to choose negative energy instead, nothing ever weights in heavier than love.

I can never control others, no matter how much I try or wish for it. What I can control is the amount of love I choose to receive from God and give to others. What if this physical reality we call life isn't real? What if it's all a game, a chance for us to practice having experiences, developing the skill of *being the love*?

I see life as a stage, where all the people are actors, and they don't even know they are acting; they play their roles so well. They are professionals—the best available. What would happen if I got an ah-ha and discovered this secret? What if I discovered that the role I am acting wasn't really me? What if I decided that deep down inside, I always wanted more? Can I honor this relationship with myself and with the others who

171

assist in my awakening?

There comes a time in every life when being out of love no longer serves, when we know we have to let go of past belief systems based on other people's fears, and start living true to our own spiritual integrity.

People are *consciously* living: making healthy choices, knowing the consequences, and the effects on self and others. And people are living *unconsciously:* reacting to life based on ignorance of the sack of lies that live within them, beliefs and thoughts that came from childhood wounds and grown-up losses.

It is a day of awakening when I realize that I don't need permission from anyone or anything outside of myself to live by the truth I know deeply within myself — that I am a creation of pure love.

Purpose of Relationships

People are in our lives to teach us and to give us the opportunity to learn to love. Thus, those of all types and appearances will come into our lives. We get to look beyond the masks and costumes and learn to see the *souls*. All are pure and perfect, no matter what they look like on the outside. We have the choice to ask and determine the situation.

Consider this message: *be not forgetful to entertain strangers, for some have entertained angels, unaware.* (Heb. 13:2) Giving of self generates a feeling of forgetting myself. As I reach out to give love and support to another, his joy in receiving expands my joy of being. It's a *gratitude exchange*, and I may have blessed and been blessed by an angel!

There are other ways to look at serving others: perhaps being giving without expecting to receive anything is actually good for me. To be considered a gift, it has to be my choice — to do it because I want to do it. Perhaps such opportunities are my practice in allowing inner guidance to lead me — working my *giving* muscles, practicing until I feel it and know its value.

The more we serve, the more we become a being of love. The more we become a being of love, the more like God we become. The more like God we become, the more we are actually like His *being*, with that substance I call light. Light attracts light. That light actually bonds us as one. In the process of serving others, we literally become one with God.

What about the relationships that are causing suffering? Notice the energy being created. Is it control? Is it victim/poor-me energy? Is it fear, neediness? Just as I ask, the energy is obvious. It is not about me and it will not affect me when I realize this truth: **all negative energy created by others is the game they play to avoid being in their own power. They create negative energy as they manipulate others to care for them instead of being accountable to care for themselves.** I will be unaffected by negatives when I container such energy and give it to God, and when I cut the cords that tie me to it, energetically and physically.

I have had relationships that confused me. Earlier in my life a therapist explained to me the dynamics of abusive people in order to help me see through the behaviors and to release the toxic effects. In time and through practice, I learned to focus on my own behaviors, to be loving and true to myself, from my own inner knowing. I have learned to cut ties with toxic energy and eliminate expectations. *No one can hurt you when you don't need something from them.* When you go to God for your identity, your purpose, and your support, you have found the real meaning of *personal power.*

I study everything about relationship from the perspective of the *energy* involved. I observe each relationship and determine its energetic description. This is done by examining the patterns of repeated experiences that occur in the relationship: what always happens? What does this person always do, or always need, or always cause me to feel in their presence? I notice how these energies have manifest in the past. I take that information and ascertain whether it is healthy and going in the direction of a loving creation. If not, I make decisions to guide it there. If I don't immediately know how to do this, I merely ask in spirit. I ask the question in my heart. I relax and wait. A very good answer always comes, making sense of the complexities of each situation and person. *With spirit as my guide, I always know exactly how to handle every relationship for the highest good of all concerned.*

The Reflection of Love

In the past several years, I have been focusing on having more relationships with others who share my life philosophies and interests. I pray for this, and sometimes I go further to visualize and feel the joy such a gift would bring. I am grateful to say that many new friends are coming into my life regularly: people who want the same spiritual awareness that I have and who support me in my dreams as I do them. With clear intention knowing it was my time to have this blessing, I claimed my desire, and heaven manifests the gift perfectly. I am very blessed to feel the love from these new, but eternal, friends—the kind of relationships that will always remain just as I left them, even when we don't communicate for a while.

When I first became a single mom, I still went to the same church, and I still lived in the same neighborhood; but somehow, I felt very different. It felt like people were treating me like I was a different person, like I had a curse on me. It seemed those who used to smile and laugh and talk to me changed their desires to do so, becoming more observant, as if they didn't know how to treat a divorced lady; I felt judged.

After enduring a few months of this, I decided to try a new approach. I was learning much about energy and spirit.

I was practicing forgiving self and others while healing my broken heart. I wanted my relationships to be more loving, more easy-going.

So using the principles of spirit, I knew that *what I send out is what was being returned.* I decided that the way others were acting towards me was probably a mirror image of how I saw myself, and how I saw my relationships with them. On a spiritual level, I was *expecting* them to question who I was, and how I became a single mom. I *expected* them to judge my situation as wrong, because I was taking a leap of faith myself, and while time was proving my decision right, I hadn't sent that energy out with my spirit as yet.

So I changed my energy. I forgave self and others for judging, accepting my situation with grace and love, knowing I was the same person they used to know, or maybe a better version. The subsequent changes in others were remarkable. It was as if they were relieved. They could approach me with love and friendliness, just as they had before. The respectful grieving period was over: as I moved on, loving my life, *so did they.*

Life Purpose

When I first met one of my dearest friends, she was telling me stories of her life, explaining some of the situations she was enduring. As she spoke, I could clearly see the common thread of her life experiences. They all included the energy of a white knight, out to save the world. That energy was manifested in everything she was telling me of her life story.

I asked if she felt like she was out to save the world, and she acknowledged it was true: she had been working in fields such as a police officer, where she was always standing for the truth. Her stories would make a great TV series! She quit that job when treated inhumanely by a co-worker who was horribly insensitive to some of her challenges, again defending the truth at all costs. The pattern continued in her next job and other relationships. She was sharing her story with me, asking for clarity and guidance.

When I asked if this *save the world* energy was the experience she wanted to have, she confessed she wished it would be easier. While she was very capable, being strong and good and caring, she was tired of that *fighting-energy scenario* manifesting over and over.

So with wisdom, she released the need to use her energy in fighting to save the world, and instead accepted that she might be more useful letting these realities come through her in easier ways. Instead of carrying the torch herself, always leading the battle forward, my friend now chooses to be more observant and allowing. She asks for angels to fight those battles for her, while she assists the divine by being there with her heart, hands, and voice. She follows inspiration instead of reacting from a desire for justice to be served.

My friend is now partnered in a joint venture with heaven, no longer feeling all the weight on herself. More than ever, she enjoys serving others, standing for the truth, and does so beautifully—with passion, joy, and love. She does this as ferociously as she rode into battle on her white horse, but with a lot more ease and simplicity now that she knows God and angels are on her team.

When we spend some time with ourselves listening from the heart, we get in touch with our own patterns and the associated lessons. Then we can make the choices to correct where needed. I know what is good and true for my life. I know what works, and I usually choose to do those things. I know what causes me problems and what my weaknesses are. It is truth that when I feel honored and loved unconditionally, I can make the choices to shift my energy to correct my own weaknesses and empower my own life. **From a place of love,**

we will always heal ourselves.

I will honor myself by choosing what brings me peace, life, and joy. I honor others for their own choices. I am here to love and allow and honor. *This very knowing is the required gift that must be developed in order to practice conscious living in every way.*

Couple Love

All people have the right to feel loved, supported, valued, honored, understood, and given the freedom to be themselves, without judgment. If more of this were happening, people would not be divorcing and suffering in other ways. Each of us came here with a purpose, and we are having the perfect *experiences* to teach us what we came here to learn.

The energy of the couple relationship is that space where two people, each in their own personally strong identity, share from their individual fullness, by *choice*. It's a choice to give love, support, value, honor, understanding, and to allow others the freedom of choice that we each treasure for ourselves. When that kind of support is unconditionally given from each partner, people thrive in relationship.

I compare to nature again. Nowhere in nature is any element fighting with another of the same element. Nature is doing what it came to do—just being the life form it is. But humans have a different energy, because we came with one thing no other species has been given, which is the gift to be able to make choices and to love. Using this ability correctly, from a space of pure love, makes life work and relationships blessed.

I know many things that would assist my husband to have an easier experience with certain situations, and he for me as well. Yet if my husband does not feel my *unconditional love in my offer*, he may feel *judged for his lack*.

177

My gift of myself is for me—to *be* me, and to honor all others to experience their learning at the place and timing which is *their* own path. In other words, I have to mind my own business. I am here for one reason only—*to be and give love.* I expect love to be given to me in the relationship, and if it is not, I don't have to stay. Love is a choice—a verb.

But first, if someone doesn't feel loving towards me, I must look more deeply into my own abilities, and check how much love I am giving, clearing the blocks in the way of allowing myself to express as love; for as we know, other's are just mirrors for our own learning.

You must learn to be more loving within and to love *yourself* before you ever decide to leave a relationship. If you don't heal to your wholeness in this one, you will have to heal in the next. Healing is the process of *becoming* the love, and you will have as many opportunities as you choose to perfect this awakening to your self as love. When you learn to accept yourself as love, then you may decide if you want to stay or go.

Years ago, after realizing I could not heal in my codependent marriage, I chose to take charge of my own healing to love, to become a stronger, happier individual. As I separated myself from that relationship and those negative patterns of neediness, I learned to love and empower myself from a one-on-one connection with God. From that strong core of unconditional love from God, I learned to give the same to myself.

Once clear about who I really was—a whole being of love, not needy for love outside of myself—I attracted a husband who loves me completely, just as I am. There is no judgment—not ever, not a word or thought. We are learning together how easy a marriage can be when both partners choose to always be unconditionally loving.

That's the simple version of a healthy marriage—**unconditional love**—and it works. And until you know that kind of love for yourself, God, and others, you should not be getting married.

Tangible Love

Sometimes I think about the essence of love, and how we share that with another person. Is it in the words? What do we mean when we say *I love you*? Love is a verb. How do I transfer love from I to you? How do I offer that *essence or state of being* to another with movements from my mouth? There must be something transferred in that expression, something more than just words. Words are the *vehicle*, but words are *not the love*.

Love is that tangible essence of energy of which the universe and I are made. How do I give that tangible essence to another? When wanting to express love, one must have some of this tangible essence first. To give that to another, you must first know what means love to that other person. You have to use the vehicle — the channel — on which they are tuned, the one they are listening to. These are the *love languages*, and usually are taught from birth, as the child hears and receives love from the parents and others, just like *word language* is taught — it's what we are used to getting. There are dozens of other languages out there that work too, but we only know the one we are spending our days listening to. **Whatever meant love to a child usually means love to him as an adult.**

If you want to have a relationship with me, you must first know what speaks love to my heart, and then send some of your *love essence* to me *through that channel*. This means you have to first be connected to the source of love yourself, and give it from that fullness. Finally, once your fullness of love is received through that channel to which I am open, I receive it. You give love, I receive love, and once we are connected with that love, we can have a *relationship*.

Relationship with God and Self

Often we hear of people blaming others for their situation—for not loving them or doing or being what they wanted. We hear marriage ceremonies advising couples to love and care for each other, sometimes going so far as to say it is their *responsibility* to make the other one happy. I cringe at such messages, for nothing is further from the truth. You cannot force or give or insist on anything happening with or to another person. Your only real work is with yourself. Who is your life about? You are a being of love, and the source of all love is God. Once you and God have met and worked out the particulars of a universe full of unconditional love—in you and for you—then no one else will be required to make you happy. If you are good enough for God, you are good enough for anyone else on this planet. With the strength of God under your wings, nothing can hold you back. *You will have the goods;* and you will want to share the goods—pure, unconditional love—it's who you are, what you have, and what you offer to others. It doesn't get any better than this! When two people bring such enlightenment to a marriage, the world moves over, and happiness abounds.

Conclusion

The whole of this life seems to be a school in mastering relationship. With all the enticing choices on our tables of abundance, we get to learn that *people* are always the most important choice. Becoming aware of ourselves and others as pure love is our test. I pray we can pass it well.

I hope to leave a legacy of my life that speaks this message: I **celebrate the innocence and perfection of each child of God,** and feast on the pure love I receive as I see this truth in all of humanity. This is my deepest belief, and my truest desire. From my perspective, to know this is the simple solution to creating peace and joy in our hearts, and our ultimate success as human beings.

Thoughts for Processing *The Energy of Relationships:*

- How do you feel people generally treat you? Can you see this as a direct reflection of how you see them and how you see yourself?
- What you are getting in relationships is directly related to what you expect. What are you asking for? Do you need to ask for something different?
- Having the heart of a child means to live in the moment. Can you do that? Can you let go of everything that would keep you from being in the state of happiness?
- How easily do you forgive others? How teachable and trusting are you?
- Let go of relationships that take too much of your energy. Open your heart, love yourself, and then expect to receive loving relationships in return. You attract what you are.
- Loving yourself requires healing the childhood wounds that made you feel less than loveable. Take some time revisiting your childhood — each place and time that you can recall — allowing loving feelings to bless you at each of those ages of your life. As you see yourself at each of these stages, be very loving and nice to yourself — just as you always wished it had been.
- Without using touch or words, practice spirit-to-spirit connection with a child — yours or someone else's. Send love messages via *spirit energy* talk. Watch their reactions. Do the same with any troubled relationship.
- When a relationship is strained, can you see past the faults? Can you choose to forgive and see who this

person really is, as God sees?

- All people in your life came as a partner to teach you something. Have you noticed what each significant relationship is here to teach you?
- Encourage your loved ones by reminding them of the good traits you see in them—at least once a day. Most need at least four positives statements to balance one negative.
- Learn the difference between truth (loving feelings) and illusion (everything outside of love). Teach this to your family.
- Do you believe in yourself? Do you give yourself wings to fly and do what you know you must in order to feel right? Give this gift to yourself and all others.
- You only have charge of your own decisions. Cut all cords to controlling others or being controlled by others. Your need to control comes from a lack of trust. Forgive all who caused you to lose your ability to trust others to love you and be there for you.
- Every person you meet is your brother or sister. Acknowledge and honor each with some measure of love.
- Be sensitive to others feelings and needs. Ask spirit to give you guidance to share when you feel the need to have a deeper connection with someone. Stay in the moment, and you will know exactly what is best to say or do.
- Notice the gratitude exchange when you obey spirit and bless another's life. As you honor another, you honor yourself.
- What lessons keep repeating in your relationships that might have a message for you?
- Take time to remember what speaks love to those in your care, and speak that language.

- Apologize when you want to create a bridge of healing. Forgive and forget.
- Love yourself by loving God and knowing your perfection in the eyes of God.
- Share that same fullness with all others truly exemplifying this message: *Thou shall love the Lord thy God, and thou shall love they neighbor as thyself.*

Chapter 8
The Energy of Meditation and Prayer

Heaven is already here,
And all you have to do is remember and ask,
Then you may enter.

In 1959, doors opened at a new elementary school in the rolling hills of East Tennessee, and I began first grade. The modern building of my new school was built with floor-to-ceiling and wall-to-wall windows on each exterior wall of each classroom, allowing me to spend the next eight years daydreaming out those wide-open spaces. Each year the view was the same: a calming vista of green grass and trees. It was the beginning of a lifetime of allowing my mind to find silence amidst the noise.

Spirit is the place of stillness where all light and truth exists. The vibrations of information from the realm of spirit — truth — are broadcasting on that plane. My spiritual well-being depends on having some of this stillness every day. If I find it early in the morning, truthful inspiration comes instantly. But if I wait until later in the day to seek out stillness, inspiration comes only after I consciously shut out the noise of the world, which takes a bit more effort and focus.

It's no wonder that over the ages, wise ones have gone to the mountains to speak with God. That sacred space allows higher frequencies to be heard and felt, away from the masses in which man's ignorance to spiritual realities can create confusion: the noise and interference of the day crowds out the still small voice of spirit, which speaks ever so quietly and never sleeps. **Those seeking inspiration rise up early in the morning, even before dawn, and retreat to nature, finding truth in the stillness of a sleeping world.**

There were years when I found it very difficult to meditate. There was little time for myself. I spent as much time as I could find in the quiet of nature, but often without finding the peace I was seeking. In those years, no amount of

187

meditation would have brought me peace, because I was in denial of my true feelings. To find peace, you have to be willing to completely open your heart to God, and I was afraid to face the consequences of such honesty.

In those years, I felt little emotionally. I would look at pictures of people and places I had been, and while I knew that technically I had actually been there, I did not *feel* it. I believe I was going through the motions with my *physical* reality, while my *spirit* was somewhere else, as if to hide from a life that endured too many negative experiences. I wanted to get out of that state. I wanted to run until I could feel myself alive. I tried all kinds of sports and exercise, but could not seem to keep going, for my body was limited without my spirit alive in there guiding it.

The day came when the baggage was too heavy to bear. I could not go on another step. As I prayed for relief, I believe God and angels knew I was ready, and doors began to open for my awakening. This began a time of intense emotional healing, during which my spiritually starved soul feasted on the companionship of heavenly guidance. I literally threw myself at the feet of God, pouring out my soul to Him, seeking relief and healing, day after day after day, for months and years, where I literally came to personally know Him.

I learned many things about God, prayer, and meditation during those years. I learned that first, the desire has to be real — *I have to want it*, and for me, that part came all on its own. I was at the very bottom emotionally, and there was nowhere to go but up.

My commitment to truth led to spending many hours alone by a creek in the mountains close to my home. I would go there every day, where I stayed as long as it took to feel God with me, which was the second thing I learned: *I had to be willing to wait on God.* He had to know I meant it, and so I poured out my whole soul and stayed until He came.

My mantra was *I am not leaving until I feel your love wrap around me, until I feel enough of your love to make me whole.* At first it could be six hours, then later on, an hour was about right. When I was in a hurry to be off to work, yet still my heart was longing for spiritual security with God, I was able to get my *fix* by just going to my sacred space for ten minutes. I discovered a great relationship had developed through my commitment to be with Him. And I know it pleased Him greatly, as He was always there waiting for me.

While it's not always possible to get to my sacred place in nature, I can always recall my wondrous moments there. By simply remembering that place, a shift occurs within me, taking me to the same spiritual connection, which is almost as wonderful as being there physically. This is the process of transformation of my spirit into the spiritual realm—*heaven on earth.* While spending all those hours and days and years alone with God in nature, I began to notice—through feelings within and the images I saw with my spiritual eyes—that spiritual beings were active and busy all around me.

On one particular day I wanted to help someone in a far away city, and as I was sitting on my rock by the creek in the Western mountains, I asked in prayer if some of the great spirits which I felt around me could go over to the east coast to help my friend in need. I had a spiritual *knowing* that acknowledged— they were honored I asked. I spiritually saw them turn their attention to the east and proceed to move in that direction, with purpose and love—an eternity's worth of power in their souls.

The blessings were felt right away in my friend's experience, just as I had requested, and I gave thanks, again acknowledging my spiritual knowing of the actuality of what had occurred. This was an example of **desire** added to **faith**, added to **asking,** added to **knowing**—creating a **miracle!**

The Gratitude Channel

It was through this school of faith that I have found it easy to believe that angelic presence is around me all the time. It is simply up to me to notice and acknowledge such. This is where *gratitude* becomes obvious. If an angelic spirit were truly standing beside me as my own personal aid, wouldn't I be excited, happy, and grateful for such a gift? Having the gratitude is the symbol of reality that the gift has arrived. When I receive any gift, a feeling of gratitude causes a swelling with joy in my heart space. This emotional reaction is a display that validates the gift is real. I in fact did receive a physical gift.

So this is the lesson: I take that same energy of gratitude and carry it within me always, and this same emotion of having already *received* is what actually *allows* heavenly support to walk with me and readily bless me, always. My gratitude comes from faith, and in faith my spiritual desires of hope increase to the point that I choose to exercise my faith with a prayer. The prayer is sent out from my heart and vibrates on the spiritual plane, where all truth already exists. It is literally tuning into the *God Radio Station*.

Once I have connected with this energy (my God channel), truthful vibrations connect with the vibrations of my question or desire. I listen openly and with peace, connecting to spiritual vibrations that are already speaking on this station. I believe they always have been broadcasting there on that spiritual level. As I remain open to these truthful vibrations, my prayer brings me an answer — the perfect answer — *spiritual knowledge*. I can see and feel and know with an inner sense — *spiritual knowing*. I have tuned into the frequency of spiritual information. From this space, I can get all the love and knowledge that I require to manage this mortality in blissful joy. I now understand why Jesus suggested we begin our prayers with gratitude. (I'm guessing there is also a magnificent scientific explanation for everything else He taught.)

It's really a very simple process to connect to the energy of spirit through gratitude. I sat on my porch this morning like I do many mornings, having some moments to connect with nature. I noticed the trees that I planted last spring, how well they are doing, how pretty they are, how much more connected I feel to my home now that I chose these trees thoughtfully and brought them home and planted them with love and gratitude. I noticed the copper roof on the bird feeder, which I also bought recently, and how it matches the large copper bowl placed between the lavender bushes, and how nice that feels to me. I felt happiness at the thought of how much I have always loved copper and lavender and birds, and here they are, right now, gracing my back yard, right in front of me! As I breathed in the cool morning air, loving the elements in that space before me, my heart began to swell with tingling.

Clarity of the particular emotion does not really matter, but that such feelings *moved* me into the feelings of tingling in my heart, which expresses as gratitude, and which shifted me into *the world of spirit.* Spirit is where I get all truth, and where I feel whole: life is good, and everything is going to be okay. This exercise — simply my morning ritual — allowed me to become filled with gratitude, which connected me to spirit, where I could ask prayers about anything and know my answers right away. Morning gratitude rituals can be experienced with a connection to any element of spirit: plants, people, pets, music, verse, sunshine, sky. Just notice something you can send vibes of gratitude towards, and then allow a loving energy exchange to envelop you.

Breathing and Meditation

Over the years I have noticed how much my breathing is a part of this retreat to stillness. In order to shift from the physical world to the spiritual, I must create stillness within my physical body, which begins with breathing. For years, my breathing was very shallow. Sometimes I would notice that I didn't breath at all for short spells—breath *holding*. Breathing is connected to spirit. **Breath *is* spirit**. How I am breathing is a signal of the level of *faith versus fear* I am embracing at the moment. When I notice shallow breathing, I ask, *what am I thinking or feeling right now?* Within a few minutes of just noticing, an answer comes. When my breathing is uneasy, I am holding negative energy, which is usually *ego based*, meaning it is connected to someone else's stuff, or the good or bad opinion they may have of me or of my choices.

To be able to find peace, we must learn to meditate, to release all attachments to other people's stuff and their judgments, as well as to our own judgments. Breathing is the first step to entering the world of meditation. Everyone can breathe, but it takes a bit of training to use breathing as a key to entering the spiritual world.

I learned to control and deepen my breathing in this way: while lying on my back on the floor or bed, supporting my body with that solid surface, I focus entirely on my breathing. The goal is to allow the air to go freely into my lungs and all the way down to my pubic bone area. I feel my abdomen rise and fall like a balloon inflating, focusing on expanding the area below my belly button.

After so many years of shallow breathing, this exercise feels really good. It's a powerful sensation to then take that full belly of breath and give it a push even further downward, like I am bearing down on it. I do that for just a few seconds, which allows the air to go even further into the deepest cavities, to places of peaceful feelings I didn't even know existed before this exercise. Those deeper places, when touched by my breath, are like erroneous zones: they make me feel really good.

I practice rhythms of breathing: in four counts, hold and

gently push four counts, then release slowly for eight counts. I do this for a while, then do a rhythm of breathing in one count, holding four, releasing for eight. Eventually I learn to take in enough air in one count to fill my body to the core. This exercise trains my body to breath deeply while I am upright again, out of this mode of a conscious practice. A few minutes a day over the period of about a month gives tremendous results, retraining the breathing to allow relaxation to the body all day long.

The method used doesn't matter, but *noticing and stilling the breath* is the most important launching place for deep meditation. Sometimes I visualize the breathing. I see the light particles in the air around me. I see myself breathing in the light, and then I visualize the particles entering my body and attaching to blood cells waiting in the linings of my lungs.

As I breathe out, exhaling, I see the healing loving light particles travel throughout my whole cardiovascular system, as if the pushing effort of my exhaling gives these particles the energy they require to move more deeply through me. I feel tingling in every vein. I imagine that the air is full of love — the essence of God, all light and truth. I imagine that as I exhale, all the darkness in my body is released in that outward breath.

I give myself a treatment in relaxation therapy by noticing my in and out breathing: light in, darkness (old useless lifeless energy) out. I imagine the light coursing through the whole complex circulatory system of my body, enlightening my senses to spirituality and healing my body as it goes.

I also use a visual technique of using breathing to connect myself to heaven and earth, which are my soul's two power places. As I breathe in, I visualize a cord of light from heaven right into the top of my head and down into my heart, as if a column over my head is open to the expanse of the world of spirit just above my body. This white light is consistently open, allowing the love light to flow from an abundant spiritual reservoir — my *spirit's source*. With every breath I take, I welcome this loving light into my heart, as if my breathing is literally drawing spirit into me. I receive the healing and swelling it brings into my heart, defining and strengthening its existence as a part of me.

As I breathe out, I imagine sending this light energy — this love — like another column shining from my heart straight down through my body, through my legs, my feet and further down into the center of the earth. The earth, being a physical element, is my *body's* source of energy, and helps me feel *grounded*. As I continue breathing in and out, I see light increasingly multiplying and swelling into me from above the top of my head, filling my heart, and strengthening the connection, as if to connect me to who I am, where I came from, and what I am doing here. This *centering technique* can be done for as long as desired to create a shift out of the mind and into spirit — the state of meditation.

Another powerful way to God is to call His name verbally over and over — God, God, God. This causes a spiritual awakening in the heart almost immediately. Studying the multitude of names in all cultures that reference God, I find it interesting how many contain a form of the sound *ah:* God, Jehovah, Allah, Abba, Father, Adonai, Yahweh, El Shaddai, and many more. *Awe* is what I feel when I imagine God's presence, so to say the name of God, accenting the sound *ah*, repeating it over and over while thinking of God, I feel drawn into a magnificent spiritual realm. The resonance of that particular sound or words of God's name seems to vibrate in such a way as to open my heart energies to feel spirit. Within seconds of reverencing God in this way, I feel the tenderness of knowing He is with me, and also knowing my own loving depths. I literally feel heaven vibrating within my body — a joyful, holy high. I do not believe it is an accident that this particular sound works to connect to spirit in this way, but perhaps this is one of the mysteries of God we need to remember and practice daily to bring more peace within.

Emptying the Mind with Meditation

In this place of stillness, thoughts may creep in wanting my attention, wanting my opinion. This is not a time for any judgment, which could negate my peaceful state. *All thoughts must leave.* That's the main job of meditation—to clear the mind of all thoughts, at which time *truth* can be recognized and revealed. In the emptiness of no judgment, truth simply appears.

To do this, I visualize my mind as a shiny, clean, empty sacred bowl, and I wave away with my hand anything that creeps into it. These invaders come as a form, a shape, and I don't have to know what each is about—just stuff—something that wants me to pay attention to it instead of the purity of that empty space. I keep my focus on the emptiness, and especially on the state of being *fully open*. A beautiful empty bowl is the symbol of being open to receiving, ready and waiting. **I must keep my focus on being *empty* of my own opinions, judgments, concerns, so that I can be fully open to *receive* the highest level of truth from God.** When truth appears, you *can't* sweep it away, so don't worry that you will miss it. When it comes, truth becomes one with who you are, abiding, so it is not going to leave—it simply enlightens you.

I visualize my own sacred space as a wide translucent, almost glowing, aquamarine bowl, with low rising sides gently lifting away from the center. It seems to be about two feet wide and maybe five inches deep. The color and material remind me of the most gorgeous sea, which is a symbol of freedom, cleansing, abundance and joy to me. I did not manufacture how my empty bowl looks. It just came to me the first time an empty bowl was suggested, and I loved it; it felt perfect, and so will yours.

Your sacred space may appear as an open heart, open eyes, or an open set of cupping hands; it does not matter. The only thing that is important is to create a space where you can remain in the energy of being open and waiting.

Do not set a time limit to this state of being. It is not a precursor to anything. **It is everything all by itself — the** *state* **of being open is what brings spirit to you.**

Meditation and Prayer

Once my meditation has taken me to a place of stillness, and I am separated from any attention to the mind chatter, I can ponder situations in my life: choices I can make, relationships that concern me. I examine them one at a time, asking for clarity. With each issue, I expect an impression to come to me right away.

I have heard some opinions that prayers are answered when God gets around to it, as if I am sending Him a letter, and He will write me back when my letter gets to the top of His *request-stack*. Such a belief confuses my inner knowing. It is inconsistent with the fact that I am tuning into *spirit frequency*, and while open to that frequency and listening with my spirit muscles, I know truth immediately. **My own experience has taught me that every word of prayer I send out while tuned to spirit frequency is attended to immediately.** I feel the connections, and I feel the answers.

I have learned to ask in the right way so that I can hear an immediate reply. I use my heart (my spirits home) as my source of inner knowing. When I am getting a positive reply to my prayer question, I feel an energy that is warm in my heart area, a glow that increases, causing a swelling of love to enter. It can be ever so slight, but a heart swelling is definitely noticed when the answer is yes, and it usually radiates bigger and bigger, like a consuming fire, when I am onto something really big, something really true for me.

However, when the answer is no, I get no feeling at all—none. It's as if I didn't even ask a question. There is no change in stillness. When this blank is drawn, I double-check, just to make sure I am right in my interpretation. I proceed to reverse the question, such as asking something like *so did I hear that right, that this is a no?* If I got it right, then I get a swelling feeling, telling me the answer to my question is yes—*yes, that was a no.*

Warm swelling feelings are a yes. No change of feelings—no swelling, no reaction—means a no. I ask yes and no questions, and I get answers every time *when I am first tuned to spirit.* This is faith—to enter my prayer space expecting and knowing there is someone or some spirit of truth in my presence or in my being, which is filled with all the answers to my every need, and happy to share them freely.

There are times when I try to rush the process and go quickly from one question to the next. This may confuse the answers because the swelling in my heart is still there from one question when I am about to ask another one, which may get in the way of a truthful response. To have perfect truth in every case, I have to chill a bit between questions. I say thanks for each response I receive, and then return to the neutral zone again, with no preconceived opinions, no thoughts, just peaceful centering, as in meditation. From that space, I begin asking the next question. In this way, each question gets its own *energetic space.*

Sometimes I pray and nothing comes. As I question this lack of response, I usually realize that I am unprepared, out of alignment with spirit. I may be in too big a hurry and not giving the proper respectful preparation. I may wait until a better time, or I may choose to take the time now to become *more* still, *more* spiritual, *more* humble, and then to begin asking

197

again.

Sometimes prayers are more critical, the needs greater. **Greater spiritual response requires greater spiritual preparation.** The value of the answers received is in direct correlation to the depth of desire. Again, it is an *energy exchange*—light begets light. If my needs are more intense, I must show the proper respect and spiritually prepare myself more deeply accordingly. Think about it: you are asking to receive very important and much needed guidance from God, and so you must come honoring the great gift you are about to receive. Your light must be shining first, and it seems the answers come back to you riding on that same energy, equal to it. When you send out big light, you get big light answers back. God, angels, and all of heaven's power attach its gifts to that energy you are sending up, and they send your blessings back to you accordingly. The quality of your prayer energy may be about the sum total of your innocence plus your faith and your belief, or it may simply be your efforts in pleading, even blindly, for much needed guidance.

At times, the greatest heavenly help comes to me after prayers offered in sadness, from a deep well of need—of grief and desperation. In these times, the desire of my heart has strong energetic vibrations, almost as if *demanding* immediate assistance, which I have done on several critical occasions. My experience shows that miracles happen as these powerful energetic requests are sent to God. **Miracles are grand responses to grand heart-felt desires sent in faith.** It happens every time: that sweet radiance of spirit is received as peaceful, still prayers are uttered from the innocent heart. Prayer is our amazing connection to our deepest, truest source of truth and love in the universe—our Heavenly Father, who is always ready and wanting to serve us.

Finding Your Spiritual Connection

Finding a peaceful centered altered state of being—meditation—is difficult or unnatural for some. Perhaps this is all new information and far from your normal experience of how life is supposed to work. There are many ways that affect a shift away from the cares of the busy world and into the spiritual realm.

Nature, being all about spirit and being a powerful connector to spirit, allows me the best transformation from reality. I may stare at a leaf or a flower petal at close range, feeling the amazement of joy for such a miraculous creation, melting into the parts of that leaf, and suddenly forget who or where I am for a moment. In that moment of becoming one with a part of nature or spirit, I have quickly transformed myself into the realm of spirit, where my heart is filled with pure childlike joy.

Any part has the same energy as the whole. In moments, I am transformed from seeing just a petal or a leaf, to feeling the energy of being one with a garden or forest, which is full of the same energy as me or the leaf or the flower—all perfect spirit energy! God made that petal out of His love and God made me out of that same abundance. I connect with God in that flower petal or leaf. In the process, I connect with myself, and I connect with all that is truth in spirit. All my answers *already exist* in such truth.

To know the voice of spirit requires a place of stillness. I have to find a way to still my mind of all the other voices that are chattering away, so that I can receive the voice of God. And what about this life offers stillness? This world is getting busier and spinning faster every year. With so much information and opportunity, most can hardly hold on for the ride, much less find a place of quiet peace.

I remember my mother teaching me that it's okay to

take a day off sometimes and do nothing. What a novel idea for a perfectionist like me who never had enough time to get it all done! She advised that when the load got too heavy to peacefully carry, that was a sign to stop *everything,* and start doing *nothing.*

It felt wrong to me. Guilt was screaming warnings of disapproval. But *stopping the world and getting off* is sometimes the only sane thing to do. Stillness is the personal gift you give yourself, and finding it gets easier over time.

Another technique to finding spirit is to listen to some peaceful music, which is a wonderful gift to nurture the soul at anytime, or to read some verses of truth in scripture or other inspired writings. This is the time of spiritual preparation for a while every day — my gift to God — honoring the importance of the gift I know He is about to give me: *enlightenment.*

The enlightenment that comes from these meditations and prayers with God is something I can take to the bank. I don't doubt it. I hold onto it with all my soul. I write it down. I have a journal for these inspirations — *my Book of Truths,* which becomes my own *personal scripture.* Perhaps this is the message given in Proverbs: *truth is to be written — engraved — upon the heart.* In times ahead, I may need to remember what God said to me about a certain issue, so I might want to engrave it permanently within. Knowing I will only be happy if I never waiver from the truth that was given, I can return to these personal revelations at any time. And once given, more truth will come, building on the first piece of knowledge, and more and more and more, as I simply trust, prepare and ask.

Prayer and Action

It is my firm belief that I must then *act* according to the light and knowledge I have been given. Do I really mean what I ask? Do I really want to move into and live in higher realms of light and truth, or was I just curious about all that enlightenment and spiritual stuff?

God and angels are waiting to see if I believe them and if they can trust me, to know that I am sincere, that I am ready to go to work and do and be as I am inspired. They want to be a part of my life, as a team, to help me more and more, step by step. Prayer is a lifeline, a conduit, a permanent attachment to my heavenly team, not just a now and then *drop in to say hello* visit. We are always working together with God for the highest good of all concerned. This is why we are taught to *pray always*, allowing those lifelines to remain open.

Inspiration is patient. Spirit will speak a few times in a row. I will get an impression, and I may get a second and third witness of that inspiration within a short while after I ask, such as hearing about a certain person or place or just a word that keeps being repeated. These *follow-up* impressions trigger that inner knowing place where I hold the information from my original inspirations. If I don't act on these revelations immediately, I will probably forget about it.

There have been times I was saddened to discover that because I ignored a message, someone who was in need may have suffered, when by following the prompting I could have made a difference. Ignoring spirit is often missing a wonderful opportunity to experience the high road to joy.

At other times, I get impressions to give something to someone. I start to do it, and then I get a nudge that says, *more. Give more.* I question it. It feels like spirit is testing me, to ask me to give *my all.* When I obey, I discover later that it had to be exactly as I was told — the exact content was required for me to be the hands of God to bless another's needs that day.

Ignoring spirit can cost you dearly, as I will explain with a true story. Once upon a time, I was traveling across the country moving to another city. I had made a promise to a friend to return to my former place of residence and help him with a design project. We would share the profits from a joint venture. As I was driving to my new residence a few thousand miles away, I had an impression come over me that it would be so nice to be finished with that place, to be able to remain in my new home and look ahead and not have to go back. The thought left me feeling a great deal of relief, even peace. *I wished it would be so easy* was my thought, and then tucked it away in my *wishes place*.

That feeling was a spiritual prompting, *divine guidance speaking*, and I ignored it as such. Assuming it was just my own wishful thinking, I argued with spirit that I had made a promise and I always kept my word. Spirit was trying to protect me from a situation that would end up in financial disaster. **If only I had recognized the *hunch* I felt strongly, and had taken a moment to ask in prayer if that thought was from a divine source.** It has taken me a lifetime to recognize that *I am always being guided by heavenly servants who desire to make my life better*, and I must always pay attention and live in such faith.

By their fruits you shall know them. What am I doing with my light? Am I acting on it? Am I being an *example of the believers?* It takes courage at times. It may be scary at first. But with practice, I find that there is nothing I am asked by spirit to do or be that causes me suffering in the end. In fact, whatever I gave up to follow spirit's guidance, either with time or goods, is replaced with spiritual gifts that last far longer and feel much better than what I sacrificed. Therein is my real treasure. The saying goes: *if God brought me to it, he will bring me through it.* Doors open. Miraculously.

I speak of applying a celestial power for a celestial lifestyle. Spiritual guidance is a free gift for all. It works based on my belief and my willingness to ask, hear, and follow, which is *obedience to the spirit.* Obedience is a high form of honoring truth, honoring God, and honoring my part in that whole. And that alone is an honor.

Remembering

I notice that many people hold their prayers within themselves, as if they own them, and holding onto them will somehow make it all better. They keep their questions to themselves, allowing the state of *wanting* to rumble through their beings eternally. Why don't we just go to God and get the answer as soon as we have the question? Is it a form of a habit — doubting God's love and desire to help us? Such lack of confidence in God's tender mercies shows a lack of belief in our own worthy relationship with Him. When this happens, we have another signal that we need to spend more time with God. The question always is, *how much time have you spent with the Lord today?*

Forgetting the Lord God is like forgetting myself. When I forget God, who am I really hurting? I know better! But *forgetting* is a product of mortality, while *remembering* comes from following a spiritual path that takes exercising the *choice* muscle. It's simply a choice, like every other desire and goal I might set. The only difference is that the choice to include God is so life changing, so its importance makes it a necessity for me — a choice to *stop suffering* and to *start remembering*.

Remember. Remember what? Who? This is the point of meditation, to shift my awareness to a deeper level, to the spiritual realm that exists all around me. If there was one word I would put across my mirror, this is it: **remember!**

I have two hazel-blue eyes that see in this physical dimension, but I also possess another eye, often called the third eye, which can see into the spiritual dimension. I learned to do this while daydreaming through elementary school, gazing out those giant walls of windows for eight years, and from spending my childhood free time in nature. I have pondered half my life away, looking for spiritual inspiration and solutions to my experiences.

203

For many years, I practiced guided meditation with a therapist who taught me how to connect to healing information through spiritual visions of my third eye. Everyone knows the feeling of floating off into daydreaming, while the physical body continues what it was doing, as if on autopilot. Connecting to spirit takes a bit of practice, but it's really very easy. **Getting to God was never meant to be for the privileged few**.

Over the years of practicing meditation, feeling His presence near, I have gained complete confidence in my ability to communicate with God. I feel love for myself because I know He loves me, and I love Him more than anything else in my life. There is a scale of love and fear that exists: the level at which we love God and trust Him, and *where we may fear man's opinion and judgment more than God's.*

Sometimes I have to check myself, my thoughts and my actions, to see if I am living in integrity with my belief in God. Examining motives is a great tool. Why am I doing this? What do I hope to gain? Where is my heart?

It is the *unconditional love relationship* I have developed with my Heavenly Father that has made it easier for me to get my answers and to guide others to do the same. It's as if I know I am welcome in my Father's mansion, that I am someone special who can go right in the door of His sacred throne room, without asking permission from the guards, walk up to Him and ask, *what do you think about this issue? Will this choice serve my highest good? Teach me!*

Well, in truth, that is exactly how it works. That is what He wants us to do. I know He loves me that much, that individually. **I am literally His child!** And He makes each of us think we are His favorite one; His love is that clear.

Asking and Receiving

When I have a question, I open my mind to my Heavenly

Father's loving presence, as if to literally look up and see His face. I ask my yes and no questions, and if yes and no aren't good enough to complete my needs, I ask for further light and knowledge on the matter. This kind of answer may take a little longer, so I remain open and wait, knowing help is on the way.

Sometimes messages come through others. Sometimes the phone rings as I get up from my prayers and my answer comes through something someone says on the other end of the line. Sometimes I get an answer by just being in the presence of someone's spiritual energy, just by noticing what that kind of energy means to me.

Messages come from experiences I witness, usually within a short while after asking. In the time just after asking for help, it is important that I remain open to everything that shows up. I may *physically* do something else, but my *spirit* remains as His audience. As I spiritually remain one with God, I always know He is with me, always communicating, always giving me my answers—my clarity. Even though I may go on with my work, I remain connected to spirit, multi-tasking.

Spirit speaks in a language each of us will understand. Symbols that mean something to the individual will show up. After receiving the messages, I return in prayer to confirm that I got it right—back to the yes and no questions, metering my impressions with my heart.

It may seem like God is sending me on a treasure hunt, and I may wonder why I can't just hear everything immediately. Some people do. Sometimes I do, though spiritual *hearing* comes less frequently for me. I see things easily, so I allow myself to close my eyes, or gaze off into infinity, noticing what images come, then asking what they mean, getting more images. When I think I know what the message is, I ask, *is this about such and such?* If my heart swells, I am right. If not, I ask for more, and wait, and ask, on and on until I am satisfied.

I also have the gift to feel—*clairsentience*. I feel calm

205

all over my body when I am on the right track. I feel *anxiety* when things are not right, like a protective wall going up, *as if to warn me*. These spiritual gifts are ways I was given to allow the spiritual realm to help me. We are all different in our spiritual gifts, but none came without some. God uses what gifts and tools we each have, giving us as much assistance as He can. Some are developing their gifts and others don't even know they have any.

If you doubt your ability to have open communication with heaven, don't! We all came with some lifelines to God. As a young person, I was unaware that all the visualizing I was doing was a spiritual gift. I expected everyone to understand spiritual matters the same way I did. Experience has taught me that we are unique in our relationship with spirit. I have a friend who hears words in her mind as soon as she asks a question. Sometimes she doesn't even know what the words mean; she has to consult a dictionary. But the words or thoughts come distinctly, as she has developed her spiritual awareness with the gift of hearing. Others just seem to *know* without a doubt, from an inner sense, which is their spiritual gift. And some simply have a feeling, and they know when they honor those feelings, things will always work out.

Everyone has their own personal routine for exercising spiritual muscles. Mine includes some practical applications of getting the *negative out* and the *divine in*. The time just before I go to sleep is spent in forgiveness, releasing to God all the baggage I may have collected during the day (if I haven't already done that in the moment), and asking in prayer for specific solutions and inspirations to what's going on in my life at the time. I may wait for the answers right away, or I may ask to receive them as I sleep.

As I go to sleep, I am free to float in a world of possibilities. I imagine that my spirit leaves my body and goes wherever it wants in search of these solutions and inspirations.

Or perhaps, heavenly visitors come to speak to me in my sleep. My dreams usually give me the answers, so when I awake, I lay very still, remembering what it was I wanted to get clarity about as I went to sleep. Usually I remember a dream, and as I piece it together, noticing how the messages relate to my questions, I find I have a wonderful bit of inspiration — perfect truth concerning my need.

At other times, I wake up in the morning and realize I don't remember any answers from my dreams. Perhaps feeling a little bit disappointed, I lie still in my bed, again pondering the question or need. This quiet place in my mind does a *scanning search* through the realms of truth in which I am floating, all relaxed from my sleep, where my inner knowing usually finds some spiritual guidance and solutions to my requests. Morning meditation works best for me — the time when my mind is quiet.

Spiritual messages come to me through songs. Sometimes I notice that a song is going repeatedly through my mind, so I pay attention to it. I listen to the words and realize it has a message from spirit. Having spent so many years studying, singing and teaching music, especially to children, music is a language that I understand, and where I have a lot of *verses* stored in the catalogues of my brain. Spiritual beings know this about me, so it's natural this would be one of the languages they use to guide me. When I acknowledge the song I am hearing, I am pleasantly surprised that the words of that song include a detailed answer to my prayer.

After *remember*, *asking* is the next most powerful word for being able to access truth. *Ask and ye shall receive.* When turning your focus towards spirit energy, it really is this simple to ask and then connect to a bit of enlightenment.

For example, a few years ago instead of stressing as I usually do over what gifts to give my loved ones for Christmas, I prayed and asked for inspiration. I simply sent out a spiritual request and waited for the reply. I remained open, expecting an answer, trusting, allowing—not forcing it. I kept the question floating about me, and some wonderful gift ideas soon popped into my awareness, showing up along my path that day, perfectly aligned with how I wanted to celebrate gift-giving that Christmas. As I gave thanks I wondered, *why didn't I think of that?*

Asking **is a powerful weapon against ignorance.** *God and angels are ready and waiting to supply all our needs.* My faith is strong in the reality of prayer, beginning with meditation. Asking serves me well in every part of my life.

A Spiritual Practice

Meditation and prayer are powerful, and in this busy world I believe these tools are *essential* in order to stay on track spiritually. Every day we tend to attach to whatever life dishes up, and we give those things power over our happiness and our sense of perfection. But in reality, it is only by letting go of the material world and embracing the spiritual realms that we can re-connect with our truthful inner being, and this is where *all real happiness exists.*

Meditation guides you to release the world's reality of self, separating from all attachment to things and people and life outside of the state of simply *being* self. I am not the body I have; I am not the people around me; I am not my mother, my job, my talents, my looks, or my culture. In meditation, I disconnect from my body, the people in my life, the beliefs of my experience, and of all my learning. *I feel only my spirit.* I allow my spirit to become one with the light that is in every part of this universe, like the air. I float in that space of pure, flowing light. I allow my body to dissolve into that light, until there is nothing *separate* about me. In this deep meditative state, I am not a separate being, but a part of the immense and powerful light of God. There is nothing but love in the light; it just *is.*

As I allow this oneness with the light to absorb my spirit, I feel tangibly healed and whole. I float in this space of connectedness to the greater whole of God's love. As I stay in such a lovely state of connection to the greater whole, I know my real being as a child of God. I feel the tingling joy of God's love all through my body, feeling the comfort of knowing all is well: **I am completely safe in His love, with nothing to do and nothing to think about.**

This state of meditation is commonly called 'emptiness'. It is *nothing* that I want to make it be from my experience and training, and it is *everything* that could possibly be, with all the powers of Heaven, God, and Love vibrating within me. **Everything is in this nothingness!** Everything is achieved when you can get to the state of not judging anything: the nothingness. Doing so creates a state of enlightenment in your whole body—an exercise which sends calm tingling energy all through your body, healing you, reminding you that life is so very wonderful, that you are never alone, that you are safe and everything is going to be okay, that love is your constant companion: truly the state of pure joy, and it's absolutely free.

For a moment, I may see myself as *that* identity— the person who has released all attachments and found enlightenment. I consider that I am one who has tasted enlightenment, which means that there are some who have *not* tasted enlightenment—us and them. The moment I think this thought, something has already taken my enlightenment away from me—*judgment.*

As I have energetically visualized this, I have seen in vision a metaphor of what judgment does. As I make that ever so slight moment of judgment, golden handcuffs attach to me—a symbol that I am attached to a belief of separation from the whole of God's unconditional love. Since I judged myself as one who has been in the light, where I noticed such a state as a separate identity from when I was *not* in the light, I have made a judgment. In that moment, I automatically separate myself from the light, because there is no judgment in the light.

The purpose of meditation is to bask in God's nurturing love: it's like lying out in the sun. Like the sun, unconditional love is radiating freely for all to come and partake of its abundance. So in that simple consideration (judgment) that I might be in some particular state of enlightenment, I will always become imprisoned—separate from the beautiful truth—the only truth—which is that I am always one with the light of God and that love is freely flowing *all the time*, and that is my only concern.

I cannot allow my mind to judge this space of *pure light and oneness with the immensity of love*. To receive the benefits of meditation, I want no attachments, even if the handcuffs are pure gold—very symbolic. *Wanting* (things) is an illusion, because unconditional love is freely abundant, spread on the table waiting for me to partake, always. Any judgment will separate me from the lovely body of pure, powerful light—that place which fills my whole awareness with exquisite joy. So if I judge, I must let it go and return to that place of pure love. I gather that body of light and love into my physical body, reminding me that this love *is me*. I bring all of the light into my body, from the top of my head to the base of my spine to the center of my heart. I *feel* it in my body. I become a *body of pure spirit*. From this space—being one with pure love—I can serve as God does, with no judgment, simply *being* in the state of pure and unconditional love.

A spiritual practice might look like this:

- Wake up early in the morning.
- Enjoy the stillness.
- Let inspirational messages come freely, without effort. Remember dreams.

- Write them down in a journal.
- Ask for details.
- Receive clarity.
- Spend time discussing my desires with God — pray.
- Confirm my inspirations by choosing to read some scriptures or other inspired writings. The messages of my personal revelations are usually validated there.
- Get the day planned according to this pure light and truth.
- Use said plan through the day, doing my best to *remember*.
- Pray as I go about the day, knowing I am always abiding in the presence of and communicating with God and angels. Ask and receive.
- Remember: heaven is on my team.
- Go, do, and be, as I feel prompted, now. Act immediately on inspiration.
- Before I go to sleep, find some quiet moments to unwind and create stillness through meditation.
- Allow myself to feel the gratitude I would feel if all my needs are met, feeling the comfort of being his only and honored child again, remembering my loving connection.
- Pray. Report on the day — the assignments and goals from the morning.
- Get more clarity as I discuss things with Heavenly Father.
- Converse about the challenges I have faced — how the experiences of the day have affected me, what my plans are, how I am feeling.
- Give to God all that makes no sense, all judgment and burdens, by specifically forgiving all that is not love and releasing that energy to Him for His care and keeping.
- Ask for help, blessings, for self and others as my heart

feels the desire.

- Imagine beautiful angels carrying my wishes throughout the universe, delivering the requests of my prayers to their recipients. With my spiritual eyes, I see the joy and healing that these blessings bring and acknowledge such, giving thanks.
- Ask for more clarity to come in the night.
- Go to sleep and dream with the angels.

Such a practice of spiritual communication will take a bit of focus, effort and organization at first, but will soon become a regular pattern for a life of living in spirit. It just takes a few weeks to recreate the new habits, and hopefully you can see the value in such a choice. It is my firm belief that this way of life will allow one to eliminate all suffering, and in fact bring great personal peace, even while living in a most unpredictable world. Such a spiritual alignment will actually give you the power to change not only your own course, but will assist in changing the course of our planet, as more and more souls choose to wake up to accept the state of enlightenment as a natural reason for being.

Thoughts for Processing *The Energy of Prayer and Meditation:*

- How deep is your desire to be one with spirit? What price will you pay? Will you be willing to face the truth about yourself? Will you be willing to lay everything on the altar to find God?
- How much time are you willing to spend with spirit? Are you willing to wait on God?
- Are you willing to release all thoughts and go into a state of pure loving spirit (meditation) in order to get the answers to your prayers?

- Have you exercised your spiritual muscles? Do you know how it feels when you get an answer to your prayers? Is your heart your tool for spiritual response?
- Notice the elements such as nature, music, and scripture that work to connect you with spirit.
- Once you have been inspired, are you willing to take action accordingly?
- Notice something that is troubling you right now. Say aloud some words expressing what you wish could be happening instead of the troubling thing. Say what you want!
- Visualize what it would look like and imagine what it would feel like if your wish came true. Allow the feelings to grow bigger and bigger, holding the paradigm as long as you can.
- Act as if this prayer is the *new reality*. Receive the gift with gratitude.
- Use the exercises in this chapter and practice stilling your breath.
- As your breath quiets your body, empty your mind. Imagine what your empty bowl looks like. Release all thoughts, opinions, and judgments.
- Stay in this emptiness, open to receiving only pure love until you feel transported to a higher, spiritual realm. You will know when you have arrived.
- After a while, when you are at peace, ask a yes/no question that is weighing on your mind. Stay in complete peace while listening with your heart.
- Stay open to receiving an answer until it comes, with no extra effort other than paying attention to potential messages.
- Don't argue with the spirit. When you think you have an answer, ask if that was the answer and then pay the price to act on it.

- Every time you pass a mirror, smile at and send some love to that beautiful precious child of God you see there!
- Are you more of a hearer, seer, feeler, or do you just know things? Become familiar with and use your spiritual gifts.
- God and angels are ready and waiting. Ask for everything you want. PRAY!

Chapter 9

The Energy of Healing

The lovely bright light of love,
That cleansing pool of spirit,
Where everything becomes brand new again.
There is no need to suffer or wait,
Just awaken now,
And receive it freely home within you.

On Mother's Day in the spring of 1985, I spent the day with my husband's extended family at the home of his parents, where jokes had been made as to which of the daughters or daughters-in-law would be having the next grandchild. My in-laws were merciless in their sarcastic humor, but they meant well. I ate some chocolate cake at the end of the afternoon and left a little later. I started feeling sick before we got home, about a half-hour away, and by evening I was in the emergency room, writhing with abdominal pain.

The next day I was diagnosed with esophagitis reflux. The endoscopy showed I had no sphincter muscle left between my esophagus and my stomach. What used to be a intricately important tool for controlling stomach acids was, from one day to the next, turned to a bloody and raw empty hole, allowing burning all the way up to my throat.

My life suddenly became a whole new story. With four little ones and the busy schedules I was used to capably handling, I had to learn new skills — allowing others to serve me and letting go of control, while I spent many months in bed healing and managing that condition. I slept on an incline, gave up some of my favorite foods, took pills to stop the acid from burning my esophagus, felt horribly weak and helpless, and tried to re-invent my life while I looked for a cure.

The doctors told me there was no cure. The only hope was surgery to affix a plastic replacement for the deteriorated muscle. The down side was that it would only open into the stomach, so if I ever had to burp or vomit, it wouldn't happen, which sounded completely unnatural and with a high probability for pain.

I had been eating fresh foods for years. I had used herbs

217

for medicines, and had kept our family pretty free of illness. So like all the other detours to my *perfect-life-plan*, I pondered the deeper meaning. What was this all about, and how was it to be healed?

For the next several years, I asked for knowledge from every medical professional I met, while I medicated myself as best I could, mixing orthodox treatments with natural remedies. I was able to keep my throat and esophagus *cooled down* by taking a drink several times a day of some special medicinal powder mixed in water. This was treating what I suspected was the underlying problem: a yeast infection in my gut.

I knew that eventually one of the professionals would have a good answer and share knowledge of a way for permanent healing. Meanwhile, I could not have any more babies, as pregnancy was impossible in my condition. But *my spirit knew* I had more babies yet to come to me. I had seen my other two daughters in vision, and I knew they wanted me to birth them. *I knew I would have these girls, so I knew there must be a way to be healed!*

When conflicting information exists, I keep searching, knowing there must be another way. The doctors said I would never be well enough to have another child, but my spiritual knowing said I would. Somebody was wrong, and *I knew it wasn't spirit!*

As I continued for several years to seek truth and to believe in being healed, the daughter of one of my best friends became suddenly and mysteriously ill, and doctors could not find the cause of her suffering. I had the impression to share my experience with yeast being the cause of all unknown and unexplained ills, (which was the best I had at the time). My friend listened to my story and considered the possibility, but only for a minute. Almost as if she didn't even hear my suggestion, she shared with me a recent discovery of her own.

She was using a new technique—a model of *healing*

through forgiveness, which had already brought some positive results. She had found a teacher of this way of healing—a doctor in a town about four hours south of where we lived.

For some reason, I fought with my friend's conclusion for hours that night on the phone. At that time, I had spent about twenty years studying and practicing the art of natural healing with foods and herbs of the earth, and now I was being asked to think more deeply.

Not knowing how to convince me, but unwilling to give up, she asked me if I would consider reading a few testimonials printed in some small pamphlets. I do not know why I fought so hard against this, or why she was so willing to keep teaching me when it was I who had called to help her daughter with *my* wisdom. Nevertheless, I agreed to read. She came right over with the booklets, and within a few hours that very night, my heart changed. I felt impressed that the concept just might work. I agreed to see the doctor on the condition that he could get me in immediately! This doctor was popular, and usually had a six-week waiting list, but he fit me into a cancellation four days later.

Healing in Minutes with Forgiveness Therapy

I took my nine-year old son with me to experience our new forgiveness doctor. I prayed for a miracle all the way there; God knew I needed one. Though he had experienced nasty allergies for years, my son had the innocent faith of a child as we took this new therapy on together. Amazing to both of us, after only twenty minutes of forgiveness therapy, he experienced complete healing of his bothersome ailments!

Next, I spent eighty minutes and did the same. We both received our miracles. Everything I was taught in that healing session was very consistent with principles I already knew were true, raising my confidence in this healing modality even more.

I will share the details of that first visit, but know that we have applied the forgiveness principles with the same success rate consistently since that first day in the fall of 1988.

Healing with forgiveness is an energetic or spiritual healing, which includes using a testing method known as *kinesiology*. Using yes and no questions and answers, this energetic testing method helps to locate the specific negative energy trapped in the body. Such energy enters the body due to false beliefs and painful circumstances which are literally the beginnings of the illness. Usually the doctor is able to discover the exact date and people involved with the original negative emotions.

The next step involves forgiving the offenders, including God and self for allowing such, and one's own ignorance for holding onto false beliefs and allowing them to fester for so long. Once identified, the beliefs are released by simply saying some words like this: I forgive (name of person) for *such and such offense.*

I actually and very literally felt the negative energy leave my body as I repeated the forgiving statements. The idea is that by no longer holding onto false beliefs, the molecules of this negative energy are able to release out of the body. If I choose to hold no judgment of it, the negative energy never returns. If at a later time I choose to judge the issue again, I must then repeat the forgivings to remove the negative energy that will return in the process of re-creating it with the re-telling of the story. This also applies to anything that causes the negative energy to come up again, such as speaking of it with emotions of being offended or re-experiencing the same negative situation. (This is the seven times seventy principle.)

Using kinesiology, this doctor was able to locate the time and place that my son's allergies began. There were two particular events that triggered his symptoms. The first one was based on his feelings of rejection from me when he entered kindergarten. He thought that I wanted him gone so that I could go swimming at an exotic pool where he *thought* I worked. A few years earlier, I had taken him on a design job with me, thinking he would like to see the cool pool that hung out on a balcony at one of my projects. For years afterwards, in his innocence he imagined that was what I did when he went to school, and that I preferred playing there to being with him — a deep form of rejection, which initiated significant allergic reactions.

The second event attached to the manifestation of his illness happened on a camping trip when he was a young scout, and somebody was offensive in some way, causing him to have fear and to feel badly. The trigger to his allergies was the smell of evergreen trees, which essence was present at the time of the offense. After the offensive situation happened, subconscious messages took over so that whenever he was in the presence of the fragrance of evergreen trees, he could not breathe. Also, whenever he would lie down at night, he struggled with breathing, along with other symptoms quite disturbing for a little child.

Once the doctor used the testing methods on him, he was able to identify the original negative energy. My son then repeated forgiving statements for the offenders, including the scout leaders and me. This verbal exercise allowed the negative energy to release from his body, taking his allergies with it, permanently. After our forgiveness healing experience, we were able to have live Christmas trees in the house again, and my son has never experienced any of those allergic reactions since.

While neither the scout leader nor I had done anything intentional to hurt him, he still had to forgive us *for causing him to feel certain emotions,* such as rejection. He had to forgive himself for holding onto such emotions, and he forgave God for allowing it. The words used in the process of forgiving are very important. They must convey the actual negative emotion experienced.

For me, the esophagus illness came from more complex issues. Using the same techniques, the doctor was able to identify the beginning of my illness in the month of May, exactly three and a half years earlier. Until that moment, I had completely forgotten the way I felt when the issue of more children had come up on that Mother's Day at the in-laws. But once identified, I suddenly had complete recall of the incident, as if the spot in my brain where the information was stored was touched, awakening the whole scenario as clearly as if it happened yesterday. I recalled the whole event start to finish. Until that moment, I had not connected the incidents of that Mother's Day in any way with the onset of my illness just a few hours following.

The doctor went on to question with the same testing technique, why this had affected me so. I learned that I had issues with the way my mother experienced life and her judgments of my life. We continued to explore these emotions further. I remembered the exact message my mother had relayed to me about her fears of me having more children. She saw me as *delicate*. She thought I could not handle more than four. She had almost died having her fifth and last baby, and in my respect and admiration for her, I could not see myself as one bit stronger than her.

All of these messages and emotions were buried deep within my psyche, completely unaware to my conscious mind. The doctor went on to explain that when I was asked about having more children that memorable day in May of 1985, my mind began searching for a solution. The mind, with its stored belief system based on my mother's issues and my lack of confidence in my own strengths, came up with a plan to *save* me. The mind held a *belief* that came from my *emotions* that I subconsciously feared dying in childbirth. Dying in childbirth had never entered my *conscious* mind, but because of all the issues with my mother, my subconscious mind—the obedient servant—had come to my defense. Clever it was to pick an illness that would keep me safe from further pregnancy but would not cause me irreparable harm.

I spent only eighty minutes in forgiveness therapy, healing completely from that incurable ailment. First I discovered how these false beliefs had subconsciously controlled me for so many years. Next, I began understanding how the ideas had been planted in me by my mother's fears. And finally I said the words of forgiving. I forgave my mother for causing me to fear. I said words of forgiving to myself for believing my mother's fears about me. I said words of forgiving to God for allowing all this horrible stuff to happen to me.

In these minutes of testing, explaining, and forgiving, learning about and getting in tune with how my body had carried negative energy from false beliefs, I released an incurable ailment that had plagued me for three and a half years! In that short time, I learned a new way of looking at life: *subconscious beliefs control the body, and forgiveness removes the negative beliefs and their effects.*

It all made perfect sense, and I never suffered that illness again—not a spot of it—not ever. When I asked the doctor how long it would take for the illness to be gone permanently and to be able to go without medication, having a normal life again, he simple asked me, *do you still need to be sick?*

The issues were forgiven. The negative energy was released from my body. I felt completely well as I spent that afternoon enjoying a picnic with my son, laughing as I ate all the foods that I had been forbidden to eat during my illness, and recounting the magic of our lessons.

As I questioned more deeply in follow-up healing sessions, I was able to understand how my mother would have seen me as *delicate*, since I was an amazingly strong and active person. I learned that what my *brain computed* was not what she

223

meant. I learned that the brain only remembers what it thought and registered at the time of the sharing of words. I had not taken a moment to consider or analyze what she meant at the time, so the brain stored its simplest, most obvious deduction of the information.

What Mother meant was that I was *sensitive and tender* in my *spirit,* not referring to my *body.* She saw me in a marriage relationship that was inconsiderate of my gentle nature, which caused her great concern. The comments she made had been interpreted by my *head energy* — like a computer, with no reasoning ability of its own. (That is why *listening to spirit* is so important!)

The message I later understood was translated by my *heart's* energy, by pondering and meditation. I was able to know the truth of her intentions and to find peace about it all. This *deception of mind over spirit* is how false beliefs get stored in the body, causing sickness.

Giving Negative Energy to Christ

I see the word *forgive,* and turn it around this way: to *give for.* I *give* my stuff to Christ *for* Him to deal with, to do justice with. Forgiveness is the literal exchange of giving our stuff to the light — to spirit. This allows our bodies to be rid of all darkness and to be filled with light, or spirit again.

Forgiveness is *giving* a certain thought, feeling, emotion — any form of negative energy — to Christ **for** His care and keeping, since He already paid for it with His loving gift of atonement. He already owns it energetically.

Forgiveness is also very powerful because by so doing, I am obedient to what Christ taught. He asked us to hold no negatives about anyone or anything. He asked us to let it go and let Him be the only judge. If He had said, *this is the way you will be healed of every bit of suffering you will ever experience,* maybe more people would accept this wonderful gift. (Actually, that is exactly what He taught.)

Christ also taught in Matthew 17 and other examples that we must rebuke the evil spirit, after which healing occurs. This example was shown repeatedly in the writings of His life as recorded in the New Testament, and He did this to show the way for us to do the same, (just like everything else He taught). Evil has a hold on us only when we are carrying negative energy, so after saying the specific *forgivings*, I repeat a statement to cast out all evil energy in the name of Jesus Christ—the *creator* of light.

Is it possible that all suffering comes from holding within us thoughts, feelings, and judgments that are not of the light—not true? Any beliefs held within that are of the darkness energy will cause suffering. Suffering-energy is created from emotions such as *somebody offended me, somebody doesn't love me, somebody caused me to feel I was inadequate, something or someone caused me to feel fear, shame, guilt, anger, frustration, doubt.*

All of these forms of energy are *opposite* to our natural state of joy, which is created from forms of light and truth, such as those Christ taught: *ye are the light of the world, with a tiny bit of faith in the light, you can heal yourselves, you can move mountains!*

It is a powerful and instantaneous method for healing when I choose to forgive immediately following any offense or negative experience, allowing the darkness to leave me, rebuking the evil forces in the name of Christ. When one believes as I do that sickness and health are *literal forms of energy*, choices must be made to forgive and cast out, allowing the spirit of love to return, which is our natural state. I believe this is the literal interpretation of the idea that *through Him*, we could remain free always.

As I learned this new and simple way of healing, it was easy for me to accept. Healing with forgiveness is consistent with the natural laws of energy, and in harmony with all of

Christ's teachings, as well as my own feelings for how I wanted to spend my time on earth.

I knew from personal revelation some of what my life's purpose included, and I knew that I could not accomplish that plan while being sick; sickness was not a part of my purpose. Deep within me I knew that. I suppose for some, sickness is a part of their overall plan, perhaps to learn personal lessons or to allow others to learn by serving them. I do not judge others choices or situations, nor what God has in mind in any case. Everyone is here to learn and to share such with others. I can only tell you what I learned about myself, and that it has always worked.

I was thrilled beyond comprehension to learn this new form of treating illness. I felt like I had been given a secret treasure. I lost no time in sharing the news with others, most of whom thought I was crazy or delusional. This kind of healing at that time was very new and mistrusted. The concept or science of *energy medicine* was in its infancy, and rarely understood. My faith in spiritual healing was ahead of the times, for sure.

But I had been healed, and for all these years now since I have continued to be healed with forgiveness, as have my children, one hundred percent of the time when we use the principles. Everything from flu to bronchitis to tumors, thyroid problems, acne, weight, rotator cuffs, mono and heart problems—you name it, we let it go and heal with forgiveness.

Healing Long Distance

I even used forgiveness to heal of a bad case of pneumonia that came on suddenly during my last pregnancy. Being so large with child and coughing constantly, I broke a couple of ribs. I was hesitant to take medicines in pregnancy, so I called my forgiveness doctor for help, which I should have done sooner but sometimes we humans have to suffer a bit to remember to choose easy!

In just a few minutes of testing by *proxy* over the phone, the emotional cause was identified. The answers always make perfect sense once you learn what the emotions are, and what or who caused them. In this case, we had a friend living with our family for an undetermined length of time, and I needed an excuse to create a change in that arrangement. It was a hard time for him, as he had a job near us while his family was living in a city over three hours away. He needed a place to stay during the workweek, and I had volunteered. We had plenty of room, and I wanted to help these good friends. My little toddler daughter adored him, and ran to the bus stop to meet him every afternoon. My son learned basketball skills from our friend and guest. He was pleasant and appreciative to have in the house.

My husband at the time was of the old school, believing that fish and company stink after three days (Benjamin Franklin). I was conflicted trying to please both men, and also wanting to have peace in the house as I prepared my nest for the birth of my baby. In this state of confusion, forgetting to ask for spiritual inspiration, my trusty subconscious mind created a way out of my conflict, and the solution showed up as pneumonia.

With this illness, I could not take care of myself, much less my guest. I suppose my brain designed that with such an illness, I would somehow run him out of the house, or something like that. Whatever my subconscious had in *mind*, I was very ill, and I needed to get better soon.

I did my forgivings of self, husband, and everything involved in the negative beliefs and emotions attached to those beliefs. I could then release all negative energy causing the pneumonia. The forgiveness doctor further suggested a healthier solution to my conflict: that it would be appropriate to find our guest some housing with one of our good neighbors. Several of these neighbors were getting to know and love this internationally known basketball coach from Europe, and begged to be allowed to host him in their homes. I was sad that they would get to enjoy him instead of us, but I knew it was the best solution.

I forgave myself for creating illness to get around the conflict, as well as forgiving others for their involvement in creating the conflict. I thus released negative energy from my body, and my pneumonia left me immediately. I don't know if the broken ribs were instantly made whole because I didn't have an x-ray, but I felt no more pain at all and my coughing stopped immediately.

Emotions Create Sickness

Miracles such as these have become a way of life for our family since the late eighties. Whenever any of us became sick, we used our new habit of quickly reflecting on what our thoughts and experiences included just prior to the onset of a given illness. Doing such allowed us to notice and identify the negative energy we had collected by buying into those false beliefs, offenses, and judgments. Then it was a simple process to say the appropriate *forgivings* and immediately release the negative energy, including any symptoms of sickness. Even while very young, my children did this easily, feeling the sickness leave and good energy returning on the spot.

I always know when I have identified and released the correct negative energy, because I immediately *feel* it leave. I know I have found the exact cause of an illness and have released it when I feel my body becomes peaceful and at one with light again. Until I return to such a state of peace, I continue to examine my feelings, forgiving all forms of beliefs, all angles of what may have caused my misery.

Such a simple formula, but it always works. Sometimes to this day we still have to be reminded to look at our ailments from a spiritual perspective to find the root causes. Sometimes we suffer a bit first. I am married to a medical doctor now, and sometimes I forget to look for the root emotional causes because it's so easy for our in-house doctor to diagnose and suggest prescriptions at the first sign of illness.

Recently my son called for antibiotics for a terrible cough that was getting him down. I recalled what I had learned from having that illness myself, and shared my understanding of its emotions with my son. In my experience, congestion typically manifests the presence of the energy of *confusion*. I asked if he was having any confusing thoughts or beliefs lately. He had an immediate reaction in the affirmative, knowing immediately what it was. He hung up the phone and spent a few minutes that evening verbalizing the appropriate *forgivings*, releasing the negative energy which had caused his illness, and called the next day to report he was completely well.

Whenever one of our family members feels poorly, the emotional strains we are under are discussed: work, school, teachers, friends, family, self. All thoughts, beliefs, and judgments are analyzed, then recognized, forgiven, and released, after which perfect health and peace returns. I have found that the onset of the illness is usually in close timing with the offense that triggers it, as was mine with the events of that Mother's Day years ago.

Repeating Forgiveness

Often when an offense is inconceivable, it continues to create confusion in your head as you continually try to understand why anyone would do such a thing. This is especially true when the offense is something you are sure you could not or would not ever do yourself. Such analyzing causes you to *think* of the offense over and over, which then causes a *repetition of the offense* in your mind as well. As you

229

are repeatedly considering it, you bring it back to life, making it real again. The energy is then like a virus or cancer, actively vibrating in your body.

Even if you forgave for this offense once, every time it rolls back into your thoughts it is *energetically* as if the first time — it's still there — back again. The brain is like a computer, which keeps recording the messages over and over again each time it receives them. So in order to *heal*, you will have to forgive again each time that message re-enters the brain memory, releasing the negative energy again.

Sometimes the same offense actually *happens* over and over as you continue to allow yourself to be with the same people with the same negative attitudes, which continue to offend you in the same ways — over and over again. Until you change your environment and reduce the possibility of these offenses re-occurring, forgiveness will have to be repeated again each time you are confronted with the same issues.

This is what Jesus meant by suggesting we forgive seven times seventy. We are talking about an actual form of energy — real matter — like a dark cloud with hailstones shooting into your body causing *physical damage*. So forgiveness — the literal *tool* to extract such a darkness — *must be repeated* every time the offense is repeated. Even if that repeated offense is in your thoughts or in your words, as you think about it and tell the story over and over to others, forgiveness must be expressed, which is one very good reason to avoid gossip. If you experience anything offensive, if you think about it or speak of it, you must express forgiveness again.

It is a literal house cleaning, and your house (mind) is to be cleaned out until you hold no memory of the offense. With this perspective, *forgive and forget* makes more sense. Fill yourself instead with good thoughts and truths. Spend time doing good things that bring you positive feelings about yourself and others. Doesn't this sound like a much better way to exist than continually dwelling on all that dark energy?

It's a personal choice to remain in darkness or to choose the light. I look at forgiveness this way: perhaps these conflicts and offenses in our lives are not really just about the offense or the offender. What if they came into our lives to allow us to practice the godly gift of personal choice? *By choosing either to hold onto offenses or to express forgiveness, we have power over the quality of our lives.* And since I believe we are the creators of our own lives, if we ignore the concepts of healing with forgiveness, we have no one to blame but ourselves for the way things turn out. *We alone are accountable.*

There may come a time in the future when we can verbalize the story of our troubles without needing to forgive. As long as we are no longer offended by it and have no more emotional attachments to the events and people involved, we may speak of it if we choose without having negative energy boil up within. This would be at a time when the healing is so complete that you won't feel the sting of it when sharing the details. I don't believe I would share anything that offended me unless I am completely healed, and only then when I feel it may help someone else by learning through my experiences. Lastly, *I only share feelings and experiences when spirit confirms I should.*

After finding healing with forgiveness and experiencing these techniques, I was led to further knowledge on the subject through books such as Louise Hay's *You Can Heal Your Life*, and Carol Truman's *Feelings Buried Alive Never Die*, which explain details of the concepts of energy medicine. There are documentaries available such as *What The Bleep Do We Know*, and *The Living Matrix*, which attempt to introduce the mind/body connections. Energy medicine is the way of future healing, and gratefully, I know it works.

The bottom line is this: *negative energy stored equals sickness. Negative energy released equals healing.* Repeating words of verbal forgiveness is the surest, most immediate form of healing on the planet. **Once you become familiar with this method, healing through forgiveness is as easy as washing your hands.**

Allowing Others to Heal Through Forgiveness

Forgiveness not only heals ourselves, but may also heal the others involved in offenses. A few years ago, I was spiritually guided to know that I should engage in an exhaustive forgiveness session with my father. While Daddy had passed on at the time, certain things about his life had left some scars.

I followed this guidance and found myself in my sacred place in nature by my favorite mountain stream. Deciding that I wanted to make this a final effort of getting everything forgiven and healed with him once and for all, I approached my father's spirit as if he were standing right in front of me. I verbally told him my intentions, face-to-face — spirit-to-spirit. As if he were right there, I expressed that I wanted to forgive everything; I wanted to be healed forever of the scars left from my experience with him.

The memories flooded my mind as I spoke to my father for several hours. I really *let it all out* that afternoon, saying forgiveness for every possible offense from him to me, or to others — every bit that I had ever been party to. I said what I wished I could have said in life but never dared. I continued verbalizing words of forgiveness for each memory, until there was nothing left. When it was over, I felt completely peaceful, and I knew I would be forever healed of any negative experiences from that relationship.

Just then I saw my father's face as it changed from the old man I had last known to a much younger aged version of him. As I watched this sudden transformation, I realized he was being freed from his prison of justice. As I had completely exhausted every possible offense, giving it all to Christ, it seemed my father was allowed to start over again, vibrant and alive as the day I was born. I felt his gratitude for the gift I had just given him. Those hours of deep and complete forgiveness allowed both of us to be free to begin all over again, as if those offenses never happened. For all these years since, I have only thought of him with a sense of comforting, peaceful love, as if that's the only relationship we ever knew. All memories of anything but love have literally vanished.

I know my father would have asked forgiveness in this lifetime had he realized the lasting and damaging affects his choices had on others. Maybe it was actually his desire to do so that was calling me to him that exhaustive day on the mountain. Maybe he had to watch from the other side for a while to really know what had happened, to know that he *needed* forgiveness.

Most of what we do to offend is done in ignorance, which is all the more reason to quickly forgive others. Usually *we don't see ourselves as we really are.* Usually we don't know the impact we have on others, good or bad. Realizing how easily this happens, I have been asking my children for years to please forgive me when they realize negative effects of the things I have done in my ignorance!

We are accountable for our own lives, including the affect we have on others, now and in the eternities. Looking at our own faults instead of blaming others allows us to not be so easily offended by their choices. *Who is your life really about?*

Forgiveness is a Choice

As with all other aspects of life, healing has become a matter of spiritual discovery for me. The more I learn about healing, the more I see its connections to all other facets of a spiritual life. Energy—*spirit*—is in everything. It is in our beliefs. It is in our reactions to all of life's experiences. This

233

is the ultimate challenge of this mortal life that will never end until death. Because we came here with the gift of choice — free will — we are always faced with the opportunity to choose between light and darkness: *what brings me joy and what brings me opposition to my joy?* Everything about this life exists somewhere on that scale.

I hope to be able to make it my nature to only choose light — what some call the state of *enlightenment* — when it becomes such a part of the whole of my daily practice that I always act from the energy of light, in every moment, in every choice.

For years, I only believed in healing with certain foods, herbs and other physical applications of nature's abundance. Then when I learned about energy medicine for healing, using spiritual tools, I wondered if that was all that was necessary for healing. But now I realize that it is important to apply the truths of all our wisdom, including advising with medical persons when your heart tells you such is necessary.

If I do consult with medical professionals and discover an issue with my body, that information is then most useful in releasing the illness through the modality of forgiveness. I love that I do have a choice and that I am not limited to the traditional methods, which often do not have all the answers, as my experience has shown.

I believe that the body can live well on just about any foods as long as the mind has no negative attachment to such. As I wrote earlier about the energy of foods, the *belief* is what holds the power, more than the actual energy within the food. Spiritual healing is about *releasing all attachment* to fears of foods and sickness and judgments. We have to release attachment to all beliefs that we have to be sick, and especially to all negative beliefs about self and others. Healing with forgiveness is about living in purity and innocence, releasing all judgments. This may be a daily, sometimes even moment to moment process, but it works to keep the life lines clear to experience perfect health.

I respect and use all physical healing modalities: herbs, essential oils, yoga, tai chi, acupuncture, reiki, cranial sacral, meditation, massage, and anything that I can tangibly feel radiating goodness, such as eating from the living abundance of the earth. These are all beautiful and sacred gifts for healing, and I feel gratitude for God's grace in providing them. But as I weigh all I have learned and experienced, I know true healing only comes through forgiveness and unconditional love. The literal energy exchange that happens when you transfer darkness into light cannot be duplicated any other way. The actual transferring of negative energy out of the body is never final and complete until you experience forgiveness and receive compassion to fill its space.

Healing Begins with Spirit

As I have shared, spiritual impressions guided me to find the truth of healing with forgiveness. Focusing on the truth through spirit will always guide us on the perfect path to achieve success. I feel gratitude that the overriding belief carrying me through years of sickness until I found spiritual healing was the fact that I knew I had *a purpose*, and I knew I could not fulfill my purpose while lying sick in a bed! As I said, for some, being sick may be that purpose, but I knew it was not so for me.

When two opposing issues show up, I have to trust spirit! For years I had been spiritually shown my life and purpose, and it continues to be revealed to me almost daily. I have been spiritually shown that I will live long and full and healthy, including being shown many of the wonderful details of how this life will be manifest, and so I know I will — it will be so! For others, learning through illness may be their path. I

235

do know that no one living by spirit will leave this earth before their time, however that is to be accomplished. In any case, I choose to focus on living as close to spirit as humanly possible, and trust the messages received, no matter what. My advice to all: before you decide you must be resigned to suffering, I suggest you check the *spiritual healing route* first.

Spirit is the power that guides the physical experience. *Spirit* is all that lasts, all that is real. *We were spiritual beings before we incarnated as physical beings.* **Everything that is physical has roots in the spiritual.** Everything that is created begins as a *spiritual* creation first, which then manifests physically. God did this with the creation of all of life. When you have a spiritual prompting, you act on that prompting by making a plan. You hold true to that plan. With love and time, that plan will manifest. That is the pattern. That is how it works.

The same is true of all illness and healing. If you want to heal something on a physical level, you can't do that by simply addressing the physical symptoms. All that appears to be physical is *not* just physical—it is both physical and spiritual. The spiritual came first, and is an integral part of the physical.

To reverse the physical creations (sicknesses, troubles) you have to find its origins in the spiritual. You have to return to and examine the spiritual energy that created the physical manifestation in the first place. **Change the spiritual (the thoughts, beliefs, judgments), and the physical will no longer be *subject* to those judgments.** The illness will immediately *heal.*

Forgiveness is the vehicle—the *tool*—that releases all illness, and love is the *essence* that heals. I actually *feel the love energy* entering my body when I forgive and release false beliefs, returning to the state of my innocence.

I can feel healing love enter my body through my husband's hands on my head, giving me a surge of his love as a blessing when I ask him to share from his loving fullness.

He has a lot of love in him, but the actual transfer of love to me comes because of my *belief* in his love and in God's love. Christ showed us healing based on faith in this energy of love. He showed it over and over as He taught that we do not judge, that we love unconditionally, that we forgive all, and that we allow Him to manage the details of justice from His omniscient view.

Christ is the generator of love—the ultimate source for healing—because He lived His life *choosing to love* one hundred percent of the time, which is *the perfection of love*. He is so connected to love because He has learned or chosen to *remember* the power of love, and He never denied these truths in His entire life. His example shows that to successfully survive mortality, to rise above our troubles, we must do likewise.

In every instance we must choose to forgive, to release all negative to the healing power of love. Doing so allows us to return to our true nature as original beings of love ourselves. Free will—choice—is the very nature and purpose of this experience we call life on earth, and *forgiveness is the absolute and essential partner of choice.* **When the exercise of our gift of choice causes suffering, we can fix it with forgiveness!**

The powerful healing energy of love replaces all negative energy and allows us to return to the state of pure joyful innocence again. Love is a *gift*, free to all. Forgiveness may sound like an undeserved requirement and an unnecessary encumbrance, but it's really a precious *gift*, and I promise you, forgiveness and love work to heal.

Thoughts for Processing *The Energy of Healing*:

- Are you suffering from any physical, mental, or emotional stress or illness?
- Can you recall the time and circumstances of when you first discovered this illness?
- Do you recall any negative or offensive emotions

237

surrounding those circumstances?

- Do you recall having expectations to be sick or to have a certain illness? Did you ever fear that you might someday become sick? Does the idea of sickness dwell in your mind?

- List all the people and events that have offended you, and one by one say words of forgiveness, releasing all to Christ.

- Remember to say specifics about what offends you and to verbalize the forgivings accordingly.

- Continue repeating words of forgiveness every time you think of it, speak of it, or re-experience the offenses.

- Can you literally feel the negative energy leave your body?

- Can you understand how important it is to get this negative energy *out* of your body, so that you can be healed, *regardless of what happens to the offenders?*

- Can you leave all judgment to God and make choices to stay out of judgment?

- Anytime you are feeling off balance, remember to forgive and then to cast out the adversary in the name of Christ.

- Remember to focus on the good things—the things you are grateful for, and to seek to infuse your life with the spirit of truth, light, and love.

Chapter 10

The Energy of Heavenly Beings

Dearest ones,
My life you share,
Honoring my moments with your loving care.
If my eyes were opened,
And I could see your breathtaking love always guiding me,
I would know heaven came to earth
And never ever leaves me to wander here alone.

In 1977, when I was just learning how to be a mother myself, I received a phone call from my mother telling me she had cancer. It was the worst news I had ever conceived of getting—a completely unexpected blow to my heart. My mother was my soul's connection to all that was good, and to me she was completely immortal.

My little one-year-old daughter, my husband and I were living in Santa Barbara, while he worked as a summer law clerk. I remember exactly where I was when I got the news, as well as how I handled the next few days. I was going to church that morning, with trauma so evident on my face, people were asking what was the matter. Everyone had a piece of advice, which only served to increase my fears of loss. This was a situation to which I had no preparation or skills to handle.

I decided to go to God in fasting and prayer. After about a day of humbling myself, turning my soul to a place of spirit, I remember lying in bed pondering the depths of my emotions and hearing this message:

"Yes, your mother is going to die of this cancer. But you will have six or seven more years with her. And don't worry; you will still be able to talk with her."

The blow of knowing she was going to die was somewhat softened by the fact that I had just been told by spirit that I would still be able to talk to her, but it was devastating news, just the same. I was twenty-three years old and had planned on having my mother around to teach me everything about raising a family. I was planning on enjoying her spoiling my children like she did my brother's little ones: building forts in the living room and climbing in with them to play for hours, making artistic creations of all kinds, baking, teaching, and traveling

241

together.

My mother knew how to make everything wonderful, and she did it all with precision and patience. My granny had told me that she never taught my mother how to do things, that she just seemed to already know how. From the time she was little, if she saw a dress in a shop window that she wanted, Mother would cut herself a pattern and make it from fabrics on hand. She made all her own clothes after that, and then later for her three younger sisters as well. I loved my mother's wisdom and her constant unconditional love. I could not conceive of life without her.

Blessings from the Other Side

For six and a half more years almost to the day, Mother struggled with cancer, and then she left. I was with her nearly every minute of her last few weeks. I watched her take her last breath. I grieved terribly at the loss, but I had hope that we would not *really* be apart, due to the promise from spirit which I had kept sacred all those years within my spirit's inner knowing.

On the day she died, I felt heavenly beings in the room. I somehow knew in which corner they were gathering. Somehow I heard the song they were singing: my mother's favorite hymn which she used to play with a few fingers on the piano and sing along — *Now Let Us Rejoice* — and then she went with them.

I was afraid of seeing dead people. I had only seen one — my paternal grandmother. At the age of thirteen, I fainted at the viewing when I saw her body and spent the rest of the evening in the bathroom. So it was not something I looked forward to when I was asked to come with my siblings to the very same mortuary to approve Mother's presentation. I don't know when I have dreaded anything more.

But I was surprised when I walked into that large,

mostly empty gathering room to feel that it was not morbid at all. In fact, I was aware that on a spiritual level, there was some sort of celebration going on. I could feel the room full to capacity with spirits — happy spirits. It was like a glorious ball. I don't know how I knew this, but I clearly did. I choose to avoid spending much time looking in my mother's open casket. I knew she wasn't in it. I knew she was dancing and laughing and celebrating with about three hundred loved ones from the other side, right in my presence. It was a sweet gift to a devastated young daughter.

Later that evening, when my best friend greeted me in the receiving line, she asked what I was on.

"Valium?" She asked.

"No, nothing," I replied. *"It's all spiritual."*

"I don't believe it," she said. *"There's no way you could be this happy and peaceful without something."*

I hope I was not irreverent that night, but I did enjoy a spiritual feast amidst generations of ancestors, for which I will always be grateful.

A few weeks later when I was back at home with my family, I spent one evening in particular joy. I was having fun playing with my four little ones, ages one to nine, and then with sweet satisfaction, putting them to bed. Afterwards, I was standing at the kitchen sink doing the dishes, feeling peacefully gratified about how the day had gone. Just then, I had a sense that someone was standing in the doorway across the room, so I turned to look. No one was there. The children were all happily tucked in bed and their father was working late. I had the sense of a presence again, so I turned a second time. Again, no one. I had a feeling to be still and listen, and then I heard my mother's voice:

"You are a really good mother, and I love your new house."

That was all. Then she was gone.

It was an unmistakable knowing. It was just what I

wanted to hear, filling my heart with love. How did it happen? How did I know it was her? I just did. It was perfect. It was enough. She was not gone. She was near me. I wanted to be a good mother, like she always was. I thought I was, but it was so good to hear it from her. I had been a great mother that day in particular. I am glad that was the day she came to visit.

Houses were important to me. I was a designer and this house was four months new to us. Mother had lived a lifetime raising her five children in the same small house. She had wondered if she should move when she could finally afford it, but she never did. She wondered if the giant electrical transformer near the street outside the house had caused her cancer and if she should move away, but she never did. She always wanted a nicer place, and the one I had would have been just exactly what she would have chosen. I knew she was happy for me.

Faith Versus Fear

The spirit of peace that she brought lasted for several weeks, warming my heart with love, reminding me that she would always be able to talk to me. And it is significant to recognize the cause of it leaving: *fear*. One of my brothers had come to visit. He had spent the day skiing at a resort about an hour away. It was late and he wasn't back. Those were the days before cell phones. I started thinking the worst: the steep canyon coming down, the weather wasn't great, many horrible accidents happen in that canyon.

Fear gripped me as I considered the possibility of losing another family member, which I knew I could not bear. My soul plummeted down into darkness. The fear took with it the loving peace Mother had brought several weeks before. My brother came home, but Mother's peace did not return so quickly.

Spirit comes and spirit stays when it finds a matching energy to draw it near, such as joy and love. But on that day, *grief* overtook the joy of the love I had been given at her passing, her viewing, and her personal visit to my home.

Several years went by with no more messages from Mother. I missed her so. It was seven years before I stopped being teary and aching in my heart every time I thought of her. I wanted to hear from her again, so I went to the mountains on solos with spirit. I sat in the woods and waited. I imagined I heard her, what she would say, but it wasn't very clear. Anything I thought I got was a bit manufactured.

A few more years went by, and I was alone at her graveside. It was a horrible time in my life, just after Daddy died and I was getting divorced. I cried over her grave, begging her to talk to me. And then I heard her clearly say,

"I am not here in this grave. I am peacefully with God. Don't be sad for me. Take care of yourself. Get up and make something of yourself."

Make something of myself? Was that a reprimand? Stop whining? I think that was the message. Over the years, I had leaned on her way too much. Sometimes I thought that was why she died so young, so that I would learn to find the truth on my own and learn to lean on God and self instead of her. If so, it worked. I knew I only had God and self to lean on now, and I knew I had to get on with making my own life happen.

Other Family Visitors

After Mother died, I became the family genealogist. I gathered all the bits of information she left, which she had meticulously researched for many years, and I began piecing together our family tree. It was a complicated job, and I felt called to do it. Since I had four young children at home, I had to organize my time and plan my *genealogy day* each week. I had a small table set up in the corner of my bedroom just for this purpose. I worked on this project, committing one day every week until it was done, about a year later.

The interesting fact so indelibly clear to me was that my ancestors were with me, attending me as I worked on their family history! I felt them come to my side, as if to watch or help the minute I sat down at that table and opened the books. Their loving spirits blessed me and guided me all day long. It was magical and delighted my heart. The moment I closed the books and got up from my chair at the end of that special day each week, my ancestors left, just like that.

Further, as I was getting more and more involved in that hobby, I was often asked to speak about genealogy. Knowing my words alone would have little impact, I always invited my ancestors to be there with me to guide me and bring the loving spirit I knew would touch the hearts of my audiences. I talked to these spirits as if I knew they were standing there beside me, though I could not physically see them. Sometimes at first I felt very alone on the stage, but when it was nearing my turn to speak, I sensed they came and joined my audiences. With spiritual eyes, I saw them enter and take their seats in an area that appeared like a balcony just above the rest of the audience, smiling their loving approval and giving me the strong witness I needed to share my story from my heart.

It was a time of knowing a connection to love that I had never known possible. The depths of my familial connections on the other side filled my heart and removed all loneliness of being without my extended family here on the earth. I felt an important connection to something so much bigger than this life or my small part in it. I felt loved by great and real people who actually cared for me, as I remembered and loved and communicated with them through spirit. So that is how we connect with loved ones on the other side: *they are with us as we remember them.*

When I was a child, Daddy bought our family a ski boat. Every Saturday, he would take us to the lake for some of the greatest times I can remember. With my love for water and trees and all things natural, being at that beautiful lake having a good time with my loved ones filled my soul. Daddy loved to pilot the boat up and down the miles of lake channels, as we children took turns skiing and trying new tricks. My sister and I loved to stretch out in the triangle of seats at the front of the boat, getting sunshine and just relaxing. When I saw Kate Winslet in *Titanic* leaning out over the bow of the boat, that was me. As a child, I was free as a bird riding in my father's boat.

About a year after Daddy died, I took my first ocean cruise. We sailed for seven days from Long Beach to Puerto Vallarta and back. Being on a boat—any boat—reminded me of those happy days at the lake in my childhood. I stood on the bow of that cruise ship, feeling the wind to my face, the dolphins jumping ahead of our course, and thought of Daddy. My heart opened to all the love I shared with him in boating over many wonderful years, and my gratitude for all that those wonderful memories represented.

I longed for him to be with me and share in the joy I was feeling, which he had been so much a part of in years past. I wished he could have been there, that he too could have enjoyed such a lovely trip. In all his life, I don't believe he ever had such a pleasure, but in the moments of such thinking and wishing, I literally felt Daddy come to me, standing right beside me on the bow of that cruise ship. How I knew, I don't know, but I did know. I felt him—his physical presence—and my heart knew too. I stayed in that very spot on the bow of the ship for a long time, feeling the joy of loving being with Daddy again.

I know that whenever I allow my deep feelings of love for them to become present tense, my loved ones are with me. My love is their *invitation*, which gives them permission to enter my space, riding in on the *energy* of that love. My emotions at the time I was on the cruise ship were not manufactured in any way. They were very sincere and natural. And that is always when it happens.

Hearing and Seeing

Through the years, I have heard spiritual messages from my mother—always exactly what I needed to hear. But that was not the kind of communication I had expected when I heard the spiritual message in 1977, assuring me of continual communication through the veil. I had expected to see her face to face, without any changes from mortal death. I thought a lot about it, and kept the wish very much alive in my heart.

A few years ago I attended a life-awakening course— weekends of intense classes where I shed burdens, fears, issues which did not serve me, and learned even more deeply to listen to my inner knowing and to honor what I knew from spirit. The program was very spiritual and enlightening, guiding towards living in tune with our highest spiritual selves. Others in the course spoke of seeing and feeling supportive loved ones and angels from the other side. I wanted to have this experience too. It had been promised.

I returned home to ponder my desire. I missed my parents. I mostly missed the unconditional love they shared with me since birth. I recalled the intense loving connection that was waiting at the airport each time I went home, with tears of joy at my return. They adored and spoiled me during my visits, but when I left amidst more tears of sadness, it was torture in my heart and theirs. My father particularly had a soft place for me. People who knew us said I was the apple of his eye. It seemed his heart was breaking each time we had to say goodbye, and so was mine.

As I meditated on this shared love, I knew the experience

of such feelings would never come again. My parents were on the other side, and the rest of my life on earth would be without that amazing powerful parent-child love that no one else could ever have for me. This was the vein of my thinking on that winter day a few years back. It was the thought of *loss* of love, but I was thinking of the love just the same. First my mind wandered through the feelings of loss, but then it became focused on just the pure agapé love itself. The more I focused on the love, the more real it became. The thought that passed through my mind next was, *what would it be like if they were alive and coming to visit me, now?* For just a moment with my daydreaming thoughts, I had transformed myself into that space where the love was alive and real and coming to visit me. The emotions of joy swelled in my heart like the grandest miracle I could ever want. Just as I allowed that feeling to be completely real, without even trying to do anything, I felt my parents running from my front door to the room where I was sitting; they literally had arrived.

As I felt them closer, I shocked myself with what I had created. The reality of this woke me out of the trance, and with that sudden awakening to my present place and time, my parents were gone. This event was a major surprise to me, completely unexpected, but I was joyful realizing that I had felt them so close, and that I had learned how to connect to spirits of loved ones on the other side: they come when we bring them with our love—our intense love—no fear or sadness. Though it may start with that, it has to flow into love, *the very essence of heaven's energy*, which is the place where we can connect with them.

Overcoming at Last

Later that year, I attended a course on the study of angels. Given by an international expert on angel therapy, my intention was to get over my fear of seeing angels. I knew I was afraid. I had been afraid since childhood when I first started studying religion. I had asked my mother about it, and I still remember her response:

"It is not something to fear or dread; people who have that experience don't report fear. It happens when you are ready for it, and it is always very wonderful. "

While I acknowledged my fears, I knew from past inspiration that I was going to be able to talk to spirits — at least to my mother's. My *fear energy* and my *inner spiritual knowing energy* were opposing forces, which did not compute, so I knew I had to make some changes.

I hoped the angel conference would give me the missing pieces. I did very little preparation. I was not a practicing therapist like many there who had come to learn how to further their work. I had read very little about this woman's program. My inspiration came from reading an autobiography of someone with certain spiritual gifts in energy work, which gave me courage to acknowledge my own. I chose to attend the angel conference with a simple clear intention to *get good at being okay about visiting with angels.*

I had attended a wonderful mind-control course twenty-four years before, where I had learned to feel, see, describe, and somewhat control what *energies* were vibrating in my own life, and then further, to *read* the process in another person's energy, to assist them in their own healing. I had also studied and practiced for thirty years to use visualization techniques for relaxation and healing therapy. I had developed my clairvoyant gift confidently, and knowing this about myself gave me the courage to include myself in such a class on healing work with angels.

From the first hour, our teacher shared the simplicity of her work. She explained that angels are always with us, ready to serve in any way. She taught that by tuning into their presence, asking for heavenly protection, and then looking for messages, we could identify certain pertinent information for our lives and others via the guidance of angels. Very quickly she put us in couplets, giving us specific assignments, and we began doing what she called *angel readings*.

The energy of the group was very tender and humble. Several hundred open hearts, all who seemed to desire to serve on this planet in the highest possible ways, shared their desires, faith and courage through their intuitive gifts. I was definitely in my heaven on earth, gaining confidence that I could magnify my intuitive skills as well. Over the course of this five-day intensive workshop, I did remarkably spiritual and accurate visualizations on about a dozen partners who did the same for me. With instructions and examples from the experiences of our teacher, I followed with faith, using my gift of *seeing with spiritual eyes*. In this setting it seemed ordinary. It was not at all fantastic, fearful, weird, or scary to talk about seeing, hearing, feeling, and knowing messages from angels.

The lessons about angels that were shared by our teacher were completely consistent with my beliefs — the information from my own training and experience that radiated as truth in my own heart. I was impressed that no angels were telling anyone anything that I would not approve of. In fact, the messages were on a very high level of integrity that is uncommon to the world at large.

I found a wonderful fondness for angels, and I learned quickly to trust the images and messages derived from visualizing the impressions they shared with me. The angel's guidance included deeply spiritual suggestions for lifestyle, such as healthy eating, abstinence from anything addictive such as caffeine and alcohol, relying instead on spiritual help for everything we would need in life.

The angels taught of spiritual cords that become connected with any ego-based relationships, and thus counseled against any sexual relations outside of marriage. This was my belief, but certainly uncommon to a group of spiritual seekers attending from all over the world. I learned to trust the angel's messages, which I saw and understood through my spiritual eyes and feelings.

It was all so easy. It was a magnificent gift to experience this shift from fear to faith. I learned to ask the angels for help with anything, and if it were for my highest good and aligned with God's will, it would be granted immediately.

God and His Angels

I wondered if it was right to talk to angels directly, for I was taught to pray to the Father, in the name of Jesus Christ. I imagined that after I asked for something, Heavenly Father delegated my request to the proper angel, the perfect one who was then assigned to take care of my need. It seemed like Father was in charge to make the decision for the details of how my request would be handled. It seemed improper to me to ask angels directly.

I realize that prayer is a sacred rite used only for God, therefore, I do not pray to angels. I pray to God to send angels according to my needs and requests. But I also consider that some of them are already assigned to me as my personal assistants — my guides — and talking to them is simply spiritual communication, separate from prayer. I also understand that we are all a part of the same whole truth, working for the same God, and nothing I ask these angels to do is going to happen without God's smiling approval anyway.

There is no time or separation of love in heaven. My childlike innocence sees no barriers to communicating with any of the spiritual realm of loving heavenly beings as I am doing God's work with spirit. I now see angels and God and loved ones on the other side as one in purpose, one in love. I see that they all have the same desire and mission: all are working together to help me find my way, with love. As such, all have the same vision and use the same techniques. They are all bound by and operating from the same truthful, eternal laws, such as allowing me my free will and not interfering unless I ask.

I learned that being with angels, acknowledging their presence, and asking for their help is a completely different exercise than prayer. The time I spend with God is sacred and personal, holy time with my Father, sharing my life and learning wisdom from His. These are two completely different ways of spiritual connection with the highest realms of existence. God and angels are different entities, but they are one in their mission and the ways that they operate. I believe there is incredible perfection in the organization of spirit work in heaven.

This principle of *all for one and one for all* is the meaning behind one God, one purpose, one love. Heavenly Father, Jesus Christ, specifically chosen angels, loved ones, and ascended beings through all time are guiding me with the same basic desire: here to serve and bless me for the greatest and highest purposes my life can become; and it works.

Application in Daily Life

As I returned home from this conference and found any relationship stressed, I immediately asked my angels to touch those persons with some *love energy*, and within minutes my heart and the other party's were changed — softer somehow. My perspective became more open to theirs, allowing me to make a personal adjustment to my opinion. It was like seeing as God sees — the whole picture. With such guidance, I knew I would become a much better person. I could feel much more comfortable in my relationships. I have even asked for angels to send some love into the hearts of my two cats that had never gotten along, and found them thriving together ever since—very sweet.

Walking and working with the angels is knowing that the power and love of heaven is here to serve me, always waiting for me to ask, and always ready to go and serve wherever I feel the desire to bless. It is being in partnership with heaven, receiving the smiling approval of God, knowing He believes in me.

This may be a completely new concept for Christians who see themselves and earth's inhabitants as less than the dust of the earth, but I know my experiences and beliefs are true—we are honored and beloved and remembered by God. I honor the holiness of God and angels, and always approach them with great reverence and awe, but I also know we are intimately connected in our purposes and must work as a team. We need to know we are not alone on this earthly ministry of learning to perfect our obedience to spirit. We never have been and we never will be.

I have advised my friends and loved ones about angel therapy. My brother, who has the teachable heart of childlike faith, found himself in a crisis and called on his angels the very day I taught him. He heard them advise him in handling a difficult situation—the exact words to say in a moment of intense stress. This was a *spiritual hearing*, an inner voice that was distinct and audible to him. He did as they counseled and everything worked out to his advantage. He continues to ask, listen, and follow spirit.

Angels are under the direction of heaven. God sends angels to attend to everything in the universe to keep things working in perfectly divine order. This system of operation is like a great business organization of networking associates with God as the boss of the company, and in this case, the product being produced and distributed is *love*. Calling upon God is essentially inviting angels to participate in your success at achieving a status of living in such love.

Anytime I ask my angels to assist, they show me things with my spiritual eyes. They show me with pictures and symbols that mean something to me, so that I will be sure to get the message. When I am confused, I ask for clarification—just talking to them as if they are standing right there—then I get more details.

We all have one or more gifts that allow us to receive heavenly inspiration, and we would be wise to recognize, accept, and use them. This was the plan from the start of creation: to live in the physical realities yet manage it all from the deeper and more powerful realities of spirit. We must learn to *trust spirit*, to accept and be joyful that spirit is real, alive, even tangible, and here to bless us from a family of heavenly guides, God at the helm.

I know that angels are assigned for all of us. I know they want to help. They cannot help me *unless I ask*, except in life and death emergencies when it is not my time to go, in which case they don't wait to be asked. They respect my right to choose. It is very important that I live my life by choice. Yet the second I ask, my angels come to my aid and to others who ask for this special assistance. I don't have to go through a maze of barriers to get to the angels assigned to serve me. I can call on them anytime. I can ask directly, or I can ask God to send them.

Since the angel conference, I have been guided to others who feel blockages in their flow to living in love. Whenever I am asked and when I feel it's right, I help them with *angel meditations*. I share my intuitive and experiential gifts, guiding others to this place of perfect love where they can receive truth as they desire it. I am merely a channel, a teacher, a way-shower, as I have learned to recognize and accept the truths of angelic, heavenly guidance.

Over the years since my first messages from spirit, things

have changed a lot for me. I no longer have to wait and plead for Mother to come. She has always been here. I am learning to just think of her, to feel her love and then start talking to her, as if she is right here, knowing she is near. I have also had the impression that she is wants me to pray to God and specifically ask for this. That's what the message meant when I was told I would still be able to talk to her. It's unnecessary that I see her face. I may, but I can also feel, hear and generally sense what she would tell me. I love her.

Mother is not alone in these heavenly assignments to guide and bless me. As I have used my spiritual eyes to see what is beyond the mortal eyes, I have become convinced of the nature of pure love from *many* angelic beings, a love that exists and which is available all around each one of us all the time. It is a whole new awareness of the loving essence of spirit, bringing peace and lots of assistance on the wings of my desires. What a great gift to know this, replacing my former state of fear of that realm! *There are guardian angels everywhere I ask, everywhere I look, and everywhere I go!*

I have realized lately that my maternal grandmother is often with me. Thinking of this, I understand something I had never thought of: we have a lot in common, and she is here to help me from her experience. Whenever we think of a loved one on the other side, we can be sure that they are near. I have learned beautiful truths and experienced great healing peace from many loved ones on the other side who openly share their inspired guidance with me.

I also have angels with me who are committed to the same goals as I have, and I believe we came into this life process together. This support in a shared purpose reveals that we are not alone, that we are a part of a great and meaningful team! The physical realm is meant to test our depth of faith—to give us choice. Being stuck on *physical realities* keeps us from seeing anything beyond what we can detect with our five senses.

The energy of angels is about great spiritual power *beyond* our mortal limitations. It is a whole other, more powerful world, coexisting along side and simultaneously with the tangibles of this physical existence. We were always meant to work together as a team — the spirit world with the physical world — *heaven as a part of earth,* just like *my spirit is a partner of my body.* I completely rejoice in acknowledging my beautiful, loving *company.*

Origins of My Belief in Heavenly Beings

My first *knowledge* of the presence of heavenly beings came many years ago, in the winter of 1972 while a young college student living far from home. I felt overwhelmed by life and had no one I could trust to talk to. My free and tender spirit was weighted with my intense academic challenges, plus the many relationship experiences I was having, which were mostly new and strangely uncomfortable situations to me. I was an inexperienced co-ed facing grown-up challenges far over my ability to comprehend and manage by myself.

Feeling such confusion and burdens overwhelming me to exhaustion, and while walking home alone from campus one starry night, I began to pray. I looked up into the sky and started sharing my pleading heart out loud. I asked if there was anybody up there who cared about me. I asked if I was on the right track, if my life even mattered. I cried out with all my soul for someone, somehow, to help me make sense of my life and to help me feel good again.

Then suddenly out of nowhere I heard a voice giving me a personal message, telling me of my worth:

"Yes, I am here, and I hear you. I love you. You are important to me. You are like one of these stars in the sky — all of these are important to the whole — you likewise are a part of my team. You are doing just fine. I am here with you always. And I love you dearly."

It was simple, but it was enough. It helped me know that

I was heard, and that I mattered, that I was on the right track, that everything would be okay. I immediately felt warmth and love all around me, which brought an intense sense of comfort.

I walked the next block to my apartment in silence. There was no one home. In the darkness of my living room, I knelt to thank God for the gifts I had just received. During my prayer, I felt loving hands resting on my shoulders, comforting me further. It was so physically real I thought if I turned to look, I would see Jesus standing there. Those feelings of loving assurance remained for many years. And it all started with simply *asking from my deepest heart's desire.*

A beautiful and most powerful spirit world exists all around and in our physical world. That spirit world is humming with activity — busy creating worlds of good. The world I know is about living *in* this earthly world, but not *of* this world. It means my physical being is here, but I see everything about life through the lenses of my spiritual eyes, always knowing there is more. There is a deeper truth and meaning in all of life's experiences, like the message I got in 1977. I heard information whispered from spirit, and I never gave up on it. The answers I received about my mother's date with death from cancer and my ability to still talk to her were real. That message was spoken by spirit to my soul. I knew it, and the spirits who gave it to me knew it. That message comforted me greatly at the time and during the transitioning years, as well as guiding me to brave furthering my education of the realm of heaven and angels. In the years between then and now, I have remained open and teachable to learning deeper ways of experiencing guidance and loving support from the other side.

This is the gift of being a believer and a seeker. Holding on to every bit of truth I receive, it becomes magnified, and in its own time, it manifests in perfect divine order. Such a gift is worth every drop of the faith and patience required in the meantime to stay true to the spirit of my inner knowing. **Truth always prevails.**

Thoughts for Processing *The Energy of Heavenly Beings*:

- Have you ever felt the presence of an angelic being with you or wished you could?
- Have you ever thought that your questions or prayers were being answered by something instantly showing up on your path when you least expected it? Begin to notice.
- Take time to meditate and ask: *who from the heavenly realms is with me right now?*
- Notice feeling them near, ready and waiting to serve. Believe.
- Notice what feelings such knowledge brings.
- Make it a goal to remember to ask for angelic help in the moments when you are struggling.
- Visualize *your people* going to work to assist your needs, immediately at your request.
- Pray for and be open to greater understanding about angels.
- Ask for specific angels or masters with specifically defined gifts that you know would help you at this time. God is very generous and glad to help. All of heaven is waiting for you to ask.

Chapter 11

The Energy of Christ

There is a gift,
And all you have to do is believe it's true:
Christ gave His unblemished life for all,
Making us perfect too,
Brand new and free again every moment of our lives,
And there is nothing else that matters.

I find awe, wonder, and amazement at the gift of knowing Jesus spent His entire life ministry teaching this one lesson: love—*unconditional* love. That means what it says: no conditions—just love. This is the highest form of energy that exists, and the power from which all life is created. Everything about how life works always comes back to this.

Love to me is radiant, warm, caring, wise, dependable, accepting, perfect. In the presence of love, I am whole and good, just as I am. I have no *need* to change anything. But I *can* change. That's up to me. I have learned that to bask in God's love leaves me feeling such joy that I *want* to spread it around, to be caring, to be honest, to be truthful, to be unselfish—in other words, *Christ-like*.

All the things we are *told* we should be, we *want* to be when we bask in such unconditional love—the gift of seeing myself as a perfect creation right now in this very moment, just as I am, doing nothing but breathing. I have studied many sources, many courses, and many opinions, but my own experience with God has taught me how incredibly free and happy I feel knowing there is no judgment in His eyes. Through Christ's loving gift of mercy, justice is satisfied, *which is the greatest truth mankind needs to learn and apply to find perfect peace.*

I consider the energy of judgment: to judge, as in a courtroom of law, there have to be two opposing opinions—two different ways of seeing things. But this act alone is opposite to the natural laws of *truth*. How can we take *truth* and separate it into two things? *The act* of separation *causes judgment*, and God wants us to stop judging others. We can apply *discernment* when a choice is to be made, but we cannot *judge others* and remain

263

in the space of loving oneness with God. At the moment we judge, we separate from love (the greatest truth). God wants us to stop judging (separating) ourselves from perfect love, from each other, and from Him. When I am one with Him, through His gift of atonement, *there is nothing but love.* I am passionate about this truth, which I will explain.

I had heard the words all my life, but until I focused on and prayed to understand *the atonement,* the literal experience was a void to me. So what is it about the atonement that I must understand to be free? How do I literally connect to and wrap my mind around this all-encompassing gift? Who has ever really taught or experienced such freedom and cleansing? At the time of my inquisition, I knew of no one, though I longed to know for myself. It has taken me years of desiring, praying, searching, and experiencing life to be clear on the subject of *the Atonement of Jesus Christ,* which gratefully now I am.

I looked at the peaceful concepts of Buddhism and Taoism, which are similar to the love Jesus taught, wondering if this was enough—just to live in love. But while I learned and greatly respect the many powerful truths in those teachings, I still felt a need to have a place to *put* the baggage I experienced (collected) through daily living.

The atonement started to make sense when I realized such a place to put the burdens of life was already created. That is what the atonement is for: to allow us to give up our sufferings and sins and to become brand new in love again. How did He do it? How does it work? This was the question that plagued me, always coming up in my questioning mind, until the time my answers began to unfold.

Learning How Atonement Works

The first and simplest explanation came in a dream, many years ago. In this dream I saw a gigantic roll of amusement

264

park tickets. You know the kind—about one by two inches in size—thousands of them, connected with simple perforations and all rolled tightly into a wheel shape. I've gone to the fair and bought these ride tickets before. I might have bought a dozen, then run out and purchased another dozen, all day long buying tickets for myself, my family, my friends. I usually buy a lot of tickets before I am finished with the fair. When I had this dream, I saw the symbolism this way: Jesus gives me tickets—unlimited tickets—as many as I want. Anytime I am suffering, lost, lonely, hurting, fearful—experiencing any emotion that is *not* love—I take one of my *free* tickets, write my *not love stuff* on it, and drop it in the box that says FREE GIFT OF ATONEMENT, which is owned and managed by Jesus himself. And then—poof—miraculously my *not love stuff* is gone.

This visual gave me the general idea, for which I was grateful, but it lacked the spiritual depths I was seeking. My heart was full of pain at the time. I was in the midst of a lot of loss, and I desperately wanted God's peace assuring me all was going to be okay. I wanted to believe letting go of all the pain and confusion could be as easy as dropping it into a special box—a place symbolic of His loving gift—but I knew there must be more.

I spent hours, usually everyday, for a period of about a year, staying in a quiet place in nature waiting for God to make me feel better. I would sit and simply breathe and talk to Him, at first not knowing or feeling that He was really there. But I would stay until I felt His presence, when a warm, comforting glow would begin to soak into my being. I wasn't sure if it was just the gifts of nature's glory or actually something bestowed into me by a heavenly being, but it was the good vibes I needed, causing me to feel joyful. It seemed to be pure and real joy from some source *outside* of me, which touched and lightened the troubled spirit *inside* of me.

When that comforting peace distilled upon me, filling

me with an abundance of love, I gave thanks and went home. I desired to keep that peace with me as long as I could in the midst of daily living. The peace usually lasted until I had to deal with something *unloving* again—any form of energy I did not know how to handle. I was beginning to know God's *abiding peacefulness,* but I did not yet understand His great gift of atonement.

Guided Meditations to Christ

As the months passed continuing in this practice, I consented to visit with a therapist referred by friends. This was a man whom I will call a *spiritual mentor,* one who had a deeper understanding of the gift of the atonement, and who could assist me in spiritually (energetically) approaching Christ and personally experiencing these truths for myself.

In one of our therapy sessions together, I was surprised when my mentor asked me where I thought Jesus was *right then,* in the very moment that I was pouring out all my sorrows. I wanted him to solve my problems, but he was using a *higher source* to guide me to my healing. When he asked this question, while holding a firm belief in his mind that Jesus' presence was right beside me, I too seemed to feel such a pure and holy presence standing beside us in the room. My mentor then reminded me of a promise Jesus gave His disciples when He left them and ascended in heaven:

"I will not leave you comfortless. I will come to you." (John 14:18)

Humbled and believing, I began a guided visualization in which my mentor directed me to a beautiful secluded place of my choosing, where I would actually meet Jesus and unburden myself of all my sufferings. All was going well until I came to the part of greeting Jesus face to face. Though I had never consciously felt I was a sinful person, in that moment the burdens I carried caused me to feel a great fear of approaching Him. I felt too unworthy. As I expressed this feeling, my mentor explained that there were garbage bins available nearby in my vision into which I could direct my feelings of darkness— construction-sized ones—as many as I needed.

That suggestion seemed appropriate and do-able to me, as I could not conceive of giving my hidden unworthiness directly to The Perfect One. I immediately allowed the dark energy to flow out of me. I saw energy releasing, thick and dark like tar. It flowed into one of the bins, and I began to feel peaceful in the process. But it did not stop; it continued to flow for quite a while with no effort of my own but to simply allow it. My burdens filled one bin, then another, and another—four total, then it was finished. I was empty, and there was no more.

I could not identify what exactly I had been holding that had manifested as such darkness, but it didn't matter. I felt so good just knowing that in Jesus' presence, at His feet, I could unburden myself of every unholy thought, feeling, experience, and belief which were definitely *not love,* but which had been leeching within my soul for some parts of my lifetimeAfter dropping my load at the feet of Christ, His love started flowing into me. Cleansed and free, I spiritually allowed my soul to fall into the arms of my Loving Friend, Jesus. I was enfolded with His unconditional love for me. The feelings I experienced were unlike anything I had ever known. It was more than freedom and love. It was *life* all before me, with powers and insights very clear, as if all wisdom suddenly opened up before my eyes and into my entire soul. This was real. This was *the truth!* Jesus' unconditional love was something that I could keep, something I could depend on.

Such joy cannot be expressed in any combination of beautiful words. It took me to the top of the world and gave me wings, protection, answers to every question, and clarity of my mission. Anything and everything I wanted was there in such abundance that I did not previously know even existed. It was pure and glorious *love*, unconditional and unlimited.

In my ignorance, I had been unable to conceive of putting my darkness onto a Being of such light. I had to witness this literal cleansing, even in a guided vision, in order to understand the goodness of it—that it is done without judgment and without spotting Jesus.

I wondered about what happened to all my tar-stuff. I asked my teacher, but he suggested I ask *our Savior* to show me. I did so and continued my vision. I saw that in a flash of a moment with a wave of His hand, Jesus annihilated all of it. He literally changed it. He made gigantic trash bins filled with a lifetime of burdens disappear into pure light. No more darkness. It was gone!

As I witnessed this, I knew that because of His love, He had already overcome the affects of all darkness. I realized that in the *Garden of Gethsemane* on the eve of the Crucifixion, He bowed in prayer, and through that long dark night alone, He allowed every bit of the sufferings of every human—past, present, and future—to approach Him. With His love, He overpowered every particle of all of the darkness of the pains of all of humanity.

I do not know if He already possessed such a depth of love, or if His capacity increased with each bit of darkness He battled. But through that night, all of the sins and sorrows of mortal life were put upon Him, and nothing was too much for *His love* to overcome. He took it all, combating everything with the *energy of pure love*, which He alone possessed and accessed. **Because of this redemption of all our darkness, He literally *owns* us, and we are His.** In the process of accepting His gift of atonement, I chose to receive the pure love of Christ into the voids of my being, and to live in that light forever. After releasing all that darkness and being filled with pure love, I knew the difference, and could never choose anything less than being one with Him.

The Energy of the Atonement

If you look at this from the standpoint of energy, Christ already bought our *not-loving stuff,* because of His perfect life and because of Gethsemane, finishing the process by giving His life and then being resurrected. Our efforts to hold onto our negative issues are futile, and will never bring us peace. Energetically, our negative *already belongs to Him.* All of our life experience that is unloving is magnetically pulling us to Him. The atonement of Christ was designed to create a literal *vortex of energy* where all sorrow has already been endured and healed with love, creating a vacuum for collecting everything that is not consistent with the state of love that is our truthful being. Though it may seem painful in the process — we will eventually be drawn to His healing waters for the only cleansing that can allow us into the presence of perfect love.

My mentor suggested I could also visualize bringing my loved ones into the loving aura and arms of Christ. I immediately watched my six beautiful children run into His arms and sit upon His lap. They held nothing back. They seemed very familiar with this place. They glowed with the joy of being home in the comfort of perfect love. I brought other family members and friends and watched all of them be healed in this same presence.

I asked about my enemies, those who seemed to want to cause me harm.

"Give them all to Jesus," my mentor suggested.

One by one I witnessed them being directed into the arms of Jesus. Kicking and screaming and thrashing they came. Jesus couldn't hold them. They wouldn't be held. He handed them off to angels to attend to them. I knew they were in His protection, and that they would be cared for in such a way as to never again appear to me as capable of doing me any harm.

I have repeated this type of meditation over and over, for weeks and months and now years, and it has become very natural to me. Whenever I feel out of the state of love by being overwhelmed, stressed, frightened, confronted with darkness of any sort, I visualize an energetic form of that negativity and then send it straight to my Savior who, always near me, banishes the person, problem — any dark energy — with a wave of His hand. He always returns my offering with a smile of gratitude. He likes me to give Him my *not-love stuff*. He is proud of me. Because of my acceptance of His atonement, we are a team, which was always the plan for our time on this earth from the very beginning.

Jesus is literally our *Savior*. As we follow His example — how He interacted with others and handled issues — always remembering to do likewise, allowing love and light to guide our choices, we are free from the sins of this world. We are saved from the negative affects of our choices and circumstances, and allowed to live in the light forever — we are literally freed from bondage.

Jesus Christ was the only mortal to live one hundred percent of His life remembering and obeying the truth and *being the love*. He took this same loving perfection and cleansed all of humanity with its power. Only He could do that, being perfect love — the Chosen One. His manifestation of love from the spiritual into the physical day-to-day living showed us the way to have power over mortality too, as we choose love in spite of earthly cares.

Practicing the Atonement Experience

In any given moment faced with routine experiences, I have a choice: I may see things with the literal interpretation of mortal human beings, including judgment, or I may shift into

270

spirit mode and trust a higher power to assist me in seeing with my spiritual eyes, as God sees.

I prayed for years to be able to see things with eternal vision. I always knew there was something bigger and better outside of me that could make things lovely. I have always had a sense that I could create that kind of utopia. Using my knowledge of the atonement, I have been able to experience an easier time with life. That's the beauty of giving everything to God and letting Him be the only judge.

Nothing is too difficult for God, who promised never to leave us. He offered, *"Come unto me, for my yoke is easy and my burden is light."* (Matt. 11:30)

I have seen pictures of two oxen yoked together. The idea is that when one can't carry the load, the other one makes up the difference. **Jesus simply offers to carry the part of our burdens we cannot carry by ourselves.**

I always know when my load is too much, as a sense of heaviness and darkness comes over me, taking with it my peace, energy, and sometimes my heart. At the time I notice such an experience, I call Jesus to come to me, giving a simple prayer. I feel Him near, then immediately upon feeling His love, I energetically hand the *not-love stuff* to Him. This may be done in the very moment I am experiencing something unloving. I spiritually see Jesus between me and the issue, and I ask Him to cover for me. I do not take it into myself, as that would not feel good, and I always want to live in a beautiful, peaceful world, *which is what He offers me!*

Over the years, there have been many issues come up that I felt incapable of successfully handling. In my practice of *giving them to Jesus*, miracles have always happened. Things simply work out. The monsters magically disappear. All kinds of parts come together for the successful, peaceful, loving solution. Usually these miraculous manifestations occur immediately or within a day or so, but they always appear.

This is as real to me as the floor under my feet.

I suppose it takes practice and time to learn to trust such a gift, something so immortal and powerful as a real, live *superhero*, ready and waiting to save me with unconditional love. To know I am *worthy* was a risk that was terribly frightening at first, but with some practice, I have learned to trust that Christ really does care for me unconditionally.

It was frightening to let go of all my previous beliefs—all of the *conditions* I was taught were necessary to come to Christ. But my hope and trust were well rewarded when I found the treasure at the end of that path. When one suffers enough, it causes him to become open to all possibilities. In my deep suffering, I was guided to the feet of the one true healer—our Savior—who blesses me to know this powerful energy of love, completely unconditional and freely given.

So is it really free like the unlimited supply of ride tickets? To all those who come to Him with an open heart, even a *broken* heart, in humility, and with a *teachable childlike spirit*, wanting truth, YES! Embracing this gift, we can literally bring Heaven onto this Earth, because of the all-knowing, all-loving, all-powerful, true, healing energy and spirit of Christ, which I am blessed to know and to share.

Receiving Unconditional Love

Once I know Christ's love, I attract nothing less. In the summer of 2001 while spending my month alone healing in the Smoky Mountains, I was given a dream two nights in a row. I saw a man waiting for me at the bottom of some escalators, like in a mall. He was confident and handsome, smiling at me with a powerful essence that sent this message from his spirit to mine:

"There is nothing you can do to stop me from loving you."

In the dream, I felt what it feels like to be loved

unconditionally. I don't know if I had ever known the feeling before. But as I went forward in my life after that dream, I knew that was the way my future husband would feel about me, and I had to do nothing to earn it—just as it is with Jesus. My job was simply to be *willing to believe and receive it*, holding myself in such a state of being open to receive the love.

About a year later, as I was driving to meet the man who would become my husband, doubt and fear began to creep into my mind. The last time I had seen him, thirty years earlier, he was stunningly handsome. I wondered if he would still find me attractive. The inner knowing kept me going, that if he were the right one for me—the man in my dream—then *nothing would stop him from loving me*. It was only a few hours into that joyful reunion that this truth was confirmed.

This pattern of unconditional love as exemplified by Christ is the gift I receive as I approach all parts of my life: if something lies within me—a hunch, intuition, a feeling in my heart, an inner knowing, even including my life's purpose—then it is already mine! It is in my spiritual memory, and it is up to me to claim it, love it, and allow it to manifest. I promise that when I spiritually recognize any gift that is mine, all doors open to allow me to enter and receive, and there is nothing I can do to stop it from loving me back, *just like the man in my dreams, and just like my Savior.*

Thoughts for Processing *The Energy of Christ*:

- You are perfectly loved right now, just as you are, no matter what you have done or what you are going through. Spend some time believing this.
- Say the words aloud as you look at yourself in the mirror: *I am perfectly loved right now, no matter what.* Smile at yourself and breath in this truth. Even if it's hard, begin now and practice. In time, you will believe it.

- Take some time in a quiet, safe place to practice unloading all negative energy into imaginary trash bins at the feet of Christ, giving all your burdens to Him. Allow yourself to be wrapped in the arms of His love. If you need help getting there, read the verses in scripture which teach of Christ's atonement, or listen to some spiritual music that will open your heart to truth. Access your own spiritual gifts and apply them. Free guided meditations to Christ can be downloaded from my website.

- Notice all the people, places, and actions that cause you to forget your infinite worth in the eyes of Jesus. In the very moment the negative messages rob you of your love of self, give these people and actions directly to Jesus. Hand them off to Him like you would toss out spoiled food.

- Let Jesus handle judgment and the methods of justice, while you separate from all judgment. Your job is to be a vessel of love to self and others. Return quickly to the truth of your unconditionally loving being as a constant.

- Allow all negative feelings to be drawn out of you by Jesus as you acknowledge His power to heal you. It's as if He is an all-powerful magnet, taking all your suffering *simply by your willingness to let it go.*

- Do a self-check several times a day: are you filled with peace, wholeness, and freedom to feel joyfully satisfied with yourself and your life? If not, do a hand-off of your negative energy to Christ. All anger, disappointment, pain, fear, guilt, shame, and unworthiness goes to Christ. Forgiveness of self and others is expressed.

- Afterwards, allow yourself to be filled again with unconditional love, breathing it in like the freshest spring air, freely abundant.

274

Chapter 12

The Energy of Being the Love

Awe is the voice of this simple truth:
Absorbed in the love of Christ,
I can have and be everything I ever wanted,
Joyfully living in my divine perfection forever.

In this chapter I give all my efforts and depth of spiritual understanding to explain what I believe is the highest form of energy: to *be* the love. Since the whole of this book is to explain *spirit energy* through the eyes of the author, I believe it is important for me to be completely honest, open, and clear on the subject before I attempt to paint the picture for others. I have subjected myself on the deepest levels to know in absolute reality how it feels to live in such a state of love, even if only in glimpses. For quite some time now I have prayed for and experienced intensive sessions of truth-seeking into the deepest levels of the *spirit* realm with mentors, God, angels, and alone, asking to know myself as *love*, and what that truly means.

When I find myself in the state of *being the love*, I am always one with God. All the darkness in me disappears in His presence. It dissolves into particles of light at His command. I always see Him loving me unconditionally and timelessly. I am a little child, and He invites me to sit by Him on a throne chair—a smaller one right next to His. He gives me my own crown, and I stay there peacefully watching the whole operation of His work with great interest.

Sometimes I notice I am older and have become more wise and capable, but I still sit on my chair next to Him, as if He is my Dad and I go to work with Him every day, or out for a walk in exquisite gardens where we can talk about anything. It always seems completely normal to do so. As I allow myself to remember this state of being as a truth, I literally see scenes such as these with my spiritual eyes, and live as if it were actually happening in a physical reality. In this place, I feel the state of profound joy.

As I have experienced this state of *being the love*, I have found a world that reveals the *perfection* of love. It has absolutely no attachments. It is pure freedom *to be.* It is innocent as a little child. Being the love judges nothing; it doesn't know you can. People are just there without any concern; everyone is okay with everything about everyone else. I want nothing. I have everything, and don't know if there is more, nor do I care. I am curious, and I feel perfectly safe. There is nothing that is required of me. This state of complete bliss makes my life very rich indeed, and I notice it is the same for everyone. It is a state of just living in *what is*, and everyone simply accepts that as the truth.

Being the love literally means to raise oneself into the world of another reality — a *spiritual* existence of pure light, peace, and truth, seeing and being and making choices as would our Creator — the author of love — God, from whose womb and bosom we were birthed. It means choosing to understand things from an eternal perspective, and acting from that deeper wisdom. Knowing myself as love is awakening to the truth: *God is our literal Father, and we are His divine offspring.* To know this in every cell of my body is a holy rebirth — a glorious state of enlightenment.

To continue to live in such a state is my goal — remembering — to literally be one with God in all my choices. Few may share my desire to attempt to live in spirit or to make these shifts from mortal limitations, yet I want to convince you that *it is possible.* As I describe this perspective and all the others in this book, I do so humbly, knowing that every human spirit has a very real and beautiful story of their own, with their own paths to enlightenment, and which are just as sacred. I honor you and everyone for even wandering along such a path, and I pray for your success, as I know your ultimate happiness literally depends on it.

As I was seeking more clarity on this concept, I awoke from a dream that was so real, and which was radiating love

278

and blessings to me. In this dream, I received a gift from my children. They were so excited about their gift to me, and were trying to make it a surprise. But I could not wait, and discovered that in my lovely flower garden, they had brought to me a visitor: my father. When I saw him there, I burst into tears of joy, and held and kissed him, feeling every drop of the lifetime of love that we had never fully shared. The intensity of that love was multiplied by the fact that I had not seen my father for the twelve years since his death, and I had not communicated with him for about ten additional years, a period in which a debilitating stroke had taken most of the life out of him, and also since he lived far away from me.

As I lay in my bed after that dream, feeling the intensity of love between my father and myself, I reflected in just a few minutes on what I had been unable to realize in all my fifty-plus years. All the walls of *how* that love should look were dissolved, and I was able to see the *pure agapé love* all by itself.

My father seemed to adore me all my life. While I outwardly enjoyed his attentions, deep inside I always had the feeling his love was conditional. Everyone in our family lived in fear of Daddy's disapproval. While others said he spoiled me with gifts and attention in a way that we both understood meant he loved me, deep inside I always knew his *perceived* love was based on my performance or my obedience to his wishes. While I came to believe I was special, and while I also learned to expect others to treat me with a similar adoration, I still did not know until my dream what was the essence of true, unconditional love. From the experience in the dream, I finally knew my father's real love for me. The concept of the *reality of love* had finally *downloaded* into my whole being!

Recognizing the State of Being the Love

To explain my epiphany further, I return to the concept of

spirit, (which is always the point of beginning for any creation.) *Spirit* is a living organism; I can sense it, taste it, see it, hear it, and really know it for myself. To share from my fullness and desires and choices, I can physically send it outward to others. But nothing in my power, no amount of pleading, no words or magical exercises of any kind can force or command or insist on the energy of love coming *to me* from another. **The exchange of love from one person to another is an exercise that happens only according to the willingness and *choice* of the individual himself.**

But the state of *being love* is not a choice. It is a *fact*. We were created from love, and we are a literal reservoir of love ourselves. The only thing that keeps the absolute knowledge of that fact from our awareness is the wall we have created around that sacred chamber, to protect it from a life that seems dangerous to such *a tender sacred reality of self.* In a world where most are blind to such a beautiful life of the safety of *being the love*, we have no other choice but to deeply hide our sacred love, protecting these powerful truths in the face of abusive actions and environments surrounding.

But sadly when such perfect love is hidden, it is unavailable to share with self and others, *and that takes all the joy out of living!*

To share the love that we *are*, we have to *re-learn* that we are the love in spite of the choices of others and the resulting self-judgment in response. This re-learning happens as we develop an intimate relationship with God, and we see ourselves as He does. With confidence in such a belief, we trust that our sacred being is always safe. God and angels will honor and protect our loving selves, and knowing that, we don't allow the opinions of others or their actions to hurt us. *If God is on our side, who can be against us?* Such strength, readily available to all, allows us to give love no matter who or what or how that giving may be received by others. As we grow in the knowledge of who we are — *the incarnation of pure love* — we make the choice to *honor* the reality that *we are the love,* even if others never raise their awareness to such a truth.

Receiving the gift of my father's love in a dream after all those years of separation, I finally have now *connected as one* with him. After twenty-two years of having no real communication, and even though he is beyond the veil of mortality, I finally understand, know, and completely *love* my father. I have this gift now because we both are coming from the space of expressing with our sacred chambers of love *wide open*; no more walls — no more hiding the truth of our realities as love.

In all those years that he lived and spoke and held me physically, we each lived in each other's *physical* presence, and we each felt *feelings* of love. But we also had some misunderstandings, some reservations, some judgments of who we were. Our loving beings were living behind partially closed doors, with *partial* access to our love stores available to share. Every now and then, we might have a moment or two when we gave up all fears, judgments, doubts, and just allowed the love energy in each of us to find its matching energy in the other and thus to connect. Those moments were there, but they were too rare. I believe both he and I wanted to have that kind of relationship, but we were unsure of the *level of trust* between us, thus limiting our abilities to feel love.

Living Without Judgment

My mother married out of her religion, which was a constant source of conflict between them. Often, I would sense my father desperately wanting her to love him unconditionally, and to receive him as *enough* just the way he was. I wanted to do that for him too, but I was conditioned by religious beliefs, and I judged him as *less than he should have been*, because of his lack of commitment to religious principles.

My mother wanted a large family, while my father had only one sibling. I would often hear his frustration at having a houseful of his own—five children born in six and a half years. He had no tools for managing such a tribe, and adding that to his financial and emotional burdens, his frustrations led to a lot of angry outbursts. I knew him as angry, and I was somewhat afraid of him. I chose to please him so that he would not be angry with me, but I did not really *know* him until the dream.

When I connected to my father as pure love in my dream, I seemed to understand all those difficult times when we were little. Five little children under one roof probably created a lot of contention—at least a lot of noise, and Daddy would often plead with us to just be loving to one another. He made us laugh when he suggested that we say sweet things (like he and his sister had done through their lives together). When he demonstrated such kindness by role-playing how they spoke to each other, we thought it was funny. We were already hiding behind the security of walled-off hearts, protecting our tenderness in such a way that it would never be damaged by anger or violence. But with the choice to *protect*, we covered up our true loving natures, and then spent much of our lifetimes re-learning how to trust others, to reveal ourselves, and to live from pure love. (In our defense, if my father had done more *walking his talk*, I believe we would have listened.)

This was the same man who I judged as scary because he chose to smoke, drink, and apparently had a lot of trouble being faithful to my mother. I lived in a world of religious beliefs that taught me smoking, drinking, and adultery were very evil things to do. Since I was not taught to understand the difference between people and their choices, I saw my father as evil, and I built walls to keep that scary bad (evil) stuff out of my life.

My father was an artist. I am an artist. Artists are by nature more connected to spirit. My father wanted to live from

282

his free spirit, but seemed very confused about his connection to spirit all his life. I wanted to live freely from spirit, but was attached to a system of judgment for my very survival of self. I was not able to heal and to live true to my nature until long after our communication was taken from us by his stroke. But now, as I am choosing to live from that sweeter place, honoring self, I am beginning to finally *know* my father.

Eternal Perspective

Such judgmental programming in my brain caused me to feel orphaned by my mother's death, as if the life my father lived made him outcast from God and thus our family eternally. I remember feeling very troubled about this state of isolation and fear of him, so I found solitude and prayed about it one day. I distinctly heard God's voice in my mind correcting my thinking with these words:

"Don't you dare judge that man. You don't know of what you speak. I love him."

In that moment, my judgment of him was shaken from its foundation. I realized my perspective was very limited. *There must be another way to look at my relationship with my father: with forgiveness and the deeper understanding of God's eternal wisdom and perspective.* It was a bit shocking at first, unraveling a lifetime of assuming I knew how things work, how God is, and how He sees and judges His children.

That one spiritual event changed the way I will look at God, mankind and life forever. From that day, I began to proclaim God's love for all of us, no matter what our experience or choices. I am not responsible for anything but my own reactions and choices to *be the love*, to choose love in every moment. In such a state, the choices of others cannot hurt me. In this state of love, I immediately forgive and give others to Christ for His care and keeping and judgment. They may suffer, but I can choose to remain out of judgment, thus *being the love*.

I know without a doubt that to be in the presence of love, there can be nothing of separation within us. None of us can be seen as anything less than pure love. Only God knows our burdens and sorrows, and we have to leave all judgment to Him. If we see as God sees, then we would be spilling over with compassion, and no judgment would enter our minds. Trusting in the abiding presence of God's unconditional love allows us to forgive ourselves and to make choices to live closer to Him.

Over the years I have learned more of my father's struggles, and with each new piece of information, I have been most humbled. I now know that in God's eyes, my father's essence as *a spirit of love* remained intact no matter what his load or how he apparently handled some of those things. I have now been given the *gift of compassion* for my father, and it is the ultimate goal of my life to see everyone from such love: no judgment—just as God sees.

Giving compassion to my child-self, of course I would see my father's lack of honor to my mother as a devastating experience and a very poor example of what loving parentage should look like. The judgments I formed and the fears that caused my heart to hide were very natural consequences of my experiences. Nevertheless, *I had to learn from the package I was dealt and overcome my separation from love through these trials*, as we all do!

Healing takes time, and in the process we learn the higher meanings of being the love. I expect that's the way this life was designed from the beginning; we each just get our own version of the same plan, meant to guide us higher and higher towards God. My devastating *loss of familial love* was the way I got to learn for myself the *truth about love*. When I learn from my experience to understand the depths of love, those experiences will no longer appear as a source of pain, but a reminder of the pure love of God in each of us. Because I have now learned my lesson about the truth of God's unconditional love for all, I no longer have to endure the loss of familial love. My father returned in my dream, bringing a lifetime of pure love to fill all my desires, enough to remove all memories of any apparent loss.

God can't do this learning for us. We have to grow line upon line, one experience and day at a time, allowing real change in ourselves in the process, becoming more like God as we choose to forgive, to overcome, and to *be* the *expression* of God's holy love on earth.

Personal Revelation

The state of *being love* is a blessed place to reside. It is the spiritual plateau where we get to practice being as God — the place where, like God, all creation begins. Being in the state of love with God, you have access to His vast stores of truth — all of it that serves you. This information is revealed through spiritual connections given via our spiritual gifts of awareness: seeing, hearing, feeling, and/or knowing. When you identify truth through such spiritual inspiration, you have information given specifically and perfectly for your own needs and situations, from the Source of all truth. This revelation is tangible, so real you cannot deny it. I trust my *inner knowing* as something I can count on to come true, to manifest. Living in spirit is *real power*, backed by the forces of God — the greatest achievement we could ever want. I will explain how and why this is true and how and why it works.

Accurate and true information may come to you through physical beings you can relate to eye-to-eye such as healers, teachers, mentors, and other spiritual intuitives. While such information may be right on the button *truth*-wise, it will make no difference in your life-plan, and nothing of it will manifest if this is the *only* way such information enters your life. When truth comes this way, such *information* is registered in your head, aligning with your thoughts, wishes, and perhaps your desires, but it has no power to call any of it forth to manifest into reality.

Power to manifest anything into reality starts with a spiritual alignment of *truth from the whole of the universe* as it aligns with that truth in you, as it relates to you. It comes as personal, direct revelation to you, and is received by your spirit. Personal revelation is information that comes spiritually, ethereally, from the Source of all light and truth—Christ. This form of energy registers in your *heart,* and resonates with your *eternal spirit being*—the place of *inner knowing* of your life-path and the truth of how everything works.

Your spirit is alive and perfectly operational as it is aligned with all true spirit—meaning God and the whole of this universe that is one with God. When your spirit is so aligned, it opens the channels that allow truth-energy to flow to you. The truth then downloads into your spirit. The feelings are so vibrantly alive and real, you cannot deny them, thus this truth becomes *knowledge*—your *inner knowings.* All creation begins and is manifest from the inner knowings of your soul, and your soul's *headquarters* reside in your heart!

Being the love means to be at one with all truth. It is a most powerful truth that we are here on this earth to make manifest many wonderful things, all of which are based in an alignment with the overall plan of this life: to learn, to experience creation, to love in the face of a lot of opposition, to eventually become like Christ, to have His love shine in our countenances, to actually physically *be* **His light.**

Divine Heritage

Most of the people I mentor are living from a physical

286

reality, living outside of spiritual truth. They do not see themselves as one with God. They see themselves as their familial identity, their work identity, their talents and gifts identity, their financial situation identity, their health and body identity — on and on. They work at being different — separate — by the way they display themselves. **People are looking for self-identity by creating separation from others — uniqueness — a very subtle form of** *deception of the truth,* **which will only bring misery.**

When I know myself through *spiritual senses,* I am able to dissolve such mortal connections to my identity, going beyond into a lovely, pure view where true joy is found — no deceptions. Using spiritual eyes, I see others as a magnificent and glorious matrix of energy that can do anything — healing, honoring, and loving everyone and everything in their path. When I share this vision of truth with those who come to me and ask, or when I go deep within my soul and see my own spiritual reality, I am in absolute *awe* of the beauty, and I want to sing praises of these glorious truths from the mountaintops.

We are literally Divine offspring, here to make manifest the glory of God in physical creations, in as many varieties as all the events of all the lives of all God's children combined.

In every moment, we are either *in love* — **connected as one with divinity, or we are feeling** *outside of love* — **the sense of being separate from love.** You know if you are *at one with love* by how you feel: are you aligned with the Divine or are you separated from love? If you have to think about it, you probably have forgotten for a minute that *you are the love,* so take time to go there now. It's simply a choice — allow the love to *be you.*

I find it takes a little time daily practicing being with God. If I do a meditation exercise of entering my own heart space, I find Him there waiting for me, blessing me in every way. I visualize traveling down a pathway, bright with a golden, pink light. It's as if I am happily going out to pick the fruits of my garden, feeling the energy of being *about to receive something good*—something I need. This is the trust gained from having a personal relationship with God for many years now. I feel the anticipation of walking towards my abundant garden where I know I will be seeing my best friend, my lover, my mother, father, my child, everything good—God himself. When I turn a corner down the pathway to this garden, there He sits—waiting just for me. Embracing Him, I rest and stay in the presence of such perfection of love.

Being with Him is a feeling of complete wholeness, simply what is—*love as a state of being.* It is literally this simple, and at the same time, full of beautiful intricacies like a kaleidoscope of possibilities—all good ones—serving me with the **many facets of love:** peace, support, healing, strength, protection, restoration, creativity, intelligence, expanded understanding, exaltation, self-awareness, forgiveness, gratitude, all possibilities, divinity, abundance, compassion, wisdom, balance, energy, flexibility, friendship, purpose, beauty, calm—indeed a very blessed place to reside.

I have learned that I must spend time opening myself to this peaceful state of love, where these qualities make me whole, strong, wise, capable, and happy—all of the facets that love is. I do this practice anytime I notice I am out of alignment, and especially for a while first thing every morning. **As I am** *waking*, **I allow** *awakening*. I get to remember the qualities of God, and I get to remember myself as those qualities. Becoming one with the essence of God within my own heart, I finally feel the connections of oneness to the vastness and greatness of all that God is, and I feel joy in knowing my connection to that magnificent whole—as the being of love *that I am.*

Tangible Essence of Being the Love

I have been healed at the hands and words of prophets, teachers, friends, and loved ones. I have been healed in sacred places such as temples, mountains, forests, and water's shores. I have found truth through books, music, conferences and personal experiences. The literal and spiritual *essence of Love* is the healing truth that comes to me *through* these people and places and venues. But I do not have to attach to the people and places and venues to bring me love, though it may be tempting and seem easier.

Love is the actual healing power, and it must be received one by one, through personal revelation. **I can't be saved by love in group therapy.** There is no inherent power to make me whole in people or places or things. Circumstances can and do change, causing my constant and immediate access to these sources to be somewhat unreliable. But there is one place and tool that I own and always carry with me, and that is my heart—the true connection to and *center of love in myself.* Love is always found in my heart when I open the door and allow myself to feel and know the peaceful, true, constant of *being the love* that I already am—always have been, always will be.

When I focus on the spiritual truth—whether or not something is in alignment with my life path, a part of me—I am looking at something that is *made of light.* When you think of an idea or a quality or a situation as *light,* you might look at it this way: it has a flame to it, which burns at differing degrees of intensity, and the more fuel I give that fire, the brighter it burns.

What I want to tell you is that every one of us on this planet is made of light, and has come here with powerful spiritual truth within our very being.

By focusing on the light that is within, allowing it to burn brightly, we generate a truthful place right in our very center, our heart space. We get to this place in a thousand different ways, but it is easy. You can be there simply by asking and then patiently shutting out all other physical (outside) realities. *Allowing* the reality of your inner spiritual being of light to shine, to burn, to generate within you, you begin to radiate pure light, which is truth—*all truth in one great whole*. I repeat: wherever you stand in the space of light, you can know all truth. So by getting into such a state of spiritual enlightenment and asking, you can know anything that is for your highest good to know!

Worthy to Be the Love

I go into the light—in nature, in temples, in my own heart anywhere that I am. I ask about everything that is going on in my life. I ask about every feeling I am having about every person in my life, one at a time. When I ask about a situation or a person while in this light, I get an *eternal perspective*— the whole truth and nothing but the truth. Something which may have appeared to me as *bad, difficult, painful* while in the physical reality will now appear veiled with love, and will have *completely different meanings*. Seeing with the eyes of God, with my *spiritual* eyes, standing in the space of *being love*, everything looks easy, better, perfect, lovely. Everything.

How do we stay in the space of love? The tool has already been given: forgiveness, which opens the way to immediately return from separation to the state of love. Remember that separation is caused by judgment---separating into parts. As I forgive, I release all to God, removing myself from any judgment, and returning myself to the love of being one with God.

When we acknowledge that *what we are going through is part of what is required for our spiritual transformation*, we change how we look at life, and honor our path rather than cursing it or allowing it to confuse us and block our progress. As with my childhood traumas, **whatever is our experience is the price we**

pay to know God, and it is always worth that price.

What is holding you back from believing? Recall my atonement experience: as I attempted to become one with the Savior, my first reaction was concerning my personal worthiness. In that experience and others since, I have learned that **worthiness issues are the source of all separation from God.** I see this pattern over and over, every time I see suffering. Separation from love comes from our own personal judgment of self, causing us to move ourselves out of the light. **It is we, not God, who do the separating! God always remains the light, always standing at our door, and we always make the choice to move away from or towards that constant source of love, to resist or to open the door and let love in.**

I am learning to know my value as a part of God. Personal feelings of worthiness may come easily to some, but *receiving* such a truth has taken me a lifetime. I was taught false beliefs that worthiness was something I had to earn, and that when I was good enough, deserving enough, *deemed* worthy, a level of worthiness would come to me, and I could be a part of the group of the *worthy ones*. This shows that the state of worthiness is decided by another, outside of the relationship of God and me, thus from a place of judgment.

This is completely backwards to the truth. First I must *receive my worthiness* — that gift innately mine. I own it already — *now*. This gift is given when I simply remember who I am—a part of God. **And when I remember who I am and believe I am worthy, I will only want to live my life in accordance with that knowing of my perfection in love.**

To know God, to know God's love and goodness is who and what I am—my birthright—to know myself in that perfection is to recognize my worth. When I recognize this truth, receiving that grand ah-ha, I will *be, act, and do as God,* thus living worthily. *The state of worthiness does not come from the outside in, but must be remembered and received, and then it will gloriously shine to others.* In every moment of my life, being one with love is my own personal choice. *Knowing that I am worthy is the greatest gift I have discovered* that sets me on my course to living the life I came to live—in joy, in peace, with no stops.

Creating from Being the Love

Whether or not I am ready, and whether or not I am consciously creating that life, the reality is that I am actually creating every moment of my life. Those bright light berries of creation are working just as I saw them, whether I know it or want it or feel prepared or not, know my worth or not, receive and give love or not. *Ignorance is no excuse.* Conscious or not, we are constantly creating, making choices based on our inner thoughts and beliefs.

How do we manage this great power of the human life? Love—the only *true* energy—the energy *that is* everything—is the channel from which to manage spirit. I find my center of love using the techniques of forgiveness, meditation and prayer, dissolving into love energy and asking spirit. In this holy chamber—my inner royal court—I feel and receive guidance. I trust it like my own life, and knowing this brings me confidence and peace. *It is insanity to live from any other reality!*

When you know that God is right in front of you, now, knows everything about you and still loves you unconditionally, you begin to humble. The façade crumbles, and you throw open those doors to allow Him to enter, to allow this love to heal you.

I ask you to do this right now, as you are reading this book. There is a light all around you—a glorious light—and this loving energy holds all the healing love you need to return you to a knowledge of your perfection, your innocence, your divinity. Just notice it. Breathe it into your body. Allow it to fill your lungs. The blood cells are waiting to take this love from your lungs and carry it to every cell in your body. Breathe it now and feel love flowing through you deeply, healing everything in its path. Air is *free*, and so is love. Air is *always available*, and so is love. Our breathing *comes naturally*, without effort, and so does love. **You are so compassionately loved!**

I honor you for opening the windows of your soul now and allowing love to enter. Allow all darkness to melt—all pain, suffering, and confusion; it all goes away as God's love fills you. When you open your whole being to allow love to bless you, never again would you choose anything less.

Feel the *spiritual energy exchange*: you give your soul to God, and He gives His healing love to you, which removes everything you thought was a burden and replaces it with joy. As you choose to spend more and more time with the Savior, eventually this out-of-body joyful experience becomes a constant. It just takes practice, one instance at a time, turning to God for His loving of the situation. No one else can do it for you. Perhaps this helps us understand the Parable of the Ten Virgins and why oil could not be borrowed from the wise ones. We must fill our lamps with oil—one drop at a time through a lifetime of choosing to *be the love*.

In the times when this *familiar* state of love is with you, helping you manage how you see the situation, as you see with the eyes and perspective of God, that is when you are *being* the love.

Awakening to Being the Love

Understanding spirit is our daily work and our daily gift. It is a process that comes one moment at a time, one layer at a time, one lesson at a time. *These lessons are the school of life, and believe me when I say there is no chance of getting excused from class.*

Once aware of this simple and all-inclusive reality of the purpose of life, I see everyone and everything differently.

We are all the same, having experiences in whatever school we choose. *There is no elite group that gets out of doing this work, and there is no lower class that has to do more than their fair share.* No one is different really—we are all headed down that same path called life, and we all have the opportunity to awaken to ourselves through whatever shows up each day on that path. We each choose the variety of the path we are on based on the experiences we choose to learn. With conscious awareness of such, we may choose to change the nature of our path anytime we want.

Awakening to ourselves as love is what we came here to experience. The sooner we wake up and know that we are God's greatest creations, the sooner we may begin to travel life's pathway with an *illuminated* perspective. Personal power over our experiences comes when we learn there is nothing but love in all of life, and also when we know our own worthiness of this love. By knowing we are the essence of love, we have the power to overcome *everything*.

The truth of knowing *self as love* is absolute knowledge to me: we are cared for, remembered, attended to, important, and we each have a divine purpose. No matter what that purpose may look like, it is an important part of the whole of creation. We each came here to *be the love* through our own individual gifts, and as we awaken to the truth, we will have the power to succeed!

Along my pathway to knowing and receiving this magnificent and glorious and truthful knowledge, I have had to learn to interpret spirit. Spirit comes as feelings and other forms of inspiration that are constantly speaking, but most of the time we don't hear these messages as clearly as we hear ourselves speaking or read our own languages. As we grow through life, we have to develop this sense of *knowing the voice of spirit speaking*. We do it one little moment at a time, and each one is as grand as any—each a prized gift. I accept each connection to spirit as a reminder of my worthiness—that I am cared for no matter what the lesson and no matter how long it takes to become accustomed to knowing this voice of spirit. **Just *being on the path* to spirit is all that matters. Being with spirit is the reward!**

As I spend time allowing myself to be still and then receive the love that I am, I am physically changed in a powerfully tangible way. It's as if by the simple act of *remembering* my divine connection, the energy of love opens up channels of light all throughout and around my body. I feel whole, clear, happy, peaceful, radiant, loving, giving, satisfied, safe. I feel deeper, yet lighter. I feel more grounded, yet more free. While the memory indelibly remains, *seeing myself as God does* **is so profoundly an *awe* that I cannot abide its brightness for more than a little while.** Perhaps in time it will become more natural to me.

With the gift of spiritual seeing, I have energetically looked at the aura, the spirit—the *real* being—of some of my associates who ask for this vision for themselves. I call them energy scripts—enscript for short. Each one is different, yet exquisite in colors, sounds, shapes, and patterns, their unique energies *scripted in spirit*. What a breathtaking adventure to see even a portion of how God sees us. For a human to see such radiant spirit is akin to worship—humbling, reverent, glorious. There is royal blood flowing in all our veins, and the sooner we know this, the sooner we will act like the spiritual giants we are, and begin manifesting creations of love throughout all this world!

I have seen my real spirit self in visions: how brave and trusting I have been, how fearless, how connected to love, how believing in God, how tender and innocent. I may not always act from this perfection, but it is my desire to become consistent in choosing to remember myself as this beautiful loving essence. I know such an evolution is possible.

These truths are the messages I have recorded in my heart that have come through spiritual hearing and seeing. The real *spirit* me, seen through meditation, is a powerful matrix of divine creation with colors of white, pink, gold, and sometimes purple, glowing translucently, the vibrations of loving perfection surrounded by angelic presences and sounds of heaven. Within me is a sacred chamber of love, which I have accessed through spiritual channels, and which is most glorious and magnificent to experience.

I honor myself as love, and I beseech all others to see themselves so beloved of God. This is the truth that will guide us to live in the house of spirit always, enjoying the perfection of being the love that we are. I invite all to awaken to these truths and to begin *trusting spirit now!*

Thoughts for Processing *The Energy of Being the Love*:

- Sit with the state of bliss for a few moments. Imagine being in such a rare state of unconditional love. Ponder it long enough to let it fill you in every cell. Notice how tension slips away, and you become lighter as peaceful energy fills your heart.
- What part of your story has caused you to suffer? What have you learned about love through these experiences? As you have grown older and wiser, can you see other's choices through the eyes of God—the eternal perspective?
- Try to remember times when you and a loved one gave and received pure love at the same time, when all judgment was put aside and you entered a place of heaven on earth. Honor such a prize.
- Do you have beliefs that keep you from being able to love unconditionally? In what way do you judge people and issues right now that cause separation from

the state of being the love?

- Think of someone who has offended you, someone you may even despise. Now, think of that person as being completely and unconditionally loved of God. Can you do the same for this person, knowing we are all one, no matter what?

- Ask to be able to discover more information that will enlighten you as to why others do as they do. As you choose to love, enlightenment will come, making sense of things. Ask for the gift of compassion for all offenders.

- What do you do to yourself for personal identity? What makes you unique? Who would you be if you were not creating separation through an outward identity?

- Don't move in the morning until you remember heaven is with you—*awakening* as you awaken. Once you connect to this truth, you and your team can begin your day together. Don't do anything until you remember this love is present to guide you in everything you do.

- Say this mantra to yourself as often as you need—all day long if necessary to make yourself believe: **I am worthy to be the love. I am the love.**

- Close your eyes and relax, imagining what your own light looks like—the colors, the shapes, the symbols and patterns. Enjoy being with your unique spirit—one with God, for as long as you can receive such an *awe*.

Chapter 13

The Energy of Choosing Love

This life is not about you and me,
Or even God and me,
But God as me – which is Love.

Once you know yourself as love, you no longer go and do anything for the purpose of *getting*. Being filled with the pure love of God in every facet of your life, you need nothing more, so every interaction becomes an opportunity to bless and serve others to feel the same, simply because you see everything as love and want to share from that fullness.

When asked by a certain man if he could help her with a financial contribution for her ministry, Mother Teresa replied something like this:

"No I don't need your money. I would only ask one thing of you. Go down to the viaduct at four a.m. and convince the man you see living there that he is not alone in the world."

What was she trying to teach? Why couldn't she just take the money? She had a lot of mouths to feed, after all. But perhaps the one who needed to be fed most was this man with all the money, and Mother Teresa knew just how to teach him how that feels to be so fed — with spiritual food that he could only receive from serving another *with love*, not money. She gave him the way to see himself as the love, as he was able to *be* the love. It appears that no matter what are our natural gifts, the underlying *purpose* of them will be to inspire, heal, serve, and bless others, and thus ourselves in return.

When it comes right down to it, aren't we all beggars? We take, we use, we ask, we give — producers today, consumers tomorrow. Each requires God's mercy and is dependent on Him for everything required to sustain life. Today you may need more, but tomorrow it may be me. Life doesn't happen solo; it soon becomes obvious: you need partners for this dance.

The highest form of love is service, and by giving to others we *honor* their being of love, *with* love. Serving allows us to remember each other as love, thus returning us to that state of perfection. We are literally *mirrors of love* to others. As we do, we recognize them on a deep level; honor recognizes royalty. We show others who they are by reminding them of their truthful being as love, which then validates our own state of being the love, returning us to the balance. When I awake to the real you, I awake to the real me. We connect as brothers and sisters, all children of God, all one. When we serve one another, we feel each other's spirits as we feel each other's gratitude for our giving, as fulfilling as if our own needs are being met.

By serving, I know I am in partnership with my Savior. I wonder which brings me more joy: to know Jesus is with me, or the feeling of allowing His incredibly powerful love to pass through me as it is being given to another soul who has passed my way. Somehow I think He knows we are the ones to do the service. We may be the perfect match to the needs of another. Being His hands in this way — His literal partner — we participate in this balance.

Love your neighbor as yourself makes sense. In a Christ-like view, in the recognition of the wholeness of our loving family of man, my neighbor *is* myself. *When you do it unto the least of these, you have done it unto me* — also makes sense. Again, he suggests that we are all one body, which must be kept in balance as the love-energy we are.

The Path to Charity

Christ taught that we must forgive, giving all to Him for His care and His judgment, not ours. It does not serve us to carry any darkness, for that is what keeps us from the light; and light is our natural and true state of being — the place where we find charity. Giving all to Christ through forgiveness is the actual tool we each have at our fingertips to instantly return us to the state of charity.

302

Forgiveness has very little to do with the rights and wrongs of our experiences at the hands of others, and everything to do with taking care of our spiritual selves by returning to the presence of God, light, and pure unconditional love.

When you hold judgment of any kind, your spirit is broadcasting an energetic message of those injustices, which actually attracts more of such to you. Whatever negative energy your spirit is holding onto, it is sending out that message as a *truth*, and will only bring more of what is already not working for you.

This state of trying to control life takes you out of the state of love and actually punishes *you* in the process, while doing nothing towards the justice you are probably inwardly seeking. Anytime you are in the energy of judgment (control), you are *choosing* to hold onto darkness, which automatically keeps you *out* of the light.

We must always admit the part we have contributed to any conflict, as we all know there is no conflict without two participants. Even though your part may have been done in ignorance, fear, desperation, or purely for survival, confession and forgiveness is an essential ingredient in the process of reaching the state of charity. Admitting your part can be as simple as realizing that you held in the negative energy for all this time, causing you to continue to attract more of it or to suffer longer. We must confess and spend as much time with our Savior as necessary to feel better. We must drop our burdens at His feet, and leave them there. We let His love take it all from us, through all our body and all our time.

Once cleaned by spending this close connection with Christ, feeling His healing as we lay down all darkness in us, we then move to the next step. This is where we accept His compassion *to fill the void*. We receive the pure light of Christ flooding into our physical beings. We feel free, as if nothing negative has ever been with us. Love permeates our being in a

303

world where no judgment enters our thoughts. This is the state of love I call *innocence*.

I recommend allowing this state of pure love to flow through you for as long as you can handle it. Your comfort level may resist at first, but soak it up anyway. This is the truth of who you are — a being of love, one with God. The longer you stay in this state, the more truth will flow into you.

As you enjoy this oneness with God, feeling that great love in and around you, notice that you have access to all truth, especially as it pertains to your life and purpose. This is where **hope** becomes your companion. As you hold onto a hope in all truth, perfect divine guidance flows into your soul, and *charity* is not far behind.

In the state of oneness with God, staying out of judgment in all its varieties (fear, doubt, anger — all forms of control), we live in the state of trusting God to not only teach us, guide us, and protect us, but to do whatever He will with us. We gave all our darkness to God, and now we are giving all our *light* to Him as we become one. We offer all to Him, asking where we should go, what we should do, what we should say, and sometimes how to do it — at least how to start, and usually the rest will come later. We have faith in Him, hope in the good things that come from Him, and know that as we go where that truthful guidance leads, all our needs will be met. In this state of being one with Him, we get our answers. We follow those answers and serve others accordingly. When we do so, we feel inner peace, joy and happiness — the state of charity!

It is in the act of *following divine guidance — choosing love* — that the state of charity arrives.

These steps of recognizing, acknowledging, and forgiving bring us into the presence of God. We cannot get to this state without the personal cleansing of forgiveness. Every concern is healed while in the state of being one with the pure love of God. When we follow those promptings, aligning our lives accordingly and acting as we are guided, we literally become *the hands of God on earth*; and that is the state of charity. It works every time.

This is the reason I teach to **trust spirit now**. Every need can be met and understood when in the presence of love, and love is ready and waiting, anytime you are. **Charity Never Fails!**

Learning How to Serve Others from Love

I recently awoke from another dream, which explains this practice further. I processed the dream as I wrote the story and truths gleaned in my journal:

There is much going on in my life, enough to completely exhaust me physically, but I keep asking for God to light me, enlighten me, and lighten me. Saying His name aloud over and over, focusing on light, love, I feel a glimmer of that lovely, tingling, blessed form of energy that sparks life into my whole being from a single point deep in my heart. Its glow brings hope, and hope springs life into my whole exhausted being. Love makes everything perfect. Thank you God for never leaving me.

In this place of feeling hope, feeling myself as love, I am asking God for clarification of my dreams. I remember seeing a satellite from space spiraling out of its orbit, coming directly towards me and my husband as we stood on a street in a city. As it came closer and closer, its magnificent light swirling like a vortex fascinated us, but all of a sudden as it appeared it would hit ground close to us, my husband took a dive to take cover and save himself from being hit, leaving me to fend for myself. I found where he was hiding, and leapt into the walled space with him. Then I awoke.

(Continuing in my journal): I was wondering what this dream means: was it showing me that (my husband) only cares for his

own life, and not for mine? So I asked if this is true. The feeling I got from images and feelings is that he wants me in his life to serve him, and may not see me outside of the relationship with him: he does not see me as a being separate from him, with my own needs, and he may not think I need his help to bless me.

My first reaction to this perspective was of feeling neglected, maybe even offended that he may not see me for who I am. But instead of being offended by this observation, I realized my dream was less of reality and more of a mirror. I know that sometimes dreams and life show us ourselves as we look at others.

I asked if I am doing the same. Do I expect that my husband is here to merely serve my needs? I did not like the possibility that this might be true. I wanted to be more unselfish than that. Just then, all the love in me welled up into an overwhelming desire to serve my husband.

By being teachable, I reversed the energy and turned my own needs to be served into a desire to serve him. In that moment, I showered him with deep love in the same way that I would want to be loved. As I did, I felt more loving than I had ever known possible. My husband's reaction of immense gratitude humbled and overwhelmed me with a desire to continue serving him in this way. (End of journal entry)

The gift of this special dream was to teach me, again, to serve others from a fullness of being the love, with no expectations for a return on my investment. *Rise above the things of this world, and be the love like God and angels. Feel the joy of blessing others lives from a space of oneness with love.*

By imagining how I would feel when receiving the love I wanted, I *did* know what that love would feel like. As I focused on feelings of love that I desired for myself, I got very clear about the energy of that love, which is exactly the kind of love I gave to my husband. This choice feels better than the way I sometimes *assume* I am giving love, which may be more dutifully or selfishly, wanting something in return. **The point** of a happy life is really to focus on and celebrate the *love itself,* and not any of our *needs* for it!

With the lessons of this dream, my love can come from a desire to be the hands and heart of God in this man's life. Besides, *the abundance of love I am able to give comes from a well much grander than my simple share of it!*

This perspective of life allows me to give love from a space of **being the love,** which comes from being one with God—a part of His team; what a team—what a feeling of perfection—what safety—no fear—no needs of my own to have to take care of. My love bucket is filled as I choose to fill others, by first dipping into God's and sharing from that abundance. *I get to taste and touch and feel the love of God in the process!*

As I realized the message of my dream—to enlighten me to how it feels to be the love—I felt the desire to stop waiting to be served, and to begin with joy and passion *to serve others.* I had a massive *energy exchange* that morning. Instead of seeing myself as lowly, beneath all things, suffering, in trouble, victimized, *in need of being healed or saved by love,* **I saw myself as one with God's love.** I had seen this before, yet I had forgotten how it feels to be *above all things* with God, and to give from that abundance. I saw it as energy located higher above where I was, and with powerful light energy—*above* other people's issues and things, as if to let love flow easily onto them.

I shifted from my former position of seeing myself *beneath* everyone else, where I was hiding my light. From that position below, I might have felt a need to hold others up to the light, (as if I could do that). But now I can see myself as a glowing image of love, one with the angels, full of love, healing myself first. This place of *being the love* from an elevated space is the truth of what we are and what is freely available and always works to allow joy to flow, never forcing or working it from a place of being less-than love.

I had asked, and I did receive in my dream, and I had

seen the truths given as I processed it afterwards. I no longer waited to be served by others, but felt so abundantly full of love, I could not help but share it with my husband. Until I shared from this abundance of pure love, I was too full to continue living in my body. That's how it always feels to be with God — too grand for this body. The more we seek this, the more our bodies change to be able to handle it, thus those spiritually reborn have the *countenance of God* shining in their faces.

The Motive to Serve from Love

Many years ago, while using my mothering skills one particular day, I made up some great musical ditties, which were very successful in getting the children to cooperate in doing their chores. Impressed with my instant success, watching my adorable children happily obeying my musical instructions, I thought, *these songs I make up are really good — very clever; I should write them down, make a guidebook, and sell them!* I went straight to my piano to play the tune I had just intuitively created. I got out my staff paper and pencil, ready to record my creations, and then everything suddenly left me: I drew a complete blank!

It seemed impossible: I had just been singing those clever songs. Then I heard the patient and adoring voice of spirit within, entertained by my enthusiasm for entrepreneurship, but giving me the message that this gift was not given me to sell. It was for my children, *to serve them.*

For years I avoided writing my books for the same reason. I felt I should not sell the things of my heart. Then in the fall of the year 2000, things began to change. I was awakened in the wee hours of the morning for ten nights in a row. On the tenth night, I decided to pay attention to spirit, realizing that someone might be trying to tell me something. I knew this middle-of-the-night wake-up call would continue until I received the message, so I sat up in bed, got out my paper and pen, and told the angels that I was ready to receive their message. I was then instructed that I should begin organizing myself as a writer.

I asked questions to enlighten myself further as to how this was to be done, since I was somewhat untrained as a writer. A spiritual presence spoke to me, showing me how to use my gift of vision to paint the pictures of my life lessons with the written word. I heard these messages in my mind and felt them in my heart, along with seeing pictures with my spiritual eyes of what the angels were telling me. It seemed my motives in life had turned from making money to the higher purpose of serving others, and I believe these heavenly messengers were there to invite me to then begin preparations for sharing my gifts with a larger audience.

A few weeks later, I received clear inspiration that I was to write a very specific book. I was intuitively given to know the title and all the chapter names. In that case, inspiration had directed me in the exact way I should use my gifts.

Ever since that day, I have been developing those gifts, learning what was needful, doing my part by writing everything I feel inspired about, and leaving the rest to God. The difference from my first desire to sell my musical creations those many years ago is that now I feel *divine* direction in exactly what I am to write. My motive is not money or pride in my own gifts, but to obey spirit and perhaps blessing the lives of others, that they may learn from my experience to know truth, allowing them to grow *with me* instead of through years of unnecessary suffering.

God has provided my financial support in other ways so I can focus all my efforts on putting a pen to the many powerful spiritual lessons my experiences have taught me, enlightened me to, and which I am excited to share. In fact, to do so brings me great peace and satisfaction. I may never know the effects my messages have on others, but that matters little to me; if spirit speaks, I obey. I know this is the true pathway to feeling my joy, my worth, my self as love — which is my purpose in life — and which is the real meaning of charity.

When I returned home from my trip to Korea a few years ago, having been greatly affected by the loving connections with my newly found sisters there and wondering if I could ever feel such sweet and tender love from friends at home, I fell into a deep depression. I lay in bed almost comatose for several days, and then I was given a gift that changed my life. A dear friend was impressed to come over and see me, bringing a gorgeous painting that she was *told* by spirit to give to me. In the composition of that exquisite piece were two women, painted as fairies in a forest, facing each other and chatting away in perfect happiness. Such an energetic expression was just like I had enjoyed with my Korean friends, and just like I had been in years past with this particular friend who brought it. Angelic beings and forests and friends were a magnificent gift to bless my heart.

I had not seen this friend for quite a while at that time, but she told me later that *spirit* told her that day to go immediately to me and bring this piece of art. She asked if she could do it later, but spirit said to do it right then! She couldn't even stop to brush her teeth and change clothes. She said she had never been so clearly instructed, both on which piece to bring (she had a fabulous collection) and the need to do it without delay.

My experiences with loving friends in Korea changed me dramatically, and were a turning point in my life. Reconnecting to my everyday life at home was not working for me until my friend obeyed spirit and brought the gift. Somehow just seeing that happy *girlfriends-chatting-away-in-the-forest* scene and feeling the love in the gift, I snapped back into my life. While I will never forget the sweetness I experienced in Korea, with that gift of art and the love it represented I was reminded I could have the same loving relationships from friends near to my home. I felt whole again immediately, and every time I look at my painting, my heart sings—remembering the love.

I don't know why spirit spoke such urgency to my friend that day. Perhaps I would have suffered irreparable damage had I stayed in that state of depression any longer. We may never know why we must do exactly what we are told by spirit, and we may never know the joy we can bring to others by obeying spirit. But on some level at some time, God repays those who follow His voice.

Though this friend may never understand how she raised me out of my great discouragement, she continues to report receiving many wonderful miracles in her family's lives, and her gift continues as she brings joy and peace to my soul every time I am with her. I know she loves me mainly because first she loves the voice of spirit—God—and desires to serve Him.

Charity as the Purpose of Life

What if this is the main reason for being? What if this concept of serving one another is the key to happiness? When I am giving love to another person, I cannot keep it from myself; love is emanating from the Source of love, through me, to my brothers and sisters. Envision the literal scientific process: **as I give of God's abundance, I am receiving the essence of love from God flowing into me, so in the process, I am connected with God, and the whole vastness of love-stores in the universe.**

It's as if I am electrically super-charged with God-energy, at least for the time I am allowing that love to flow from me and towards another, being God's instrument, and for some residual time afterwards. My experience shows that being connected with God has very long lasting effects. Being one with the Light is powerfully healing. Some reports of having been visited personally by Christ have healed those present and

311

also many generations following. The effects of being touched by God's love will actually change our lives too, which is why I say, *a visit with Jesus Christ is the only therapy we ever need!*

Jesus came as the perfect example and taught that we should follow Him. This perfect example of love was always forgiving, always loving, always serving others, always showing examples of faith, healing, and especially honoring the light within — teaching to follow your heart without fear of what might happen to you in the process. With Him on your side, everything always works out. God's example, His very Son — one of us mortals at the time — offered His life to show us the way to serve each other, to bless lives, and thus to be in integrity with the truth of who we all are — *like Jesus, children of God.*

If you will accept this reality that we are literal children of God, as was Jesus, you will know the power of living as He did. As He gave His life on the cross as an example, so we may choose to allow our weakness and sins to die in His grace and mercy. As Jesus rose from death, so we can be raised from our daily feelings of suffering. As Jesus reigns with love and healing in His hands, so we can rejoice in serving others and self by *being the love* — thus *being* His loving, healing hands.

Where Spirit Is Found

We mortals tend to spend most of our time taking care of our own basic needs for survival — in other words, *getting.* But all the gathering of material possessions can never bring any joy. **Material things have no spirit in them, no life, no energy of love!** These things may be nice, but *things* are only *illusions* of what is real.

The only thing that can bring us true joy is by gathering **love — spirit —** through our choices to *be the love* — remembering, asking, and being an example of the believers. *The richest man* *in the world could not buy this!* This is the oil in our lamps story again. Every act of *being the love* creates more of light within us, which is literally another drop of oil — the very oil that lights the way for Christ (love) to come. And He can come to each of us, right now, as we choose to take these actions of being the love. There is no need to wait for the end of time to be with the God of light!

Jesus taught His disciples to go without purse or script. I believe that meant that they were to focus on deeper matters, and leave the arrangements for the small stuff up to Him. Food and housing were always provided. Inspiration for who and what to teach and where to go was always clear. What a simple life plan from which to live: *follow spirit, do what spirit says, and leave the rest up to God.*

Gifts of Being the Love

God promises if we will give our all to Him, in service, He will give his all to us. This is part of His Atonement — we do what we can, and He does the rest. **That is an amazing deal — my all for His all.** As we serve, we enter that balance with the light, that place we might call *holy territory*, which alone is an adventure worth exploring.

Next is the idea that with serving — being the love — you are gathering more of the *substance* of God within you. The more of that *substance of God* you have in and around you, the more He is attracted to you energetically. Or to put it another way, you are more *like* Him — more of the same *substance*, thus more *bonded* to Him. **We literally bind ourselves to God by choosing actions to be the love.**

In the act of serving, we are filled with divine love, or perhaps it is the reverse: only those who are filled with love have enough compassion to go forward and serve others.

Looking at more of this more closely, note that we

don't just *become* the sons and daughters of God. We wake up to *remember* that we are the Sons and Daughters of God. This is who we are! And then when He comes, because we have energetically **brought him here with our awareness of the love that we are,** (like attracts like), of course we shall be *like Him!*

It is my motto that **if something can't be done with love, it is not to be done.** If something would rob you of the ability to be loving, it is not worth doing! The gift of divine love within is so much better than anything that would take its place. So when you feel it slipping away, just stop; let all that is *not love* go, let love center your heart, and then begin again.

I know what it feels like to have the Savior's love touching my shoulders, wrapping around me, body and spirit. Such loving presence has the power to heal everything, and to last for many years. Nothing of man can compare in the least. I want to be like Him. I want to be near this great love. I want to soak in it, bask in it, and *be* it. That is why I serve—from an inner spiritual knowing. It is the same in all of life: nature feels so good because it is doing what it came here to do—being the love; and this is why angels are angels—simply choosing to enjoy being the love.

So when spirit speaks and I follow, whatever I am doing is *charity*. This is the literal meaning of my life: the pure love of Christ is then flowing through my soul—the glory of God is upon me.

Charity Is Obedience

Charity is being true to spirit—honoring the inner knowing feelings. Sometimes that means to serve others and sometimes it means taking care of self—whatever spirit directs. If spirit tells me to go to work everyday so that my family can have the necessities of life, then my work is *charity,* and should bring me joy knowing I am following divine guidance and being in the presence of the divine in the process.

Following spiritual guidance is literally being the hands of God, even if that means to do something that is serving and loving self, because **to follow the guidance of spirit is always** *charity.* I know this, innately, and we read in scripture that even if I feed the poor and give my body to be burned, unless I have charity, it profits me nothing. (I Cor. 13:3)

What does this mean? *Giving* or *sacrificing for others* is not necessarily charity. It seems that charity is something *outside* of the gift itself.

Obedience to spirit is what I am talking about. Being so completely connected to spirit and making choices accordingly is the true essence of charity. *God is obedient to spirit, and everything of spirit is obedient to Him* – an amazing and beautiful reality – to know you can trust spirit.

Is it possible that the difference between God and we humans is that he *knows* and lives true to the essence of spirit energy and is using it to fulfill His purposes? *God is love* is more than a simple saying – it's a tangible essence, which He and we have complete control over through our choices.

We have complete choice to *recognize* (**remember**) and *allow* (**ask**) and *become* (**receive**) love energy – spirit. The very essence of love – spirit – is what each of us *is*. Our eternal nature is based in love energy – spirit. **Even this present life experience is an act of charity, a mortal mission to *exercise* our spirit through choice.**

To know spirit is to know eternity in the present. We know that we are happiest when we are true to that spirit, following spiritual guidance. Going to the deepest level of this understanding, knowing that every one of we humans are spirit – all one – what if our true purpose were to be one – *one in spirit.* What if our purpose is to learn to abide together in this holy recognition of being one in spirit, honoring each other in every way? What if that were the highest purpose for being? What if our alignment with that truth—serving one another—is what makes us like God? *Isn't God's life about serving unconditional buckets full of love to each of us?* **To be love is to serve**! We must be ever more gentle with one another!

The Epiphany

The truths I am teaching in these lessons are not just about cooking to bless my children's bodies or correcting the alignment of furniture to generate good vibes. The real message of all this *spirit energy talk* goes so much deeper—all the way to those mysteries of God I mentioned in the introduction! Can you see how everything is connected to truth from the reality of spirit?

Spirit is always the same, no matter what you call it or how you see it. In every chapter of this book, there are lessons in recognizing spirit. In every case, whether coming from the abundant elements of the earth and its people or the loving spiritual gifts of heaven, spirit is forever vibrating the energy of love, opening the lines of communication to truth from God.

Notice the parallels in each of these chapters explaining some of the many applications of spirit: first we *remove all negatives*—from the things in our homes that take our energy to what we put in our bodies and our closets, our relationships, our false beliefs, our own fears, releasing all through forgiveness.

Whether for our homes or our lives, these principles are the same. When anything does not feel right, we have to examine everything to discover what is out of alignment. We may feel sorrow that we have allowed any darkness into our circumstances, that our choices allowed us to suffer or that we caused problems for others.

This feeling of regret allows us to make other choices in the future, and hopefully gives us the *desire* to seek more of what we have learned about spirit. We forgive self and others in order to release all dark energy. Spirit—love energy—can then flow into us through prayer, meditation, asking, remembering, and being open to receiving.

After removing all negatives, we are open to *receive spirit*: into our houses, our foods, our relationships, the alignment with our inner knowings, our peaceful existence, our own healing.

The final piece of this epiphany is that in all applications, we make choices to place things that will **keep spirit alive and flowing,** there to bless and serve us in every way—from the arrangement of our décor to the patterns of our daily spiritual practices. With our precious gift of choice, we manage everything about ourselves in such a way that allows spirit to remain alive and flowing within us. *It is from that fullness that we bless and serve ourselves and others with spirit!*

As I wrote this book, I described what I knew about the evidence of spirit in several areas of my life: life through my eyes—an energy intuitive—one who sees and feels light and darkness in most sensitive ways. As I finished writing and noticed the parallels, the truth was undeniable: spirit works the same in every application in life. *Negative energy must be cleared in order for the light energy to abide. Choices must be made to continue creating from the light, which then allows the light or spirit to continue to remain and bless.* This continuation of the presence of spirit fills your capacity to overflowing, which is the part we freely give to others.

As you can see from my epiphany, giving to others does not decrease our own share of spirit. It is a blessing to manage our lives in such a way that we can receive such a fullness of spirit, and then to allow it to flow through us like a lighthouse, showing others the truth, giving hope as we let our own lights shine.

As we *live* in the peaceful abundance of spirit, we *send out* an abundance of radiant, all-knowing, all-caring love. God has been trying to tell us this in every language, in every culture, from every prophet, in every book of scripture: **if we want to feel good, to feel peaceful, to be happy—we have to be** *giving.* No wonder that the counterfeit is going to show up big time—selfishness—making life all about *getting,* which is the illusion; as always, here to test us and give us choice.

Knowing Ourselves as the Love

I remember the exact last words my mother shared as I left for college, when I asked her advice about guys: *Don't spend your time worrying about who is the right one for you. Spend your time becoming the kind of person that the kind of person you would want, would want, and everything will work out perfectly.*

Mother's message is not just about dating—it's about priorities. This is what Jesus taught with His example—*seek first the kingdom of God, and all these things shall be added unto you.*

Seeking the kingdom of God is about knowing ourselves as beings of spirit—love, *knowing each other* as love, and *honoring* each other as love. That means we take care of one another. We don't hide our love from our own recognition or from being that love to each other.

I must spend my lifetime becoming and being all I came here to be. No more hiding my light under the bushel, pretending I am less than I am. *I Am* is God! No more hiding my love. To be happy, to feel good, I have to be and give love—some every day. I stand on a hill, holding the torch of all I know *about* love and all I am *as* love, lighting the way for others to do the same.

"It is a serious thing to live in a society of possible gods and goddesses, to remember that the dullest and most uninteresting person you talk to may one day be a creature which, if you saw it now, you would be strongly tempted to worship." (C.S. Lewis, The Weight of Glory)

318

My belief is that we are not *possibly* gods and goddesses. **We are gods of our own lives now, with God's DNA in our veins, and we don't have to wait until that one day to see each other as such!**

Trusting Spirit is *a course in charity,* a re-alignment system for allowing perfection in life to manifest now. It's a match for what I mean when I say *everything begins from a spiritual knowing.* Everything you were meant to do will manifest when you *know you are the love!*

There is no need to separate from love. There is no need to feel exclusive or unique or special or different than others. All of us are the same in one way: **we all are the love**. It's a fact! Recognize that the only choice you ever need to make is to choose love.

There is a scale of love and fear that exists — the level at which we love God and trust spirit, contrasted by where we may fear man's opinion and judgment more than God's. We have a choice to fear physical consequences and act in survivor-mode, or choose to trust in *miracles*! We get to choose between light and darkness: what brings me joy and what brings me opposition to my joy. Everything about this life exists somewhere on that scale. This *spirit-scale* is the meter for life, and we were all born with this system already installed — simply our right and opportunity to choose.

Darkness may come and threaten your success, telling you it can't be done, this stuff isn't true, and that no one cares. But it *is* true. You *do* matter. Love is *what and who you are,* so forget yourself and let the love flow. It is absolutely safe, and the more you believe and do this, the more free you will become. Let go and fly, as you live from spirit! I want to always know myself as love, and to be bonded to God in that awakening. I want to know joy in all my mornings. I pray the same for you.

With all my love and faith — your sister, Judy

Epilogue

The reality of spirit is so real I can swim in it; I feel it full of everything I love about life. When I have those dreams about swimming underwater, forever breathing through my own gills — that pool of water is *spirit*. I can breathe freely in spirit. I can feel myself alive. It's the place where life is created, life happens, I *happen* — perfectly. Living in spirit is my favorite state of existence, and I hope by reading this book, you find your way into that lovely condition and find yourself where you truly belong. Truth is that beautiful.

The soul of man must become a fine-tuned instrument. The spirit and body must learn to work together as one. Spirit is the master, and must know itself, which is what I hope you have discovered in these pages. The soul — body and spirit — can live and grow and work perfectly well through anything that comes, because spirit is connected to all truth and love and guidance — God, and *that* source, *that* master mind, *that* omniscience can safely guide you through anything.

Everything about this life is a maze, perfectly constructed for our highest good. The body simply follows spirit's guidance, and everything works out for the best. Heaven and earth are one — working in perfect balance, and our own spirit and body must learn to work together as one in order to create the harmony that will heal our existence.

If you stop and be still for a minute and listen to these truths, you will find a world of joy and love, power and abundance that makes everything so much easier and so very pleasant. Whether or not you want to believe me, these things are true, and someday you will know for yourself: *the world of spirit is waiting, right now, to bless you with everything your heart desires.* The amazing grace of spirit is simply waiting for you to tune in, look deeper, wake up, and trust: *Trusting Spirit Now* is ready and waiting for you.

About the Author

Judy Rankin Hansen is an energy intuitive who sees life through spiritual eyes, believing that there is so much more than what we observe and experience in the material world, and so much power over our circumstances when operating from a system of spirit.

Those who have experienced her gifts call her a spiritual guide, a peacemaker, a lighthouse, and a visioner, as she has a keen sense of seeing energy or spirit with inner eyes. Judy first sensed her spiritual gifts as a small child spending long hours in nature which surrounded her Tennessee home. She has continually studied about natural living from spiritual truths throughout her life, developing her gifts from leading doctors, scientists, and spiritual mentors.

Judy has a BA in design and adores remodeling spaces according to the elements of the energy in spirit. She has enjoyed a successful career in free-lance interior design for over thirty years, including contracting and land development. She has identified the literal elemental energy that makes everything work perfectly in design, as well as in the rest of our lives—the element of spirit. She has a passion for teaching others to use spirit to heal anything in their own lives that is less than love, and to do it now through many ways of getting your life into the light.

Whether you're a strong believer in Jesus Christ or a person who has become disillusioned with organized religion, Judy shows how to achieve an intimate relationship with your Savior—the Source of all love, light, healing, and forgiveness—and whom she esteems as her very dearest friend and most perfect mentor. In a world that predominantly uses natural laws and creative energy to manifest material possessions, Judy shows you how to use the power of connecting to spirit to find greater satisfaction in living according to the higher laws of God, serving your fellowman as you live your divine purpose.

In her younger years, Judy participated in the Miss Teenage America Pageant, which brought her some wonderful opportunities to share her beliefs. She was also honored by Seventeen Magazine as one of the outstanding young women of the year. In the January, 1972 issue, along with photographs of Judy, it was printed in that publication that her greatest desire was to raise a large and loving family, and to *'get on a universal loud speaker and tell the world to stop the hatred and war--what a utopia we would live in.'*

Judy is most grateful that now thirty-seven years later, the dreams of her youth have come true. She enjoys a loving, happy life with her large family and many others who are an intimate part of her life. While computers and internet were unheard of when she was quoted in Seventeen Magazine with the desire to create peaceful living, Judy feels that her voice through TrustingSpiritNow.com is in some ways an answer to that deep inner desire of her youth to encourage peaceful living universally, beginning with self.

She does her best to follow regular spiritual promptings to explain her beliefs and experiences through articles and recordings, along with several enlightening books and guided meditations. Experiential training is available in her workshops and in one on one consultation.

Judy strongly affirms that, when we choose to create from and live a loving coexistence by trusting spirit in our own lives, the time will come when we will indeed hold hands in peace throughout the world.

Judy currently lives in the Southwestern United States. She loves people and enjoys international travel and the study of all cultures and belief systems. She will probably be spending the rest of her life writing and otherwise sharing her vision of the joy that comes from living in every way from *spirit*.

If you need assistance with any of this process, free guided meditation recordings are available on her website, and personal mentoring and group workshops can be arranged. http://www.TrustingSpiritNow.com

About the Symbol

While searching for a symbol to use artistically throughout the book, I found this piece that looks a lot like a tree. As you now know, I am very connected to nature and especially to trees, which represent life and strength, creating new life as they reach upward towards the light. Seeing tree symbols throughout my book gives me happy vibes as I feel this energy of also being lifted up into the light.

The symbol represents a ladder shape as well, showing the pathway of migration for the soul's pilgrimage from this earthly existence upwards towards a better life in paradise. Paradise used in this sense represents the state of living in the light while yet in the body—again a reminder of the main message of this book.

During the sixteenth century, the symbol was used to signify levels of increased awareness of one's evolution towards spiritual enlightenment. Seeing it throughout this book is also a symbol of enlightenment as I am reminded over and over again of the reality of spirit as the basis for the creation and successful management of literally everything we experience.

This particular symbol is also one of many representations of the cross of Christ's crucifixion used through the centuries. When I look at it from that perspective, I see the gift of His life and death showing us the way to heaven on earth as we follow His teachings.